D0342740

TEENS in
TURMOIL

VIKING

75 years

Carol Maxym, Ph.D., and
Leslie York, M.A.

TEENS in TURMOIL

A Path to Change

for Parents, Adolescents, and

Their Families

VIKING

VIKING
Published by the Penguin Group
Penguin Putnam Inc., 375 Hudson Street,
New York, New York 10014, U.S.A.
Penguin Books Ltd, 27 Wrights Lane, London W8 5TZ, England
Penguin Books Australia Ltd, Ringwood, Victoria, Australia
Penguin Books Canada Ltd, 10 Alcorn Avenue,
Toronto, Ontario, Canada M4V 3B2
Penguin Books (N.Z.) Ltd, 182–190 Wairau Road,
Auckland 10, New Zealand

Penguin Books Ltd, Registered Offices:
Harmondsworth, Middlesex, England

First published in 2000 by Viking Penguin,
a member of Penguin Putnam Inc.

10 9 8 7 6 5 4 3 2 1

LIBRARY OF CONGRESS CATALOGING-IN-PUBLICATION DATA

Maxym, Carol.
Teens in turmoil : a path to change for parents, adolescents, and
their families / Carol Maxym and Leslie York.
p.   cm.
At head of title: Reclaim your life; restore your teen's future.
"Includes extensive descriptions of resources and programs to meet
the needs of every family."
ISBN-0-670-88754-4
1. Parent and teenager—United States.   2. Teenagers—United
States—Social conditions.   3. Teenagers—United States—Family
relationships.   4. Adolescent psychology—United States.
5. Parenting—United States.   I. York, Leslie, M.A.   II. Title.
HQ799.15.M372   2000   99-38963
305.235—dc21

This book is printed on acid-free paper. ∞

Printed in the United States of America
Set in ITC Garamond Light
Designed by Kathryn Parise

dedication

To all the parents who courageously and lovingly decide that life just doesn't have to keep on being the way it is.

—CM

To all the Toms of this world and their parents

—LBY

Contents ✹

Authors' Note ✿

The families you will meet in this book may well remind you of your own family or others in your community; however, all the stories and examples are fictional and do not depict any family we have worked with.

Although this book is the product of our combined personal and professional knowledge and experience, the use of "I" specifically reflects Carol's work as therapist.

—CM and LBY

TEENS in TURMOIL

Prologue 🌀

Because I am a psychotherapist who specializes in work with adolescents and their families, I like to characterize my work as treasure hunting. My task is to help uncover the now-hidden treasure in teens who find themselves in turmoil. My job is to aid them back onto the path to joy, connection with their families, and to a future filled with love, hope, and success. Commonly referred to as "troubled teens," the kids I work with are good kids like yours, more or less lost in a morass of depression, anger, failure, drugs, alcohol, risk-taking, rationalization, and intimidation. They have lost track of themselves, their love for their families, their hope, their future, and most of all, themselves.

Although, of course, each family is different, I find that what really matters is not the details of what the teens are doing, but rather the underlying fragmentation of hope that characterizes them and their families. My first task, then, is to help parents and teens exchange their fear, worry, and desperation for hope and action.

When I work with teens and their parents, I am tough but gentle. I don't mince words. I listen more than I talk, and I have learned the value of patience in the process. I know I will never be able to help any teen rediscover his or her passion for life and for a future unless I have his or her trust. I also learned a long time ago that I cannot earn an adolescent's trust by allowing myself to be lied to, manipulated, or intimidated. I do not get caught up in causes, blame, or guilt. I keep in mind that I must always "return to the things themselves." The emotions I help clients to deal with are sometimes raw, usually intense, and always fraught with meaning.

My relationship to you the reader is the same as it would be to a client in my office: I am never the doer in a family's process; I am merely a guide. I will never give up believing teens and their families can change and rediscover their love for, and connection with, each other and their hope of a future.

I wouldn't trade professions with anyone, and yet it is one of the great sorrows of my life that I work in what could be called a growth industry. How sad for our families and communities that so many of our youth are so confused, terrified, lost, and angry! How sad that they turn to drugs or alcohol or violence when at their core, almost all are wonderful human beings. How necessary, then, to work to alter that situation.

Although there are a number of books designed to help parents "manage" and "parent" their difficult teenagers, there has been no book designed to guide parents through the difficulties of being the parent of a teen who is in turmoil. This is the book you have in your hands. Early on I realized I could broaden the book's perspective by combining my professional experience as a therapist with the personal, "lived" experience of a mother of a once-troubled teen and of a woman who is now an educational consultant specializing in placements for teens such as her son once was. Leslie York was that person. Together, we offer you a process to help your family come together in joy again.

Leslie has "been there." As you can see from her story, it is possible to make the changes you and your teen need. It is possible to get through this difficult time to find that hope and the promise of a joyous future.

Leslie's Story

"Thank you, Mom and Dad," Tom said. "Thank you for not giving up on me, no matter how much I tried to make you. You never did, and that's why I am here today."

My son was graduating high school. I remembered well when that seemed the impossible dream. He was sobbing, and, of course, so was I. In a moment all the pain I had suffered for five years was gone. It was like giving birth to him all over again, except this time he had done his own work. For the first time in years, I could feel deeply and honestly proud of my son and profoundly joyous about my life.

As his and my family's troubles had mounted, I had stopped believing I would see him graduate high school, but he did. I had stopped imagining he could live independently, but he is doing that now. I had stopped hoping I would see him smile his special smile, but I see it all the time now. I had given up hoping to have my whole family together at Thanksgiving dinner, but I've had that now, too. For years I ached with the fear he would never hug me or kiss me again, but now both are plentiful, and I treasure each and every one of them.

Our most difficult years with Tom began when he was fifteen and lasted until he graduated from high school at nineteen. During that time I sacrificed more and more of my own life for my son, thinking that by doing so I was the "good mother," focusing my energy to watch over him, but was really trying to live his life for him. Worry about my son droned underneath everything I did or thought. My last thoughts every night were a prayer he would just survive. I forced myself to keep hoping. I would not speak the unspeakable—that my son might become a school dropout, a druggie, or die from an overdose or in a car crash. It was the reality I avoided by never saying it, yet it was the reality he seemed to be trying to make happen.

I stopped talking to friends because of the fear I would have to eat my words if they were too optimistic or that, God forbid, they might be prophetic. I withdrew into myself. My husband, Dick, and I supported each other, but always just beneath the surface was the unspoken agreement that neither would say anything too negative about our son. We bravely kept up a united front, vowing to remain on the same page in everything relating to our son, but our usually unspoken terror of what Tom might do next kept us emotionally distant. I lived on automatic pilot, and I became all too good at it.

Slowly, over the years, my inquisitive, bright, loving, sensitive son became withdrawn, depressed, angry, and deceitful. He stopped talking to me, and he pulled away from our family. He changed his friends, his grades dropped, and he became verbally, emotionally, and physically violent. I did not realize it then, but—having always been Tom's excuser and rescuer—my determination to get him out of the mess he was making of his life turned me into a master excuser and rescuer extraordinaire. I never wanted to believe that he could be capable of doing the things that deep down I knew he was doing. I never allowed myself to face up to how I was becoming ever more involved in his downward spiral. I chose not to let myself know what I knew. It seemed to be the only way.

With each crisis Tom created, panic would overtake us. We knew we were losing him to a life where love and warmth were replaced by drugs and alcohol, anger, despair, and failure. We didn't know what to do, but we kept trying. We hoped we would find the right professional or program to create the miracle and get him "cured." Over the course of three years, Tom bounced from program to school to program—twelve in all—until he finally hit bottom, and we were used up. Our home and our community were no longer safe for our son. We knew that residential placement was our only alternative. It was then that we began to realize that for our son to change, we would have to change, too.

In our first family meeting with Carol, only a month after Tom had been in an emotional growth program, she posed the question that catapulted us into facing some tough issues. "Do you want your son to grow up to be a boy or a man?" she asked. In that moment, we realized it was time to let go. It was time for our son to grow up. Tom was in a safe environment, he had connected with his therapist, Carol, and she was not going to let him get away with his old tricks, lies, games, and infatuation with failure. We realized we had to find, articulate, and stick to our bottom line. It was painful, necessary, and simple: Tom could not come home unless and until he changed.

As the months went on, we could see Tom beginning to discover the courage to find himself again. I wanted to believe in it, but Carol always reminded me that change is a process—for Tom, and for Dick and me. We had to walk a fine line between patience and no patience because a process cannot be hurried, but there was no more time to sit back and wait.

As Tom was learning how to grow up, I was making changes too. I knew I needed to reclaim my own life—and that I had the right and obligation to do so. Carol provided a powerful catalyst for me to do that when, after several months of working together, she asked me during a therapy session, "Leslie, how's your sex life?" I was shocked, but in the discussion that followed, I understood she wasn't looking for details, but rather that she wanted me to see how I had narrowed my life into being just Tom's mother. That question made me begin to recall the woman I used to be, to see the woman I had let myself become, and to think more clearly about the woman I wanted to be. That was my first inner shift. For me, the change process had begun for real.

Another catalyst came from Tom. He called one afternoon to tell me he had messed up yet again and would not be able to come home for Thanksgiving, his first visit home in nearly a year. For the first time in years we each had our own, appropriate emotional reaction: Tom was ashamed; I was furious. Something in me snapped. In an instant I knew I was no longer willing to be the mother of an irresponsible adolescent. Tom was no longer in control of me or my emotions. If he chose to be irresponsible and self-sabotaging, it was not my responsibility. For the first time I knew I could no longer even attempt to rescue my son. I meant it—from the very core of my being. I felt liberated.

I began to rediscover my life, and it was exciting. Over the next several months, with Carol's guidance, I increased my understanding of the issues I needed to deal with in relation to my son and myself. I discovered I did have the courage to be the mother of an adult son. I stopped solving his problems; I stopped thinking for him; I stopped trying to live his emotional life for him.

In the meantime, living and growing emotionally in the residential program, Tom was sober, beginning to do well academically, finding friends worth having, and able to have real conversations with his father and with me. He was ready to plan his future and act in ways to make it happen. Tom was growing up. He had done it, but I had let him.

I can say with pride that my son has become a man, and we are friends as well as mother and son. When, three years ago at his graduation, he apologized for putting us through the anguish and pain that he had caused, the only hope and dream I had allowed myself for so many years had come true. My son was not only alive and sober, but he was emotionally healthy and happy. He was back in his life, living with energy, passion, and focus.

I have a life now, too. My marriage is stronger than it has ever been. A fulfilling career for myself as an educational consultant in private practice allows me to help families like my own once was. I know what it feels like to live in despair, and I know how possible it is to exchange it for hope and joy.

Tom has his own hopes and dreams for a future now. It is up to him to fulfill them.

This book is the product of Leslie's and my personal and professional experience. It is about how to make change happen because your family life is not anything like what you thought it would be, what you want it to be, and what you have every right to expect it to be.

We like to think this is the ultimate "self-help" book, because its object is to help you help yourself and your family. Because neither of us knows you personally, we cannot offer solutions tailor-made to your situation, but we can offer you something even better: a process through which you will be able to clarify your situation, focus your energy, make the changes you deem important in yourself, and thereby become a catalyst for change in your teen. You might think of what we offer as being similar to the Chinese proverb "Give a man a fish, and you feed him a meal; teach him how to fish and he can feed himself for life." We do not offer a formula that will solve the problems in your family, but we show you how to find your own solutions.

Clarity about your family situation combined with newly discovered courage and focus will direct you toward knowing what you need to do and how to do it. You may find that you can handle the difficulties you are facing with the support of your spouse, family, and friends, but you may also find you need professional expertise or to locate different professionals from the ones you have been consulting. You may come to realize, as Leslie did, that you must consider residential placement for your teen, but you may not. No matter what you decide, this book will help you find and ground *your* decision and *your* ensuing actions.

This book is thought provoking, and while overall its focus is hopeful, parts of it may be very painful to read. There may well be times when you will hear yourself saying, "But not my kid . . ." When you do, step back and remember the reasons you bought this book. Be kind and patient with yourself. Do not rush to judge yourself or others. Give yourself the gift of time and some patience to let yourself know what you know. Facing your reality will bring you the courage you need to act decisively for the welfare of your whole family.

The book is divided into four parts: Part I focuses on teen culture both outside and inside your home. In this section, you will be guided toward developing your first clear picture of your family, your teen, and yourself in the context of all that influences your teen to be the way he or she is.

Part II focuses on stories of families that may remind you of your own. Reading and reflecting on their stories and my accounts of how I worked with them will help you to clarify your picture of how teens and their parents become involved in downward spirals—and how they can alter those patterns.

Part III helps you to bring your increased knowledge and insight into the realm of practical, everyday change. Part III is where you will begin to develop your own ways to take important, positive steps on behalf of your teen, yourself, and your whole family, whether you do that on your own or seek the help of professionals.

In the final section of the book, "Where Else to Go," you will find a guide to making decisions about selecting appropriate placement programs for your teen, if that is what is needed. The guide will help you sort through the issues involved, including legal, medical, and educational issues. It also provides a thorough explanation of the types of programs, schools, rehabs, and interventions you may want to consider for your teen and what to look for when you are checking them out.

Some of the resources may be appropriate for you and your teen now. Others you might think of as an "insurance policy"—there just in case you might need them some day. Just knowing they are there will give you comfort and security as you embark on this new path to create a better future for you and your family.

You may choose to read through this book quickly, or you may prefer to let it stay on your nightstand for weeks, reading just a few pages every night so that you can digest it slowly. If you and your teen are not in crisis, that can serve you well. If, however, you know already that your situation is dire, we suggest you go directly to the Resources and Programs section and begin immediately to locate some combination of the appropriate professional help and/or placement for your teen.

As Leslie and so many other parents have discovered, you will need patience for the process ahead, while at the same time, you must remember that the time to act is now. You may want to start a journal in which you can record your thoughts and feelings as you work through your own process of rediscovering joy and peace in your life and in your family's life as you require your teen to change his or her behavior and attitudes. You may also find that you want to buy yourself a talisman to wear around your neck or as a bracelet. Something you wear every day will remind you that this process, though difficult, will be worth it. It will remind you that you are courageous and that you have faith in yourself and your child. It will remind you that you can and must make it through this process.

PART I ✹

Understanding Where
You Are Now

Chapter 1 ✿

What Is Happening All Around Us:
The High Stakes of Teen Culture

It is obvious to us all that parents and teens face a national crisis. One need only read the newspaper, watch a TV newsmagazine or talk show, listen to the radio, or even just walk down the street to know that. We all realize that younger and younger kids use drugs and alcohol, but what many parents do not realize is that the drugs kids get today are more potent, varied, and virulent than even a decade ago. Typically, kids experiment with lots of different drugs until they find the one they like best. In a mindless frenzy just to get high, some kids, usually the younger ones spurred by peer or media pressure, seriously endanger themselves by inhaling one or more of the approximately 100 everyday substances kept in most homes.

Teens spend $122 billion annually, mainly on "badge items," designer clothing, shoes, and sunglasses, just to fit in. Nowadays kids begin to be sexually active when they have barely entered their teens; AIDS and a host of other sexually transmitted diseases remain only one mistake away. Gangs have come to the best suburbs as well as to quiet rural areas, and they have brought their guns. Nice kids carry weapons to school—and perhaps keep them in your house. The U.S. Senate has investigated the music teens listen to, the movies they watch, and the video games they play to try to determine their relationship to teen violence and suicide. Millions of teens are labeled with various disorders, many of them are prescribed various forms of powerful psychopharmaca to combat depression, anxiety, and difficulties with their attention span, and many of these kids are using their prescription medication in combination with street drugs.

These are our realities. They are not pretty, and no one likes them. It's no wonder kids are frightened. It's no wonder parents are frightened.

We all look for the causes of the reality we deplore: Are they cultural, a product of parents' disenchantment and cynicism from the sixties? Of the new rules and mores of the seventies? Of the affluence of the eighties and nineties? Do more kids spin out of control than before? No one has the answers because the questions are too global. Parents can only address these questions in a family-by-family way. What we do know is that the crisis is real and that parents approaching, near, or in crisis do not have time for theoretical solutions—and ones that will take years to implement. Hundreds of thousands of parents like you find themselves caught in a very personal crisis—one that threatens their family and their teen and his or her future.

Language, clothes, behavior, and attitudes have all changed, and parents' fear and confusion trying to understand isn't just about a generation gap. Some of it, of course, can be related to the special need teens have to fit in to be accepted. Parents can accept some of that, but it becomes different when they must wonder about their child's safety and future as he tries to fit in, be accepted, be popular, and grow up. The stakes for teens are higher nowadays than they were even half a generation ago. What kids have to do now to be "cool" is not only more costly, it is simply far more dangerous than it used to be. We dare not look for quick and easy answers because our children's wellbeing, and even their very lives, may be at stake.

"In Control" Teens

Many teens make their way through adolescence without getting trapped in a cycle of failure, loneliness, and despair. They are able to use their strengths to avoid serious problems or to manage them successfully. If your son or daughter gets in trouble sometimes, it does not mean you have a crisis on your hands. At the same time, it doesn't mean you should ignore your teen's behavior. One rule of thumb for deciding if your teen may be in or heading for trouble is to notice whether he or she learns from mistakes. The teens who insist upon repeating the same behavior and displaying the same attitudes that got them into trouble before are the ones whose parents need to pay particular attention.

Among professionals and laypeople alike, there is no commonly used, accurate term to denote the broad spectrum of teens whose parents will be reading this book. Because many of these teens have worked with counselors and therapists, they often have been labeled as having one type of problem or another: attention deficit disorder (ADD), problems with attachment, difficulties due to adoption, etc. But Leslie and I have both observed that when the parents we work with describe their situation—whether or not their teen has been labeled this way, whether or not their teen is just beginning to cross the line from acceptable to unacceptable behavior, or whether or not their teen has already moved way beyond the line—they all share one thing in common: The *teen* controls the family life and their parents' lives. We often refer to these teens as "in control." (In fact, the concept and reality of kids in control of the family is as applicable to toddlers and their families as it is to teens—and I have met more than one family in which it was still true when the child was twenty-five, thirty-five, and even forty-five years of age.) Changing who is in control in the family is one of the crucial issues parents need to deal with.

No More Safe Places

Home should be the one unconditionally safe place in everyone's life. But when a frightened adolescent is in control at home, then home hardly feels safe. It becomes characterized by a potentially destructive combination of entitlement, resentment, immaturity, fear, and self-centeredness. Home becomes a sort of war zone, characterized by chaos where teens view parents as the enemy. The result is that security and safety stop being a part of a teenager's life. Instead, home becomes a place where tension and anger, hurt, recriminations, lack of trust, and scant belief in anyone's honesty, loyalty, or love permeate and infect the atmosphere. No one feels secure and safe.

When that happens there is no absolutely safe place in the whole world, not for teens, for their siblings, or for parents. When home stops being the place where things are just okay, where love is a given, and where understanding and caring happen as a normal part of life, then everyone begins to feel tight, tense, and unhappy. Unhappiness breeds unhappiness. Parents of teens in turmoil generally describe an atmosphere that feels always charged, like living in a thunderstorm that pauses, but never stops. In one way or another everyone in the family is waiting for the next explosion, the next lie, the next catastrophe. Everyone walks on eggshells, trying to avoid the next confrontation, the next argument, or the next slammed door.

Unfortunately, the other traditionally safe place in a teen's life also can no longer be taken for granted. For kids today school can be a threatening place—even the "good" ones in the "good" neighborhoods. Can a place be called safe when there are police in the halls and/or metal detectors at the doors and when some kids carry weapons? Is it a safe place if girls and boys report verbal rape or assault, and kids are afraid to go into the bathroom?

Too many schools are now places where gangs recruit and drugs are sold and used.

With no place that feels completely safe, and with no adult whom teens trust, many teens find living responsibly hardly inviting. For teens what makes sense is the immediate and the tangible: having fun, buying something new, going to a concert, taking risks, getting high, or getting laid. Odd as it may seem, those behaviors and attitudes are experienced as safer than trusting adults, the future, life, and themselves.

Dreams of success, honor, and respect are distant because they require perseverance, diligence, and the courage to keep on caring. I think of Jeremy, who had always wanted to be a marine biologist; but in the second semester of his freshman year, his biology course required more work than he had ever done; he became scared he couldn't do it, so his answer was to cut class, telling himself that he hadn't ever really cared anyway. I think of Cathy, who was fourteen when I met her. She was smart and pretty, but she lost track of her dream of being a teacher when weighing only 100 pounds became all she could think about, talk about, or do anything about because it was a more immediate and realizable goal. And I think about Randy, whose best answer to his profound existential questions was to avoid them by sleeping through life, sleeping through his future.

When I talk with teens like Jeremy, Cathy, or Randy, they give scores of "logical" reasons why seeking positive goals doesn't make sense or why those goals no longer matter to them. But no matter how they may pretend or protest to the contrary, on some level most teens do remember their dreams: wanting to be a doctor or a teacher, helping others, or traveling the world. Sadly though, those dreams become less and less achievable as kids lose themselves in their own personal downward spiral.

The Downward Spiral

Everyday adolescent life is a fast-paced confusion of fantasy and reality that teens, by virtue of being between childhood and adulthood, naturally lack the experience and maturity to negotiate, either psychologically or emotionally. It is no wonder that many of them spin out of control: They have almost no firm ground beneath their feet.

As these teens watch their opportunities melt away, their attitudes become more and more paradoxical. Kids I have worked with realize on some level that they are making their own opportunities disappear while on other levels they seem oblivious to that fact. That is when some of them seem to want to fail with a vengeance, skipping school like Jeremy did, or quitting the cross-country team as Randy did, or, like Cathy, exchanging her meaningful activities for drinking and drugging as though there were no tomorrow. Thousands and thousands of kids all over the country do similar things. Others—and I have worked with so many of them—pretend to, or even try to, pull it together, working hard in school for a couple of weeks or even a month or two, until something difficult comes along, and they give up, rationalizing all the way. It reminds me of Paul, who said, "If I had tried, I could have, but . . ." followed by the hundred excuses why it was better to give up because there was always another time, another chance, or at least the possibility of saying, "I didn't really care anyway."

Often and unwittingly parents help their teens rationalize. Jeremy's parents told each other, "School is so hard these days. Kids need to have some fun, after all. Freshman grades don't really matter all that much." Cathy's mother could not help but think her daughter really did look great in a size 2. Randy's parents took him from specialist to specialist, trying to find the cause of his malaise, never thinking it might be fear combined with laziness.

As teens begin to spiral downward, often taking their families with them, they start intimidating parents or teachers or siblings, acting even more entitled and defiant. Somehow, it seems, the mess that is his or her life must be someone else's fault. Taking responsibility is overwhelming partially because it implies living in everyday reality. And everyday reality is boring (a favorite teen word used to describe almost anything they don't like or can't handle), but even rationalizations have consequences. Teens like Jeremy, Cathy, and Randy don't like to acknowledge that.

As life spirals downward, the future begins to look increasingly ominous. Teenagers tend to react with anger or depression or both. Parents do, too, and it affects everyone else living in the house, not to speak of the teen's future, the parent's career, and everyone's belief in life. As one problem begets another, families feel as though the spiral is whirling faster and tighter, and escape begins to seem impossible. But, strange as it may seem, the spiral downward can become if not exactly comfortable, at least familiar. When just about everything in life is uncertain, familiar ways of behaving and experiencing the world have the advantage of being, well, familiar.

Chaos

Sometimes family life begins to feel as though it is structured only by chaos. Chaos is wild and full of energy, but it is an energy that just scatters in the wind like leaves in a late autumn storm. In the whirlwind of chaos emotional numbness seems protective, feelings hardly exist, and that seems better. Because it is so powerful and self-propelling, chaos helps parents and teens avoid noticing how bad things are. The teen tries to drown out bad feelings by creating more chaos, and again, wittingly or not, parents often end up playing into it, perhaps even helping to create it. Sometimes it plays out like a melodrama, as in sixteen-year-old Allie's family, where tears and accusations of "You don't even know me!" punctuate daily life. In other families, like Jeremy's, explosive outbursts divert attention from his impending failure. An eerie quiet prevails at Randy's house because no one is sure what is wrong, but everyone is afraid of disturbing Randy. No matter what the manifestations, chaos always feels about the same in the gut: tense, anxious, foreboding.

Chaos becomes a metaphor for the way many adolescents feel about life: It's more than they can handle, it hurts, it betrays, it's menacing, yet its energy is seductive. Chaos and all that it brings can become a sort of addiction unto itself and can take on a rhythm and momentum of its own. The ultimate distraction, chaos makes it easier to quash the feelings of hopelessness, depression, despair, guilt, shame, anger, failure, and loneliness.

Acting Out, Acting In

Some teens direct their inner conflicts and their frustration about the world as they perceive it outward, and some direct these feelings inward. This acting out or acting in manifests in three general ways: anger, wild behavior, and/or depression. Most teens display aspects of each, but the trouble starts when the anger, outrageous behavior, and/or the depression take over the teen's personality, until parents and even friends feel they don't know him anymore.

Angry kids get right up into everyone's face to intimidate; wild ones intimidate with their energy and defiance of all caution, and depressed ones by maintaining a cold, dark, and silent distance. These three manifestations of inner turmoil may look different, but they usually overlap in some way. An angry adolescent is usually also depressed; a depressed adolescent is usually also angry. And all of them are wild and defiant in one way or another. I understand that parents crave the now-elusive peace and family pleasures of earlier years.

Because the manifestations of the problems define their teen's life and their family's life, many parents seek mainly just to eradicate the most obvious symptoms, such as poor school performance, drug or alcohol abuse, apparent depression, uncontrolled, irresponsible behavior, or disregard for family rules. Often parents resort to trying to control their teen's behavior, attitude, and worldview in the vain hope that it will make their teen change, *really* change, and become once again that kid they used to know.

However teens act out their feelings, parents and professionals often mistake the manifestations of the problem to be the problem itself. They often believe that if they could get the symptoms (bad grades, undesirable friends, foul language, use of alcohol and drugs) to disappear, the problems would vanish. Consequently, parents, professionals, and even the teens themselves fight the smaller battles and ignore the larger issues. For example, Jeremy's problem was not that he began to skip school—that was the manifestation of his deep belief (read: fear) that he really was not intelligent enough to realize his dreams. Cathy's problems were related to her self-image and her fear of her own extraordinary potential. Randy began to doubt himself and the meaning of life, and instead of actively seeking new answers to these profound existential questions, he became demoralized. While his parents and the professionals they consulted dealt with Randy's symptoms—sleeping all the time and appearing depressed—they missed the deeper issues.

Teens in turmoil often substitute short-term conformity for real changes in behavior and attitude, further confusing their parents and the professionals who work with them. Boys like Jeremy may begin to go to school regularly and improve their grades, but their newfound energy often falters once the going gets rougher. With some counseling, girls like Cathy may turn their obsessive interest in their weight and sexual relationships back to their future in order to regain the privilege of using Mom's credit card, but they will not have changed their worldview or self-concept, and then they quickly revert to the old behavior. Randy may agree to go to therapy and take (or pretend to take) his medication, but he will not have begun to seek the real answers to his questions about life and its meaning. Short-term conformity is too often mainly a convenient way to "get my parents off my back!"

Behavior is a metaphor, a way teens have of acting out the real problem. The real problem is the teenager's attitude toward herself, toward others, and toward life. However a teen is acting out, beneath the surface of the actions and attitudes lurk the teen's self-doubt, self-disrespect, and self-hatred, providing the rationale for behavior that is self-sabotaging. These teens accomplish the unstated and unconscious goal of finding reasons to hate themselves by engaging in a wide variety of behaviors along a continuum that can range from innocuous to outrageous, self-destructive, and very dangerous. The behaviors can be as small as not completing a paper for school, or as large as having unprotected sex with several partners.

Self-doubt, self-disrespect, self-hatred, and a strange sort of self-indulgence become part of a vicious circle in which, because the feelings are overwhelming and define a teen's inner reality, she must do things to make those feelings make sense. She feels as though she has to be still more hateful and self-destructive, stifling her better, truer feelings in order to be who she believes she is. In the ensuing vicious circle, self-sabotage breeds failure, and failure breeds loneliness, despair, and anger, which breeds more self-sabotaging behavior. The circle pulls tighter, engendering resentment toward rules and life in general, all nurtured by the feelings that keep the circle in frantic motion. Hard as it may be to accept, this "rationalizing" process makes inner psychological sense to the adolescent caught in the vicious circle of self-perpetuating self-hatred.

The Rush

One of the favorite ways teens try to drown out the irrationality, inconsistency, and deep-seated unhappiness of the vicious cycle of being hateful to justify feeling worthless and then having to lie and manipulate to cover it all up is by seeking the rush. The rush is a passionate search for a single moment of feeling intensely alive, in tune, powerful, ready, and able to experience life as no one has ever done before. The teen looking for that rush seeks risks to challenge the very meaning and essence of being alive. Using drugs and alcohol, having sex, driving fast cars, and seeing how far the rules and the law can be pushed all contribute to achieving the rush and that feeling of being invincible. Even if a teen feels worthless, surviving self-destructive attitudes and acts like driving drunk and surviving or having unprotected sex and not getting a sexually transmitted disease or pregnant is also a rush. It fools kids into believing they really are in charge, invincible, and immortal, and for some kids, that risk taking is the same as being heroic. It's a modern version of Russian roulette played by kids who don't believe there is such a thing as the future and surely couldn't trust themselves if they got there. For kids who don't really care about their lives—or are afraid to admit they do—being self-destructive (and that includes lying, manipulating, basking in self-hatred, seeking failure, etc.) yet surviving is a tremendous rush.

But no matter how good the rush is, it never lasts more than a moment, and then depression, alienation, and loneliness suffuse the teen's soul.

Common Threads

The irrationality of the vicious circle and the teen's quest for the rush is often hard for parents to understand, but recalling similar feelings from their own teenage years helps. Underneath the behavior and attitudes there are some threads common to all teens having trouble negotiating their growing up. Teens in turmoil take it to a different level, and although it is sometimes hard to admit, their parents know their teen is doing or feeling all or most of the following behavior-attitudes.

COMMON BEHAVIOR-ATTITUDES OF TEENS IN TURMOIL

1. They don't like themselves.
2. They feel like failures.
3. They are demoralized and react with an I-don't-care or "fuck you" attitude toward school as well as other things.
4. They are frightened and resentful.
5. They are self-absorbed, self-centered, and self-indulgent.
6. They lie.
7. They manipulate.
8. They test limits.
9. They are struggling with profound existential questions.
10. They are sabotaging themselves, their future, and their family.
11. They are self-destructive.

Of course, no parent wants any of these behavior-attitudes to be true of his or her teen. It is tempting to rationalize or cover them up by means of rationalizations, excuses, and explanations. But it is fear, not reality or truth, that leads to the rationalizing. And it is fear that makes teens—and their parents—act in ways that seem to justify behavior and attitudes that everyone knows cannot be justified. But kids change, and parents can be the catalyst.

Clearly, outrageous, self-destructive, sabotaging behavior needs to be stopped, but teens like Jeremy, Cathy, and Randy can't stop their self-sabotaging behavior until their attitudes change. But changing attitudes without eradicating self-destructive behavior is virtually impossible. It is a chicken-and-egg scenario—in which it isn't ever possible to say exactly whether the behavior begets the attitude or vice versa. In either case, though, kids can make positive change with parents as the catalyst.

But in order to change, parents need to recognize and acknowledge the part they have played in creating the feelings of unbounded entitlement in their kids. For so many kids who grow up believing Mom or Dad can and will bail them out of life's scrapes, when they have to start producing on their own, life becomes too challenging. Like Jeremy, who gave up once the going got tough in high school, many kids do fine throughout elementary school, maybe even into middle school. But when diligence, perseverance, and some maturity need to be brought to the table as the work in high school becomes more demanding, they don't know what to do because they have no experience to guide them. The focus on self-esteem has schooled many teens to believe that rewards and praise need not be won by hard work and real achievement. It is easy to understand why a teen like Randy, who preferred sleep over seeking answers to his questions about the meaning of life, turns tail and runs emotionally, psychologically, and in reality, blocking out life when it seems too demanding.

The reality that success and happiness come from hard work, honesty, perseverance, and self-discipline strikes many teens as old-fashioned and unfair. Designer clothes, loud music, medication, street drugs, and rationalizing unacceptable behavior will never give any kid hope, but many teens don't want to believe that. Cathy uses the mirror and pseudosophistication of promiscuous sex as her way to seek hope. She manipulates men even much older than herself into believing whatever she wants them to believe. She just doesn't understand that she never will find hope in promiscuous sex or the momentary rush or transient sense of power she gets from it.

So much of what teens hate and fear is the product of hopelessness combined with fear and more hopelessness, fed by peer pressure and the commercial adolescent culture. Some teens, however, remain connected with their families and the friends they have known since they were small, and navigate the difficult years almost without a hitch. Others make mistakes, get frightened by their own behavior and the results of it, and change course quickly and effectively. But some kids don't. Some kids just keep on doing the bad stuff and the crazy stuff until someone notices, intervenes, and forces them to stop.

When adolescents find that the last bauble or the last high didn't alleviate or even mitigate despair and questioning for long, those feelings quickly mutate into fury: rage born of feeling betrayed. Somehow it must be someone's fault, they believe, so they yell at parents, siblings, teachers and blame the world. Often enough, to get the anger and despair out before it suffocates them inside, they destroy things—their room or other parts of the house, sometimes a car, sometimes a relationship. What they are really trying to destroy is the self they have become. But it doesn't solve the problem. Often it is a loud cry for help.

Is Your Teen Asking for Help?

The behaviors listed below can be warning signs. Do not let yourself rationalize, justify, excuse, or ignore any of them. A decline in their teen's grades is one of the most common reasons parents come to us for help. When we begin to talk, we find that several other issues were also at work in the teen's life.

If your son or daughter has sent you even one or two of these messages, he or she may be in more trouble than you think. It is now time for you to get more information about what your teen is doing. Consult with teachers, school counselors, a therapist, or clergy. If you feel your situation is more urgent, see "Red Flags" on page 51 and consult the Part IV section for more information about professionals and programs to help your teen and yourself.

Pay close attention when your teen:

- Wants you to buy lots of Gatorade, mouthwash, aerosol products, or household cleaning agents. These can be used to cover up drug use or as recreational drugs themselves.
- Begins to stay up alone and late at night.
- Comes home and hurries to his/her room.
- Is glib or evasive when you ask about unexplained charges on the phone bill such as calls to 900 numbers.
- Leaves drugs around where you can't help but see them.
- Leaves incriminating letters and notes open where you will find them or has incriminating phone conversations within your earshot so you can't help but understand the content.
- Binges or eats secretly.
- Changes appearance abruptly: hair color or cut, clothes, jewelry, body piercing, tattoos.
- Shows consistently and increasingly poor school performance and correspondingly poor grades.
- Gets suspended or expelled from school, especially if it happens repeatedly.
- Asks to be home-schooled.
- Is ready to settle for a GED or tries to convince you it would make sense (or the school counselor suggests it as an alternative to staying in school).
- Suddenly quits a sports team, drops out of clubs or activities, or changes friends (particularly if this happens in conjunction with any other items on this list).

- Stays on the Internet for hours.
- Suddenly loses or gains a lot of weight.
- Appears with lots of new things (jewelry, clothes, and so forth) without having asked you for money or incurring any credit card charges.
- Is physically threatening you and/or siblings.
- Exhibits a change in behavior toward the family pet or other animals.
- Has unexplained scratches, burns, or bruises on his or her body or always wears long sleeves and trousers, even in warm weather. (This may indicate self-mutilation.)
- Starts seeing a man or woman many years older than herself or himself.
- Spends hours alone, especially in a dark room, maybe writing depressing or even suicidal poetry.
- Listens to music which glorifies suicide and/or death and/or violence.
- Uses the Internet for sex.
- Is being sexually promiscuous.

A New Understanding of Failure

One of the most indistinct but heartwrenching cries for help is a teen's frantic search for success, taking the need for success and the success itself to absurdity, moving nonstop from more honors classes to being the best in several sports and president of a club or two. These teens strive to be not only the best at everything but also truly "perfect." They need to be the best dressed, have the perfect body, be the most popular, and seem completely in control of everything in their lives. Watching them can leave you breathless—and wondering what they are running from and to.

The drive for perfection that permeates these kids' lives may come from outside, but just as often it is self-imposed. High ambitions aren't wrong or harmful, but striving for perfection is, by definition, a self-defeating, self-destructive project. The push toward perfection can begin early in a child's life, as he strives to meet every challenge until one day the proverbial straw breaks the camel's back. Greg, for example, had always played baseball, been involved in his church youth group, and been an A student. Early in his eighth-grade year, he forgot to study for an important quiz and failed it. "I felt so ashamed," he told me, "I never did any homework again. I quit baseball and just kind of gave up. It made sense to me, then. I felt like a failure, so I had to become one."

Aaron didn't seem to need Ritalin (or any other medication) until he was sixteen, but then, worried he could not cope with the pressure of SATs, Advanced Placement courses, college applications, and basketball, he hoped a little extra boost would help. Anna was fourteen when she decided it would be okay to use speed to lose that last eight pounds she felt sure she needed to shed. Lara was always the star of everything until her senior year when she began to feel overwhelmed by the pressures of getting into college and the prospect of having to keep up the work at an Ivy League school. She rationalized that cocaine would help her through exams, and she promised herself she would use it only when she "absolutely needed it." Unfortunately, that became more and more often, and before she had even heard which colleges had accepted her, Lara had a serious drug problem to deal with.

Sometimes a divorce, parents' separation, or a death in the family can be the catalyst for kids to give up. And sometimes there is no discernible catalyst at all.

The pressures involved in being the best of the best in different and possibly conflicting spheres is enough to convince some kids that giving up altogether is a much better, or at least a more achievable, goal. After all that striving, finding themselves unhappy and unfulfilled anyway is devastating. Feeling betrayed, fearing they cannot be the best of the best, they may become overtly resentful. Some kids then choose instead to be the worst of the worst. Sometimes this drama plays out in a family context. Ted had three older sisters who were athletic as well as academic stars. Afraid to compete, he reacted by giving up when he was only thirteen, choosing for himself instead the role of class clown. Dora, afraid she might outdo her older sister, first quit playing piano, then stopped playing tennis, and eventually settled for Cs in school. Hank, realizing he could never be an all-state football player like his brother, opted instead to be the wildest, biggest failure the school had ever seen. Failing, after all, isn't that hard to do, and teens usually don't see the risks to their future that failing implies.

Some kids find that the only thing they can do really well is to be the class clown, the biggest screw-up in the school, or the most depressed and lonely kid ever. Some kids who are failing at school are mainly bored by it, either because they are very bright or very lazy or because school really is boring. These teenagers seek their challenges elsewhere—getting over on parents and teachers, breaking the rules, procuring drugs, being secretive, being a dealer, playing the gangster. All of these behaviors and attitudes provide interest, excitement, and—above all—risk in what otherwise seems like a very boring, bland life. It seems easier to be the kid with the new gear, the drugs, the newest CD, or the newest information from the Internet than to write up the chemistry lab results or finish the English paper. The satisfaction is immediate, and teens generally aren't looking ahead to the longer-term consequences.

Teens who are caught in any of these downward spirals prove time and time again to themselves and to everyone around them that they will fail—in school and in relationships. No matter how far anyone lowers standards for them, they still manage to fail. The goal they have set for themselves is failure, and their failure paradoxically becomes a measure of success. The whole project, obviously, is inherently irrational. Able to trust themselves only to fail, they apply their self-imposed standards to the rest of the world. As these kids reach the age where growing up and taking responsibility is the next step, they don't believe they can handle it. In a way, of course, they are right. Anger, depression, and looking for someone or something to blame for the state of their lives are common, easy responses. These kids expend enormous amounts of energy blaming everyone else without really examining and experiencing feelings, meeting responsibilities, or overcoming challenges.

Failure can become a sort of addiction, and like all addictions it begins to take over the lives of the teen and his family as everyone in the family becomes involved in excusing, rationalizing, and trying to stop the failures. But rather than try to "fix" the teen's failures, it is far more important to recognize the meaning of the failure and to see it for what it is: a self-absorbed, self-indulgent, and self-centered act borne of fear.

Self-Centered, Self-Absorbed, and Self-Indulgent

Whether we look at the kids who are striving for perfection or the ones who are striving for failure, whether they act in or act out, are depressed or angry, they are almost always self-centered, self-absorbed, and self-indulgent. They have learned to regard themselves as the center of the world. Considering how narrow that world is, it is little wonder how confining and boring they find their lives and how desperate they are for outward excitement, novelty, and drama. They act entitled to everything and more, hiding their feelings of self-doubt and self-hatred with the incantation, "I want what I want when I want it, and I should get it because I want it."

Using one means or another, these teens try hard to stay in control of their situation. They are ready to tantrum, threaten, cajole, and intimidate until they get what they want, and their experience is that it almost always works. They turn their well-meaning parents into well-trained givers who would never think of saying no or of wanting, much less requiring, reciprocity.

Many parents and professionals describe the adolescent years as inherently self-centered, self-absorbed, and self-indulgent, but I don't agree. Many teens remain as considerate, interested in others, and generous as they were as young children. Some teens show a few signs of becoming thoroughly egocentric but pass through it like a stage. Other teens seem only to have learned to consider themselves to be the center of the world. These teens rarely know or care what their parents do, where they come from, even how old they are, and surely not who they are as individuals. Perhaps the best example is someone like Robert, a fourteen-year-old who would never bother to remember his mother's birthday but would be resentful, furious, and hurt if she dared to forget his! Self-centered teens can't imagine that parents don't want to hear their music or let them use the family car whenever they want.

Self-indulgence applies especially to feelings. One mark of teens who are in control of their families is that they are very concerned with their own feelings and rarely consider how their words and actions affect others. They often feign coldness and an I-don't-care attitude, masking a self-indulgent and self-centered oversensitivity. Beneath the self-indulgence and self-centeredness, they are actually hiding a deeper truth from themselves and from the world: that they are warm, good, kind individuals desperately afraid of being hurt.

Adolescent self-indulgence is most obvious when the teen acknowledges parents' feelings only when they interfere with the child getting or keeping something he or she wants or wants to do. Sarah told me, "I always get what I want," and I knew she was telling the truth. I asked her if she knew when her mother's birthday was. She looked at me with a blank stare, not comprehending the underlying meaning of my question. Doris and Mike, her parents, were too intimidated by the enormous sense of entitlement they had instilled in their daughter to expect her to remember their birthdays, anniversary, or other special days for the family.

Even teens who know, at some level, that their parents don't have much money and cannot afford to buy them a $400 prom dress or $150 sport shoes will throw a tantrum and threaten until they get what their parents can ill afford. All too many parents, especially single mothers, put themselves far into debt in order to keep their child clothed in designer merchandise they don't even approve of. The parents do not know how to say "No," or they are too afraid of the repercussions from their teen if they do.

Testing Limits

It is hardly a news flash to say that teens test limits. What is important is not that they do, but the meaning of the testing. Most teens trust their parents, unless their parents have given them reason not to. The testing so common to the adolescent years is really a self-testing, although it plays out more like testing of adults. *Testing limits is a way of finding out what adults think, feel, and expect. It is a way for adolescents to try to fathom how they are supposed to act, think, and create and maintain relationships once they become adults.* It is a way for teens to begin to find their own moral and ethical code. It is a way to establish standards. Note I didn't say it was a nice way or even a very direct way, but it is clearly an important way teens find out about the boundaries of their world.

Anger, depression, and blame-placing sometimes function as ways to test parents, therapists, teachers, and fate. By their actions, teens are asking, "How many times will you believe my lies?" "How much can I mess up and know you will still love me?" "How much can I hurt you and know you will still be there?" "How many times can I fail and know you will step in and make everything all right?"

Often it doesn't seem to matter how many times a parent or anyone else passes the tests by still loving the teen, still caring and being there. The testing will continue until the cumulative effect of the testing results in the teen beginning to trust herself. It may seem that teens want parents to give in and do or say whatever it is the teen seems to be asking for, but it really isn't that way. Teens desperately want their parents to maintain high standards and continue to love them. "Passing" the tests means not giving in.

Carrie began testing her mother before she was twelve by coming in just a few minutes late. When her mom, Deanna, complained, Carrie would give her that "you're so annoying" look, so Deanna stopped mentioning it when Carrie was late. Soon Carrie was testing limits more and more, yelling at her mother, threatening to get a tattoo, using language she knew Deanna hated. Finally, during an argument, Carrie yelled, "You don't even care about me. You don't even notice when I come in late!" Deanna was shocked. I explained that by means of her testing, Carrie had been trying to find out just how strong and committed to her principles Deanna was. So far, Deanna had failed Carrie's tests.

Jeremy's professor father failed the tests too. When he finally agreed that Jeremy should take fewer and easier classes, in Jeremy's mind that meant his own worst fears for himself were accurate: He was worthless, a born failure, helpless, hopeless, and, most important, much less intelligent than the father he worshipped.

Every time a parent lowers his standards so that the teen might meet them, the parent fails the test. Hard as it may be to believe, teens want you to pass their tests. They need *you* to prove *they* can succeed and be loved.

Manipulation

When teens lie, cover up, and fear the truth about themselves, it makes sense that they don't trust themselves. And because they know better than to trust themselves, they manipulate. Manipulation is a sign of desperation and lack of belief in oneself. Kids manipulate when they feel they cannot get what they want or achieve their goals by more straightforward means. They manipulate when they feel weak, helpless, powerless, or when they are in a silent but vicious competition with adults to prove they can get the better of them. Such teens manipulate each other, their teachers, their counselors, their therapists, and, above all, their parents to get what they often know to be inadvisable and unreasonable.

Not only do kids manipulate their parents into doing things like extending curfew or allowing them to smoke, kids also manipulate their parents into doing their schoolwork for them or talking to the teacher to excuse them. They manipulate parents into doing their chores for them and into cleaning up after them. They manipulate parents (especially mothers) into feeling their feelings for them. Parents may rationalize that they are just trying to help out, but, in fact, when kids manipulate their parents, they are getting their parents to help them fail.

Perhaps the ultimate manipulation occurs when teens ask their parents, "Don't you trust me?" It is hard to give the answer: "No, of course not because you have not earned it." Sometimes, however, that is the honest and correct answer.

When a teen (or anyone else for that matter) manipulates someone else, they manage to get that other person to be, if not dishonest, at least disingenuous. Manipulation is one way kids get what they want or what they think they want. Another way is by lying—first cousin to manipulation.

Lying

No parent wants to admit that his or her child lies. However, most teens who are even just beginning to test your limits will lie. Teens whose lives are in turmoil lie for reasons similar to why they manipulate, fail, seek the rush, and do all the other things you know are not in their best interests.

One common method of lying used by teens is to create confusion. They retell a story enough times, changing it just slightly every time, so that after a few minutes the truth becomes elusive. When their parents become confused, the teen takes control. (When parents feel confused, they need some time, even if just a minute or two, to sort out what is going on!)

How to "Boil" a Family or How to Boil a Frog

"How did things get to where they are now?" Every family asks that question. One way to think about it is through the following metaphor, which will be familiar to many from their professional lives. Applying the concept of the Boiled Frog may help you to understand how you got to where you are today.

How to Boil a Frog: Recipe

1. Place frog in large pot of cool water. Place pot on stove.
2. Continue to heat slowly, being careful not to increase heat too rapidly. (Frog will acclimate itself to the temperature and does not seek to escape to save itself.)
3. Continue cooking over slowly increasing heat until thoroughly cooked.

CAUTION: Dropping the frog directly into boiling water will cause it to jump right out to save itself.

How a Teen Boils a Family: Recipe

Using low but constant heat, agitating ever so gently:
1. Intimidate and bully parents.
2. Making certain not to bring to a quick boil, carefully combine lies with manipulations. Add a pinch of need-to-be-rescued.
3. Making sure to keep parents unaware of the increasing confusion, pit parents against each other until they explode. Be sure to allow parents to justify, excuse, and rationalize the increasing chaos, unhappiness, and failure.

CAUTION: If you act too precipitously, your family may realize what you are doing and react.

The first lies may seem harmless enough. Jeremy, who got scared in freshman biology, started by lying to his parents about how much homework he had and how his schoolwork was going. Greg, the eighth grader who stopped doing his homework when he failed a quiz, told his parents that the school was conducting an experiment with his class, so they didn't get grades anymore. Because Greg had always been such a trustworthy boy, months passed before they discovered his lie. Cathy, the fourteen-year-old who obsessed about her appearance, told her mother that the prices in the cafeteria had gone up, so she needed more lunch money, which of course she used for speed.

But I love to tell the story of Paul, who used to lie straight to his parents' faces with the most sincere look. It was his direct eye contact, combined with their desire to believe their son, that made Paul's parents go along with whatever he told them. I will never forget the day in therapy when Paul had one of those great revelations: "If I don't lie, I don't have to worry about who I told what to. That makes life so much easier!"

Russ is only twelve, but he already knows how to use manipulation and lying together. "Aren't you proud of me that I told the truth?" he had asked his father, who told me the story with a degree of satisfaction. Unfortunately, I had to reply that I do not find honesty something a father should have to acknowledge in that way. "Honesty," I told Sam, "should be a given."

Most parents know when their teen is lying, but they find it hard to acknowledge. That isn't surprising. Once parents acknowledge one lie, they raise the question of just how many lies there are underneath it. That can be an ugly, disturbing moment. But it can also be the first step toward reestablishing the truth as a standard in your family.

The Paradox of Your Teen's Life

Teenagers today ask the same questions teenagers have always asked. They seek the meaning of life, they wonder about their soul or spirit, and they try to figure out what their place is on earth and in the cosmos. Their questions are age-appropriate, but the ways teens go about finding the answers nowadays are too often fraught with danger. The urgency of their age-appropriate existential questions can overwhelm many teens who lack the patience and wisdom that only years of life experience can bring.

Perhaps the most profound but least-recognized question teens face has to do with fitting in. It seems banal on the surface, but I don't think it is. Attempting to fit in—or not—implies questions such as "Am I okay?" "Am I like other people?" "Do I want to be?" "What if I am different—what will that mean for the rest of my life?" It is all too easy to criticize teens for trying to fit in, forgetting that we adults do it, too. For teens, fitting in is accomplished in a series of stages that can and often do help an individual define and re-define him- or herself. Sometimes, however, fitting in results in an almost complete loss of self.

As adults we often remark how little concept of the future teens have. However, it may be more accurate to say they have not yet created their own inner rhythm and inner context—an integrated identity—that underlies and guides their actions, thoughts, beliefs, hopes, and dreams, and this, too, is age-appropriate. An identity based upon an inner context provides the means for acting in the world, for feeling confident enough in oneself and one's motives to believe—not so much in something but in belief it-self. Teens often imitate their concept from their parents' identities or beliefs; other times they seek to do exactly the opposite of what their parents do and how they do it. Many teens only need time and safety to create their own inner context. Others may self-destruct before they get there.

Life is not easy for a teen who whirls like a toy top in a dizzying paradox of feelings, convinced of his utter invincibility and immortality and his total fear of growing up. His life is full of the everyday tension between acting good or acting bad, between doing drugs or not doing drugs, between being sexually active or not, and between being cool or not being nearly cool enough. He has become trapped, stuck in a complicated web of failure and bravado, reality and fantasy. His trap is mainly self-imposed, but fear, peer pressure, entitlement, and the ensuing resentment, adolescent culture, and the downward spiral of repercussions at home and school tighten their grip. Kids usually need help to find the freedom they delude themselves into thinking they have and have not.

Teens try to escape the everyday challenges and realities of their lives by imitating what they see in music videos, on TV, in advertisements, putting on the trappings of being grown up. For many kids, becoming the next millionaire rock superstar or athlete seems almost real and realizable, but then the everyday reality of an algebra test, a rewrite of an English paper, being grounded, or not having enough money from allowance to buy the latest "necessity" interferes. Then the lived comparison between the media fantasy and everyday reality jars terribly. For teens who are somewhere on the continuum of a downward spiral, the result is demoralization, anger, failure, deceit, and self-sabotage. Many notice they are lost, but sadly, most of them will continue on the downward spiral until someone, usually a parent, steps in to stop it.

For a teen struggling with the realities of growing up in our culture, parents' love and the security of a home and family life can seem boring, banal, and definitely not cool, but it isn't so. In the end, home, security, and love are what kids want—and need—in their lives.

Chapter 2 ✿

What Is Happening in Your Family: Beginning to See with Clarity

You remember so well your wonderful child, the bright-eyed kid who ran off to school by herself, the boy who wasn't very good on the clarinet but a star at soccer, the one who was always first in the class, the one who worked for hours to color a birthday card for you and who wouldn't go to sleep at night without your kiss. How could that be the one who just told you to "Fuck off and get out of my life!"?

Your memories and your everyday reality barely seem to be of the same child. Nothing you ever did or thought prepared you for how you are living every day. You come home from work in the evening, wanting to smile and to laugh with your family but instead you hear yourself yelling and threatening, using language you despise. Too much of your time and energy is spent being angry and depressed, but your resolutions not to be are brought to naught again and again. It feels as if you, too, are becoming someone you don't know and someone you don't like very well. There is a nagging feeling you have lost control of your adolescent, but even more than that, you suspect you have lost control of your own life and your family's life.

Buffeted between being afraid *for* your child and afraid *of* your child, you try to make sense out of the turmoil that characterizes your daily life, but it doesn't work. Nothing in your life has prepared you to live this way. You know you haven't earned it. You can't escape it, but your fear foretells the consequences of your teen's behavior. Fear breeds more fear, and it feels easier to escape into a bubble of denial or under a shroud of resignation than it does to confront your teen every day, all day long.

It's as if you hardly know your child anymore, and in a way, of course you are right. But in a more fundamental way, in spite of the behavior, the attitudes, the language you hate, you do still know your child. Some days it may feel as if you have lost your child completely, but all that has happened is that you have lost touch. You can't help but wonder what you don't know about her, why his grades keep going down, where she goes when she leaves the house. The way she dresses, the way he speaks to you are painful. Perhaps you try to intervene; perhaps you don't even try anymore. You suffer alone and silently because you don't want anyone to know, and you don't believe anyone could understand anyway. Somehow there is the feeling that if you don't tell anyone about it, maybe it isn't as bad as it seems.

Maybe this is just normal adolescence. Maybe you are blowing things out of proportion as your teen claims. Probably not.

We tell parents to remember: Using foul language and taking drugs may have become "normal" these days, but you don't have to like or accept either. Lying, manipulating, acting depressed, giving up, taking life-threatening risks may have become a part of "normal adolescence," but you know they don't make for happiness, success, and fulfilling relationships. You know all that, but it is difficult to figure out what to do about it when the rest of the world seems to be accepting, even encouraging, what you cannot. *You* can become a catalyst for change in your teen's life. You are not powerless.

The treasure that was his or her golden spirit is still there. It is hidden, but still it is there.

It Isn't Your Fault, But It Is Your Problem

The first step toward change is making the decision to change. It happens when parents like you realize, for whatever reason, that life just cannot go on like this. When they say, "I cannot live this way, and I cannot watch my child compromise his or her future any longer," then they are ready. That decision has enough potential energy and power to begin to enact change.

Because you cannot change your teen—indeed, no one can ever force change in another person, no matter what their age—you must begin by making changes within yourself. Making important changes within yourself will help you to establish the firm ground you will need in order to become the agent of change for your teen and family. Here are five things you can begin to do today. Accomplishing them may seem impossible just now, but try to have faith that as you work through this process, the benefits will become clearer and deeply personal for you.

1. Burst the bubble of denial that surrounds you—let yourself know what you really do know about your teen and your life, both the good and the bad.
2. Stop being afraid of your teen.
3. Make a commitment to yourself that guilt, blame, and shame can no longer define or even influence your actions.
4. Allow yourself the luxury of talking about what you are going through, how you feel about it, and about life in general. Find support from a spouse, friends, relatives, clergy, professionals, and other parents who have been or are going through this.
5. Promise yourself to exchange the desperate hope of lowered expectations and simple solutions for real hope for the future.

Denial Doesn't Change Reality

Denial is refusing to see, in spite of an inner, better knowledge, that the very reality you fear is indeed your reality. Denial only makes a situation get worse.

Our work with parents, therefore, usually begins with helping them realize that knowing what their teen is doing and how much trouble she may actually be in is better than not knowing, no matter how startling, how frightening, how unpleasant the truth may be. Parents who have changed their family life from their teen being in control to the parents being back in control tell us that getting rid of their denial was an important first step. Without that, they say, they would not have been strong enough to help themselves and their child. Turn back to the list of the behavior-attitudes typical of teens in turmoil on page 19 and check off which statements really do apply to your teen.

Facing the truth about your teen's actions and attitudes can be deeply distressing at first, but be assured that with this knowledge, your fear and uncertainty will turn into a decision to begin a process of change. When you stop minimizing, softening, or avoiding the truth, you will finally be free to take new steps that can catapult your family into positive change.

Denial may seem to provide comfort, but it is false, short-lived, and often the mother of regret. The longer you remain in denial, the deeper your teen's problems can become. You may be trying to convince yourself that things are not all that bad, and meanwhile, your teen may be suspended or expelled from school for her behavior. She could find herself caught in situations involving violence, drugs, promiscuous sex, or crime—situations way over her head. As your teen continues on a downward spiral you don't want to acknowledge, she may lose the last of the decent friends she has, fall deeper into drugs and alcohol, or even flirt with violence. For some kids the bottom of the spiral is a suicide attempt; for others, it's never really growing up, and at age forty they are still fighting adolescent battles with you—and the world.

Perhaps worst of all, when you finally wake up from denial, there may be years of remorse and guilt over what you *didn't* do, what you *didn't* allow yourself to see in your child. If you summon the courage to face your reality, and then do everything you can to foster change in yourself and your child, at the very least, you will know you did what you could.

Prisoners of Love, Prisoners of Fear

It is hard to admit that you are afraid *for* your child. It is harder still to admit you are afraid *of* your child. But, like an ominous, omnipresent drum roll, fear of one sort or another permeates your life. How could it not, when you don't know where this is all going. And how could it not, when you believe you can't do anything about it.

You may have felt that flip of fear in your gut when the $20 you put in your wallet this morning was gone after your son left for school. Maybe you feel it when you ask your thirteen-year-old daughter to unload the dishwasher and she rolls her eyes and doesn't do what you asked. So it seems easier not to confront your teen, and you convince yourself you must have been wrong about the money or unfair to ask her to do chores, even though in your heart you know you were right. It is easy to rationalize why you shouldn't confront your teen—and it stems mainly from being afraid. If you feel that kind of fear, it means your teen is in control.

One word parents often use to describe their situation is "prisoner." They don't dare go out of town because they can't leave their child alone, much less with a relative or a baby-sitter. They are called out of meetings to speak with school counselors. Their other children stop inviting friends home. The whole family has become a prisoner of fear—*for* the teen and *of* the teen.

Fear of your child and fear for your child are so intertwined they are hard to separate. Because your teen is frightened himself, he tries to "protect" himself; to do that, he feels he cannot allow you to come too close. He keeps you at a distance by intimidations, manipulations, lies, and threats. Of course you feel frightened, but if you remember that your teen is also frightened and trying to escape his own self-image, it will be easier for you to realize you dare not be afraid of your teen. Of course you are frightened for your teen because you can see how he is compromising his future and his own self-respect. That fear can motivate you to do what you can to begin to change the situation.

Guilt, Blame, and Shame

Even when parents finally let themselves "know what they know," they may still look for a simple explanation or solution to the problems in their child's and their family's life. You may be thinking, "It's her friends," or "It's ever since we moved," or "It's the drugs." Perhaps you tell yourself, "It's ever since he started wearing those clothes," or "It's the school, his girlfriend, peer pressure." Maybe you say, "It's her father, that stepmother. . . ."

You may not want to admit it, but realize that other parents may well be attributing their own child's downward spiral to his association with your child. In fact, the new friends, new lifestyle, and new attitudes and behavior are more *symptoms* of the problem than the problem itself.

Most parents experience some guilt for what their teen is doing or not doing. Questions, excuses, and recriminations follow one upon the other: "What did I do wrong?" "It's my fault!" "I should never have gotten divorced." "Is it really as bad as I think?" "He didn't mean to hit me." "Why can't the school do something?"

Try to remember this: You did not tell your child to stop going to school; you did not put that joint into her hands; you did not encourage him to drink and drive! It wasn't you who encouraged your child to give up on doing her homework, test the contents of your liquor cabinet, or start a fight in the middle school cafeteria. *But every time you make an excuse for your teen, you release him from taking responsibility for his own actions.* Each time you accept the guilt for her behavior, you send the message that you will make things okay that are not okay. Each time you wonder what *you* did wrong, you deny your teen the chance to grow up.

Oversimplifying complex problems will not lead to meaningful answers. More useful is to rethink your assumptions and reframe your questions about the situation you are in. Look at this list of questions and phrases parents often hear themselves thinking or saying. Are any of them familiar to you?

- "If things don't change . . ."
- "If she doesn't graduate high school . . ."
- "If only he wouldn't . . ."

- "If he is arrested . . ."
- "Why is this happening to me?"
- "Why does she do drugs?"

Sentences beginning with "if" and "why" are born of desperation and cannot bring you meaningful answers. The intent of "if" and "why" questions is to ascribe guilt or blame and imply a belief that history can be changed, but we all know better than that. Answers to "if" and "why" questions generally result in feelings of shame, blame, or guilt. "How" and "what" questions, however, immediately focus attention on what is really going on and on discovering how it can be changed or stopped.

Try reframing your phrases and questions about your teen into a "how" or "what" structure.

- "What do I do that plays into my child's craziness?"
- "What is the meaning behind my child's behavior?"
- "How do I make things change?"
- "How do I excuse, rationalize, justify?"
- "How do I let my child manipulate me?"

Parents usually tell me that when they force themselves to reframe their questions and statements to begin with "how" or "what," they suddenly find themselves feeling they can function and find solutions rather than feeling helpless and hopeless. Although it's only a first step, you may find that making this one simple conceptual change will help you to reorient yourself in a positive way to being your teen's parent. You will have taken a big step away from feeling like the embarrassed victim and prisoner—away from being the one who is to blame and the one who has to excuse and rationalize unacceptable behavior and attitudes. Instead, you will become the one who takes charge, who realizes that change in your teen can only happen if you change yourself first. It takes determination to focus your courage and resolve and make changes in yourself. But once you do, you can leave the place where your teen is in control.

Coming Out of Hiding

Being the parent (or stepparent, grandparent, or guardian) of a teen who is in turmoil is difficult and painful. Because parents tend to associate the teen's behavior with something they themselves did or did not do, they feel guilty. Because they love the child, they feel afraid. Because they feel guilty and afraid, it is easy to feel helpless, hopeless, and embarrassed. Conversations with friends at a cocktail party, business lunch, college reunion, or family gathering may make these feelings especially acute:

"Oh, yes. Elizabeth got 1480 on her SATs. She was just accepted to Brown, Early Decision."

"Chris? Oh, he's doing so well. He made all-state basketball as a junior."

"We're so proud of Jennie. She's only thirteen, but she's started to earn her own money by being a mother's helper."

Each comment is like a knife in your heart, turning slowly. Your mind races, trying to think up something to say if anyone asks you about your daughter. "Meagan? She's fine . . ." you manage to say with a vague smile. But in your mind's eye you are picturing your once-beautiful daughter with her eyebrow ring and terrible clothes and the boyfriend whom you don't want in your house but whom you can't stop your daughter from seeing, much less from sleeping with.

"Matt? Well, he's just started at the alternative school . . . but we think it might work out better for him." Of course, you don't mention that this may be his last chance because he has been suspended so many times for fighting. And you don't say that you are extremely worried because he spends all his time playing violent computer games, and you don't know what else he may be doing.

How can you even think of introducing your middle-school child to anyone when he looks so ridiculous and his language is unbearable? How do you explain to someone whose respect you value that your daughter had to be sent to a program for "troubled teens"?

Remember: Your embarrassment is grounded in pain, your fear in the reality of the situation, your shame in anguish, your hurt in sorrow. None of those feelings makes you a bad person or a failure; they only mean you are living with a teen who has taken control of his family and lost sight of his future. That can change.

I think of Melody, Robert's mother, who told me she felt mortified to have to "confess" to her old friend and college roommate that her son was at a program for troubled teens. "Then Ginny looked at me and smiled vaguely. 'Really,' she said. 'So is my daughter.'" Keep in mind that someone else at your convention, gym, or swim club, someone else jogging along the path next to you with less energy than he wants to have, is going through what you are going through. The details of your situations are different, of course, but the feelings are similar. When you allow yourself to give up your denial, your guilt, and your embarrassment, you will find many people who know what you are talking about and who will sympathize, empathize, and support you as you make your decision to change life in your family. Beginning to talk about what is going on in your home will not help to change the situation immediately, but it will ease your pain. It will help you to clarify your thoughts and gain courage. It will help you focus your energy. It may also help you to locate the professional help you and your teen and family may need.

It takes time to let yourself know what you know; it takes courage to stand up to your teen. It takes inner strength to give up your fear and let yourself act instead of react to your teen's attitudes and behavior. You can do this.

The Paradox of Loving But Not Liking Your Teen

It took Marianne, Randy's mother, several months of therapy to be able to admit that although she loved her son, she did not like him. Considering what she had been living through with him, I could easily understand her feelings. Parental love may be unconditional, but liking, admiring, and respecting your child are not. Those feelings must be earned. It was important for Marianne to realize that her son had not earned her good opinion for many months and that what she really disliked so much were his behavior and attitudes.

Of course, the paradox of loving but not liking your child is fraught with complications and deep emotional pain. Admitting those feelings to yourself frees you from a terrible inner conflict; in fact, it is probably healthy for you and for your relationship (especially in the future) with your child. It makes sense that you don't like what your teen is doing! Keep in mind that your child's behavior probably does not mirror his or her real self—that now-hidden treasure you miss so much. The behavior and attitudes you see are covering up and overwhelming the loving child you remember. It is this awareness that can allow you to make the necessary differentiation between "loving" and "not liking" your child these days.

Changing Desperate Hope to Real Hope

No matter what your situation is, feeling truly hopeful probably feels about as realistic as climbing Mt. Everest. How often do you sigh to yourself, "If only . . ." or "What can I do besides hope?" Those kinds of statements reflect that you have taken on certain aspects of your teen's worldview. You, too, have considered giving up. What that means is that your teen is in control—not just of the family, but even of your own emotions. Your love and the real hope you still harbor, perhaps secretly, can serve to propel you to do what you have to do for yourself and, ultimately, for your child.

I think back to families I have worked with and the desperation parents have felt, desperation that made their love almost stand in the way of achieving change. Margaret, who was a corporate executive but who could not stop crying the first time we spoke, told me she would do "anything, *anything*," for her son. I recognized immediately her love for him, but I told her that she had to give up her desperation because it robbed her of most of her energy and all her personal power. Her desperation gave her son Sam all the room he needed to lie to her, to manipulate her, and most of all to propel himself along his self-sabotaging path. Jim, a teacher, confided that he was terrified his son "would go down the drain, just like his mother." Jim had become so desperate for a solution that he would have accepted almost anything anyone had offered him as solace.

But if you can overcome the desperation, the rewards will come. As I sit here writing these pages, my phone has rung seven times with kids on the other end just wanting to say "Hi" and to tell me how they are doing. Each is in college, when once their parents despaired they would ever graduate high school. They all have friends who are honest, caring, and ambitious like they are. They do their work because they have the courage to care about themselves, their futures, and their families. How I remember when I first met each of them! Heavens!—how they looked, how they talked, how they acted! And how much fear and emotional pain they felt. How desperate were their parents!

No one besides yourself and those you love and who love you can restore real hope and a belief in the future. Both are crucial to beginning to act now.

It Happens in Good Families, Too

Many professionals and laypeople say that "good" families don't produce "bad" kids, but my experience does not bear that out. Many families really do "do things the right way" with their kids. In these families there is a strong family structure and connection, no matter what the makeup of the family: two-parent, single-parent, latchkey, or blended. Drug use, excessive alcohol consumption, foul language, dishonesty, and disrespect are neither practiced nor tolerated. Chores and responsibilities are equally divided. Actions are met with consequences. Home is filled with love. Still, one child somehow takes control of the family and perhaps even begins a downward spiral.

Psychology is sometimes seen as the science that relates past to present, cause to effect. My own education and experience, however, have taught me to be wary of those ideas. Yes, we are all the products of our own personal, family, and cultural histories, but those histories can never completely explain why or how any of us become who and what we are. Neither you nor anyone else will manage to find the clue to the mystery of exactly what, if anything, caused this child of yours to be the way he or she is now. There are always too many factors involved to allow you to be able to find a direct, clear, provable cause-effect relationship between family situations and resulting behavior. Yes, as a parent you made mistakes—didn't we all! You also did a lot that was good and right. But now, how you got to where you are makes much less difference than where you go with it.

You Are the First Agent of Change

Change frightens many people, but as you admit to yourself the reality of your status quo, then change must be welcome. Even if your teen, no matter how old, is just beginning to cause you concern, your status quo is not the family life you had hoped for. If your teen is already falling into a downward spiral, then change must be better than the turmoil you and your teen experience every day. Life in your family need not go on the way it is.

In order to change, you must define for yourself how you play into your teen's games. There are many possibilities. You may be too permissive, you may be helping your child to play the victim, allowing your child to intimidate you, getting your child to act out your anger for you. Perhaps you are always excusing her actions, never obliging her to take responsibilities, or most of all, not letting and requiring your child to grow up and take responsibility for his or her own actions and attitudes.

Change is a process; it takes courage, work, patience, fortitude, and belief in yourself, in your teen, and in the future. At the beginning of this new phase in your life, change will depend more on you than on your teen. You are the first agent of change.

Here is an image that has helped many people resituate themselves in the context of the chaos and fear that define their lives and their kids' lives as they begin the process of change. When you watch a video and you press the "pause" button, you find that the actor, stopped in midsentence, has a distorted, outlandish expression on his face. It's no wonder, for you have stopped an emotion, something that is by its very nature in motion. As soon as you press "play" again, the distorted expression moves and becomes real again and therefore excited or sad or frightened.

Because of the way you are living now, you may feel you want to hit the "stop" or "pause" or "rewind" button in your life to make your life less painful. Even if you could press such a button, you would only produce a distorted picture of reality. Pretending that there is a "stop," "pause," or "rewind" button in real life is fooling yourself in a dangerous way. You are in a process that has no "pause" button, no "rewind" and no "fast-forward" button. It is frightening because you don't know the end or how long it will take to get there. From where you are now, all the "futures" look ominous.

Sometimes people say that kids have to hit rock bottom before they will agree to change, but I think not. And it surely isn't necessary for parents. You don't have to wait until your whole family is in crisis, your career is on the brink of disaster, and your emotional life is in tatters before you act. You can decide to act at the first signs of trouble with your child. When you first begin to wonder who is in control of the family, it is time to act. When your teen begins to seem like someone you don't know anymore, it is time to act. When you no longer trust or respect your child, it is time to act. When you know life in your family is not okay, it is time to begin to change what needs to be changed in your life and in your attitude toward your child. If you do, you may be able to stop the downward spiral before it goes too far.

Using Your Feelings to Help Evaluate the Situation

No matter how recent or long-standing your concerns about your teen, no matter how moderate or serious your teen's behavior, the sooner you accept *your* reality for what it is, recognize how you play into it, and then change your actions and your perspective, the sooner you will find that life doesn't have to keep on being the way it is. Our experience is that most parents really do know and understand the situation in their family, but admitting it to themselves and to others in the family takes on a power all its own. It may be hard to face the truth about your teen and your interactions with him, but that is your best option right now. Clarity and honesty about your teen is vital. Remember: Pretending things aren't the way you know they are saps your energy, clouds your judgment, and keeps you locked in your status quo. In order to be able to initiate change, you must understand the situation as clearly as possible. This checklist will help you do that.

CHECKLIST FOR PARENTS:
HOW DO YOU FEEL? WHAT DO YOU DO?

Check the box next to each question for which your answer is "yes."

☐ Do you hate your kid's friends?

☐ Does the way your child looks embarrass you? Anger you?

☐ Do you think your child is using drugs? Alcohol?

☐ Do you feel as though you are supporting an industry of professionals such as therapists, tutors, counselors, etc.?

☐ Are your other children scared of and/or embarrassed by the problem one?

☐ Are you missing work time, meetings, or activities with your other children to go to school conferences, talk to teachers, guidance counselors, social workers, therapists?

☐ Do you jump every time the phone rings?

☐ Are you and your spouse or partner fighting more often? Is everyone in the family fighting more often?

☐ Are you scared *for* your child? Are you scared *of* your child?

☐ Have you or your spouse become a policeman in your house?

☐ Do you feel as if your home has become your prison?

☐ Are you missing money, jewelry, and other valuables, or liquor?

☐ Do you feel as if you are walking on eggshells to avoid confrontations?

☐ Is your phone bill suspiciously high? Are there 900 number calls?

☐ Do you often find your child crying alone?

☐ Is your child destroying the house, especially his or her own room?

☐ Do you have trouble sleeping because you are worrying about your child?

☐ Do you worry about your child's sexual activity?

☐ Does your child refuse to let you enter his room? Do you avoid entering your child's room?

☐ Do you obey your child? Does he or she obey you?

☐ Do you shell out more and more money each week? Do you know where it goes?

☐ Have you lowered your expectations for your child?

☐ Do you think or feel that you are overreacting? Do you accuse yourself of overreacting? Do others accuse you of it?

☐ Do you feel threatened emotionally or physically?

☐ Do you believe your kid is trying to get caught?

☐ Are you afraid to leave your teen home while you go on a business trip or vacation?

❏ Do you often feel stressed, dazed, confused, anxious?
❏ Do you feel you just don't have the concentration and energy to do your job?
❏ Do you second-guess every thought you have or every move you make concerning your child?
❏ Do you feel that you are an intelligent person but that nothing you say or do ever seems right?
❏ Do you find yourself wondering if your teen's problems really could be everyone else's fault?
❏ Does life seem out of control?

Review your responses. The emotional answers to each question may be different from the intellectual ones. For example, you may feel frightened *of* your child, but rationalize it by telling yourself you are only frightened *for* him or her. Think about your answers, and then change those you need to so they more accurately reflect your feelings and the reality of your situation. This is not a test, just a tool to help you build a more realistic picture of your family as it is now. Letting yourself know the truth is a crucial early step in your process of change.

Once you have reviewed your answers, you can evaluate what they mean. If none of these questions bothered you and you found yourself asking "What?" over and over again, or if the concepts seemed irrelevant, then your situation probably isn't particularly serious.

If, however, many of the questions made your stomach flip, your heart pound, or your thoughts race, or if you could hear yourself saying, "Yes, but," then pay attention! Whether you felt frightened or infuriated, please do not ignore what you thought and felt as you read these questions.

If you worked on the questionnaire with your spouse or someone else close to you and your child, you may find your answers are very different. Talk about it, but if you find yourselves arguing over your differences, that should tell you something important: This kid is good at creating tension and division.

Now add up your responses. Keep in mind that this is not a scientific study, but an opportunity for you to clarify your situation by seeing your feelings and actions as they are. If you checked 5 to 10 boxes, you should be concerned about your teen. Pay close attention to what you see, think, and feel in all your interactions with your teen, so that you will begin to develop a new, more honest picture of your situation.

If you checked between 11 and 15 boxes, there could be real trouble in your family right now. It is probably time to take some direct action, such as checking in with your teen's teachers, counselors, or clergy. You may want to speak to the parents of your teen's friends as well, to see how they are doing and if a united effort among all of you might help all the families get back on track.

If you checked more than 15 boxes, there is no time to waste in making changes in your family or getting help for your teen. We would advise you to turn to Part IV to begin finding a program for your teen.

If you have found the checklists in this chapter upsetting, it is probably because it is difficult and painful to admit to the truth of what your teen is doing and what has happened to your life and your family's life. But please take comfort in knowing that you have made an important first step in changing those things. Now that you have begun to face what you know, you can discover the courage to look at more of the picture, and then see how to change it.

Chapter 3 ✺

Taking Stock:
The Big Five of Acting Out

A clear understanding of your teen cannot be complete without a discussion of five of the ways teens act out, causing constant distress and concern in most parents. Of course, you know what they are: using drugs and alcohol, sexual activity, the use of four-letter words, the "images" that teens take on to try to seem to be someone they are not, and depression. Like thorns in your side that are a constant source of pain, these five kinds of teen behavior can come to define your life, because they define your teen's life. Increasing your understanding of the meaning of these five behaviors will help you to see how to help your teen give up these ways of acting out.

You live with a teen who is The Good, The Bad, and The Ugly, all rolled into one being. The Good is mainly the part you remember from her childhood. The Bad and The Ugly are who you mainly live with now. Part of what makes your life nowadays so painful and exhausting is the discrepancy between what was, what is, and what you know could be.

Leslie and I find that, whether seeking therapy or educational consulting, parents we work with generally want help with each of these as isolated problems, believing that eliminating this or that behavior will make life better. We each believe that these "problems" are more accurately understood as symptoms of the kinds of deeper teen issues discussed in Chapter 1: search for identity and feelings of failure, demoralization, and fear. Drug or alcohol use, new "images," the implied violence of most four-letter words, sexual promiscuity, and depression are rarely isolated behaviors of otherwise well-functioning teens.

Drugs and Alcohol

You don't need to hear the same litany of diagnostic criteria you can find in newspapers, infomercials, or from your local PTA to determine if your teen is drinking or doing drugs. You know the basic idea: If everything in your child's life is going well, if you and your teen communicate on a variety of topics in many ways, if your teen seems healthy and happy, and if school is going fine, then drugs and alcohol are probably not a problem. It is true that some teens seem to be able to keep alcohol and/or drug use in perspective, occasionally drinking a beer or smoking a joint at a party while maintaining order in their lives. Some parents and teens seem to function well enough in that lifestyle (although it is against the law), but it is important to remember how quickly and easily something harmless can turn unsafe. Drinking or using drugs combined with driving is always a dangerous mix. When teens (or adults) are even a little bit high, their judgment about any number of activities, from sex to driving, is not as solid as it might otherwise be. I have met many parents who were comfortable with what they thought was their teen's "experimenting" with alcohol and drugs, only to be shocked when they found out just how much of each their teen was really doing.

There is no measuring stick by which you can determine for sure if your teen has a problem with drugs and/or alcohol, but there are signs that can tip you off that your teen's use of alcohol and/or drugs (including household products such as inhalants) is a real problem. If grades suddenly plummet, friends change, money is missing from your wallet, or your teen's behavior becomes strange, you and your teen face serious problems that need immediate attention. Probably the best indicator is if your teen somehow begins to seem unfamiliar to you—not that kid you always knew—something is probably up, and yes, it may be drugs, alcohol, or inhalants.

You probably know already that simply saying "no" isn't a solution. Prevention programs and ads are seldom useful in scaring or deterring teens from experimenting, and some teens react by becoming more interested in drugs and alcohol! Some programs give teens information and advice they distrust, and some teens decide to try drugs out of spite.

The one thing no one seems to want to tell you when they advise you to "talk to your teen about doing drugs or alcohol" is that kids are likely to lie about those subjects. Kids lie that they have done more and harder drugs just about as often as they lie that they don't do drugs at all. There is a joke among professionals that you don't ask an alcoholic to tell you about the amount of his or her alcohol consumption. To ask someone who is embedded in dishonesty to give the details of the lies he or she protects most in the world just doesn't make any sense. The same principle applies to teens and drug, inhalant, and alcohol use.

If you feel you have to ask your teen about his or her drug and alcohol use, expect a lie. If you feel you have to ask your teen about his or her drug and alcohol use, you already know the answer. If you already know, there are professionals and programs to help him or her and you deal with the problem. (See Part IV.)

If you are still trying to determine whether your teen's use of drugs or alcohol is occasional or is a bigger problem, here are a few of my rules of thumb: If you are in communication with your teen, you will be able to judge if there is a problem; if you are not, become concerned. If you are concerned, there is probably a good reason to be. If someone in the community has talked to you or warned you about your teen's drug or alcohol abuse, take that information seriously. If you feel or think your teen is acting secretly or suspiciously, don't ignore it.

You may feel fairly sure your kid isn't doing drugs, and you may be right. You also may be wrong. Many parents decide to try drug testing to determine whether their teen is using drugs, but that is not a very good way of finding out. First of all, as soon as you announce to your teen that you plan to test her for drugs, you have acknowledged you are not in control, which, of course, you and your daughter knew anyway. Second, if your son readily agrees to testing, it's quite possible he is trying to manipulate you out of actually doing the test. (Sure, you can try the "surprise" tactic, but if you have to resort to that, you already know your answer!) Third, drug testing just isn't all that accurate. (I remember Helene telling me that her daughter had warned her that she had been eating lots of poppy seeds, so the drug test might be positive. "But you know the truth, right?" her daughter had cajoled.) And fourth, kids have lots of ways of flushing out their systems so the drugs won't show. I have known teens who have passed drug tests even when they were high at the time of the test.

Teens try to dilute or mask drugs by drinking large quantities of Gatorade, Golden Seal, tea, vinegar, and even just lots and lots of water. Amy gave her father some nice, cold urine out of the refrigerator to test, somehow thinking he would not be the wiser (fortunately, he was). I have heard that "clean" urine is available to buy—even by mail order. If your teen uses drugs and doesn't plan to stop, testing won't stop him either. It will just make him go farther underground. Testing for drugs does not bring sobriety!

Street drugs and beer are not all there is to worry about. If your child wants lots and lots of whipped cream, he may be doing "whippets"—getting high by inhaling the propellant gas in the aerosol can. Some kids even drink cough syrup or mouthwash to get an alcohol high (that happens at boarding schools, we hear). If you find a stack of dust masks in your daughter's room, she may be using hallucinogens and trying to intensify the effect by simultaneously inhaling Vicks VapoRub. Experts estimate there are as many as 100 substances in your household that kids can use as inhalants. Getting rid of the cough syrup or the household cleaner or forbidding their use won't solve the problem because your teen will likely as not find another way to get high. Remember, the "problem" is more likely the symptom of another, more profound problem. Kids who want, or believe they "need," to get high will find a way to do it.

If you notice your teenager buys or asks you to buy extraordinary quantities of any particular product, he or she may be using it to get high or to cover up that he or she is using other drugs. If you find drug paraphernalia, it probably means your kid is the one who is using it; she is not storing it for someone else.

If you use drugs—even just smoke marijuana occasionally—or drink too much alcohol, your child already knows or will find out. You will have a hard time explaining why it is okay for you but not for him. And if you get high or drunk with your teen, she will not take seriously your advice that she should not get high or drunk with her friends.

Within teen culture, using drugs is cool, having drugs and being known as someone who has drugs is even more cool. Dealing is really cool. Kids sometimes try to "buy" friends by being the one who always has drugs. Getting into the drug scene can change a kid's rating on the popularity scale. Lots of girls use drugs to be skinny-thin. Kids use drugs to get them through exams. They drink to get over their shyness, to be able to be sexual when they really don't want to. Teens who are secure in their identity and relationships don't need to use drugs.

You want your adolescent to be sober, but let's think through why that is such an important goal. You may think that if your teen would just stop using drugs everything would be okay. It isn't so; whatever made your son think he needed to be more "cool" or convinced him to start drinking or dealing drugs remains a problem until it is solved in real ways. Neither drugs nor alcohol can get rid of whatever was making him churn inside (maybe it helped him not care so much, for the moment, but that always wears off). If your teen lies and manipulates, doing drugs and drinking is a part of it, and the lies and manipulations support the drug or alcohol use. If your teen is failing at just about everything he tries, then the grandiosity he feels and portrays because he has drugs, as well as the drug-induced high (or low) can easily convince him that doing drugs is the cool, the expeditious, and the "right" thing to do. If your teen is sacrificing relationships with you and others he cares about to get drugs or alcohol, he is in trouble and needs professional help. Just getting him off the drugs or alcohol cannot bring him or you enough to create real, internalized, and lasting change. He needs to become sober in his heart if he is to remain sober in behavior. Just raising his self-esteem, especially in ways that have little or no substance, will not solve the problem.

Your teen needs to be sober. Until he or she is sober, there can be no real change in the way he or she is living. Sobriety is more an attitude that influences behavior than it is a thing unto itself. There are no quick and easy paths to sobriety for a teen (or an adult) who does not want it with his or her heart and soul.

Kids who smoke marijuana occasionally and do well in every other aspect of their lives do not need to go to rehab. Often a serious conversation will be enough to help that teen gain a deeper understanding of the meaning and implications of illicit drug use. But for kids for whom drugs, inhalants, and/or alcohol have or are becoming the be-all and end-all of life, rehab can help. Unfortunately, however, enrolling your son or daughter in a rehab program does not guarantee or even imply sobriety. Often kids agree to go just to get their parents off their back or because a school, college, or the courts have mandated it. It is easy enough for them just to sit it out or comply outwardly. Sobriety is a commitment to oneself. Rehab can be a means toward that end but cannot do the job without your teen's commitment—and yours.

The only way to get kids who are abusing themselves with alcohol, inhalants, and/or drugs to recognize that they are abusing themselves and that it isn't necessary or better to do so is for them to get sober first. Physical sobriety is easier to attain than emotional and psychological sobriety. Rehabs try to use physical sobriety to get the teen ready to become honest and begin to deal with the more profound issues. Sometimes kids just need to grow up, but waiting to find out can be dangerous—too dangerous by a long way.

The first step toward sobriety usually has to come from parents. It is a rare exception when a teen mired in the self-destruction of drug and/or alcohol use admits he has a problem, needs help to solve it, and focuses his will and courage to overcome it. Remember, kids lie about drug and alcohol use. They also need to create a structure of lies to support their lies and their problem. You do not have to buy into that house of cards. You may find that your child yells, screams, and threatens you if you do not agree to believe the lies any longer. Never mind: Drug and alcohol abuse ruins futures and kills kids both spiritually and physically. Sometimes the kids are too scared and too lost to ask you directly for help. But you can be the catalyst. Your teen may well be looking to you to be the parent, the one who says, "ENOUGH!"

Your own integrity and self-respect are your best tools for catapulting your teen into an attitude that makes sobriety an absolute part of his or her life. It is true that one's actions speak louder than words.

Red Flags:
Warning Signs You Must Not Ignore!

The following feelings you experience as well as behaviors and attitudes you observe in your adolescent are signs that he or she may have serious, even life-threatening problems. If this list defines, or even suggests, your child, you should immediately seek the help and advice of a professional such as a member of the clergy, counselor, psychologist, or psychiatrist.

IF YOUR TEEN:

- Suddenly changes friends, and you get a bad feeling about them or your teen won't let you meet them
- Loses all interest in school and his/her grades plummet
- Runs away frequently, sometimes for days at a time
- Significantly changes his or her sleeping and/or eating patterns
- Exhibits a "don't-give-a-damn" attitude
- Spends hours and hours at the computer—especially on the Internet or playing violent video games
- Suddenly loses interest in everything
- Displays sudden bursts of violence or rage
- Changes his or her behavior toward the family pet or other animals
- Procures a weapon
- Writes dark, depressing poetry or songs or draws pictures depicting death, suicide, and/or violence
- Begins self-mutilation (cigarette burns, cuts, carving words or symbols on his/her body, self-tattoos, self-pierces) which he/she may attempt to hide with long-sleeved clothing, even in warm weather
- Begins to give his or her possessions away
- Engages in suicidal and/or criminal ideation, talk, or action

OR IF YOU:

- Find evidence of torturing animals
- Find evidence or even suspect fire-setting
- Find that money and/or jewelry is missing or that the liquor cabinet is empty
- Feel your gut flip every time you talk to your teen
- Feel that nothing makes sense any more

   Get help immediately. Do not ignore, excuse, rationalize, or justify these important warning signs!

Images—Or Are They Costumes?

There is nothing particularly unnatural about having an image—we all do. An image serves as a mediator between our inner selves and the person we present to the world. The problem for teens begins when they use the image to barricade themselves into an emotional fortress, suffocating themselves emotionally and psychologically, never articulating or even acknowledging real feelings. The image is a teen's first line of defense created to keep the world and feelings at a "safe" distance. Understanding its meaning can be valuable information for you and for the other adults in your teen's life.

The costumes teens wear are image-specific (skater, gangbanger, etc.). Teens use their clothing to show what sort of music (sometimes even which specific bands) they like, which then sends silent messages to their peers. Images are a way teens have of avoiding the risk of personal self-definition as well as a way of keeping someone who seems threatening at a safe distance. Kids who feel intimidated by one group—for example, jocks or gangbangers—may feel some security in being known as one of the "alternatives" or "skaters."

The costumes teens wear tell more than they often realize. The outfits and their trappings (chains, studs, certain haircuts and colors, etc.) announce to the world: "This is what I want to be" (physically bigger than I am, threatening, sophisticated and wealthy, already grown up, too cool for anyone, don't need to care about anything). Sometimes, however, they also say, "This is what I am and hate" (promiscuous, slovenly, a failure, a clown, an outcast, alternative). The costume says a lot, but at a more profound level the message is a far cry from what a teen means it to say. The real message is "I am afraid. Keep your distance." The image is a costume, and so an illusion. Like all illusions, it lacks substance, permanence, and context.

All too often adults buy the image package and believe the chimera to be the real thing. Too often adults are too intimidated by the costume and the energy the teen uses to maintain it to look beneath the wrapping for the person hiding there. Often adults accept too easily kids' statements that they are seeking their identity and individuality, forgetting that there is little individuality or personal identity in looking just like everyone else in that clique. There is little individuality or personal identity in being a hanger-on or a groupie. Worst of all, though, is when the kids themselves begin to believe in their images and lose all connection with who they really are as individuals.

For many parents, the image their child now projects is the most unnerving aspect of living with their teen. It is the costume and its concomitant attitude and language that makes your child distant and unfamiliar to you. The costumes are more immediate and obvious than the lies, manipulations, or even drug use that your child may well be able to hide, or nearly hide, from you. The costume is right in front of you. You have to look at it every day—and you probably paid for it!

Many parents have even helped their child design the image they later learned to despise. Rick's dad began by wanting to help his son "fit in," and treated him to the new clothes and a tattoo Rick convinced him were essential to having friends and being accepted. The eyebrow piercing was a reward for some small accomplishment no one could even remember later. "But now," as Rick's father put it, "my son looks like a clown."

Allie's mother, Gretchen, gave in and bought her the tiny tank tops and skimpy shorts because she was simply worn down by her daughter's constant browbeating. Gretchen told me she thought things would calm down if she bought them. But in my office, she admitted her rationalization had gotten her nowhere, and all she could do was cry about her beautiful daughter who now looked so ugly and so cheap.

Adolescence is a time when almost everyone feels too tall or too short, too thin or too fat, not smart enough or too smart to be popular. Kids acquiesce to peer pressure based upon an imaginary set of standards set by some amorphous someone who is equally unsure and seeking acceptance by the group. Adolescent images create, fuel, and are the dupes of an industry that feeds off the age-appropriate desire to fit in. For some kids the pressure becomes so intense that the drive to look a certain way becomes the goal of their lives. I remember Emily, who, at fifteen, shaved most of her head and dyed blue the bits of hair she had left. Why did she do it? "I hated who I was," she told me. It made sense to her, because being softly beautiful on the outside was intolerable when she felt mean, ugly, and selfish inside.

In our culture it's hard to be a boy who is small of stature, not to speak of sensitive and perhaps artistic instead of athletic. Boys almost never like to talk about how much teasing they have to take if they don't happen to be physically large and athletic, but they suffer a lot of it. So do large girls. That they want to find some means to escape the teasing makes it easier to understand why some work so hard to change their appearance. With the proper haircut and clothes, a few chains, studs, piercing, and maybe a tattoo, even a relatively small boy can look sort of menacing. With the right hair color, jewelry, and a short enough skirt, a tall girl can pretend she is really a model.

Prohibiting your child from dressing the way he believes he must is not likely to be successful. You won't gain anything by making her sneak the clothes out of the house and change at a friend's house or at school. Trying to reason with your child is rarely more useful because his perceived "need" for the image is not really rational. The need is grounded in his lack of a real and individual identity. He does feel threatened without his image as a "protective shield" against the world, and in a strange way, he is right.

The costume becomes a first and favorite battleground because it is right there and it has come to symbolize something for you, too. As the costume becomes more elaborate and more costly—and in one way or another you are paying vast sums for something you can't stand—you notice how much it has taken over your child's personality. Suddenly you begin to feel its intimidating power, too.

But if you say how much you hate the costume, or worse yet, say you are not willing to buy anything else for it, you may be screamed at and told how little you understand. You can refuse to buy anything else for the costume, but you may have concerns that your daughter would steal the clothing or steal the money for it from your wallet or someone else's.

If your teen puts extreme pressure on you to buy more and more for the image, that is your clue that the image is taking over his or her identity. At that point, it will be hard to withstand the pressure your daughter or son will put on you because from inside the emotional fortress the teen believes he or she needs that image. But your son or daughter also needs you not to buy into that.

If everything else in your teen's life is in order and the image is not taking over his or her life, it may be okay. You will have to determine just how important the image is and what it means to your teen. Again, your relationship to your teen and your ability to communicate are the keys to knowing whether or not your teen's image is a serious concern.

Depression and Demoralization

When parents see their child desperately unhappy, apparently sad to the core of her being, and almost unable to function, their anger at the teen's behavior usually dissipates. Most parents would do anything—*anything*—to make that child happy again. Seeing the pain of depression is not something parents can rationalize away like outlandish clothing or even foul language. It is no wonder that parents of depressed teens are among the first to seek professional help for their child.

We can deepen our understanding of depression if we recategorize it as a symptom of a problem rather than the problem itself. If, as Swiss psychologist C. G. Jung suggested, the psyche, like the physical body, seeks to heal itself, we can think of depression as a profound expression of a deeply felt realization that the way one is living life is not okay. Depression in an otherwise healthy and recently well-functioning adolescent can be a sign that at some level, the teen recognizes he or she is in trouble.

If we rename depression demoralization, we see a more optimistic picture. Looking carefully at the life of a demoralized teen, we can see that it makes sense that he acts in ways that we think of as depressed. Martin, for example, was depressed, and had good reasons to feel that way. He was failing in school, unable to deal with peer pressure, overwhelmed by family pressure, and feeling lonely and terrified of his future. Caught between his actions and inaction, his falling grades and run-ins with his teachers made his life more ominous daily.

Depressed—demoralized—teens take all the wrong routes out, lying, manipulating, feeling resentful, and using drugs, sex, and anger to alleviate their pain and suffering. Ironically, the demoralization is the most real and honest feeling in their lives. Changing the way they have been living and relating to their world and their families and friends rarely occurs to these teens, but it would be the best solution to their problems.

It is difficult, if not almost impossible, for a parent, caught up in the fear and chaos of living with a depressed teen, to recognize that anger, depression, and wild, out-of-control behavior are not very different from each other; they are simply different ways of manifesting similar feelings. Many very angry adolescents appear to be depressed, and some overtly angry kids are deeply demoralized. Some wild, wild teens are trying to drown out their feelings of demoralization by seeking one rush after another.

Whether meeting a teen as a therapist or educational consultant, I am glad when a teen who is trashing his or her life recognizes the situation for what it is and has the appropriate symptomatic response by becoming "depressed." It tells me that she is somehow aware of the meaning of her actions and attitudes. Amy, weeping almost uncontrollably in one of our first sessions, made it immediately clear she knew how demoralized she was, though she denied it at first. She did not know how, nor did she have the courage, to express it directly. Her solution had been to keep her life moving at a fast enough pace that she hoped not to have feelings or at least not to have to notice any. It took some time and effort for her to recognize how she had used her focus on dieting and promiscuous sex to try to escape her feelings.

Within the context of the family, depression has still another equally debilitating characteristic. Depression is powerful and controlling. A depressed person often controls the whole atmosphere and emotional life of the family, whether she does it consciously or not.

Many teens find that depression is a wonderful means for hiding and indulging their feeling and fear of being fragile and incompetent. Everyone becomes afraid of the depression itself, afraid it might get worse, afraid of what it might lead to and standards, expectations, and hopes for the demoralized teen are lowered and lowered.

When I first met Allison and her father, David, it was hard to tell who thought her more fragile. However, as David began to describe life with his daughter, I could see how she used her depression to control her environment and her father. She even threatened him with it: "I won't be able to stand it if you . . . I'm so scared I might . . ." She had learned she could make her father panic by threatening another bout of depression. No one could reasonably expect very much from someone like Allison, who seemed too depressed to function!

For many teens, depression becomes a great way to remain helpless, which also means hopeless, and to keep people and feelings at a distance. It is a great way to avoid the anger that churns inside and frightens teens who worry what violence they might do if their anger ever surfaced.

Four-Letter Words

If your teen really wants to get you angry, to intimidate you, to hurt you, he or she is probably going to tell you to "Fuck off!" Most parents agree that they experience being told to "Fuck off!" as insulting, but if you think about it, what it really expresses is your teen's inability to say what he or she means—and that may be because he or she really doesn't even know. Fuck is such a wonderful word because at once it can mean anything—and everything—and nothing. But it isn't so much the word (or even all the others you hear) as the tone. I cannot remember ever hearing a teen say "Fuck" and thinking it sounded like an endearment.

Because most parents object to these epithets, kids who feel powerless think they can gain an edge on you by using the language that offends you, that will cut you to the core. I often think of Michelle, who asked me in our first session if kids were allowed to swear. I laughed and answered, "Fuck, no!" I had informed her, in two words, that she couldn't intimidate me with her language. That is not, however, a method I would recommend to parents! Generally, it is not useful for you to mimic your teen's vocabulary—and that includes words like "dude," "phat," or "wicked," and especially drug jargon.

You don't have to like the language your teen uses or even pretend that you do. However, if you react to swear words every time your teen uses one, you are encouraging him or her in a small act of defiance because you demonstrate she can get to you whenever she chooses. Dolphins are trained by ignoring bad behavior and praising good behavior. You might want to try using that technique on your teen. Many four-letter words have more or less entered our everyday vocabulary; considering what else is going on in your home, you may be best advised to concentrate your energy elsewhere.

You do however, have the right to say that you do not wish to hear four-letter words all the time. A teen who is just trying to act grown-up or cool will probably respect your wishes. A teen who is using this to test you will probably continue to do so. A teen who doesn't care about very much beyond being angry and making you angry will do what he or she must to create conflict. The four-letter words may be reflective of your teen's level of frustration and anger. You must decide how to react based on your own situation and how much you dislike the words.

There are two other "four-letter words" in teen language that I find to be distressing: "like" and "just." Those two words are the great minimizers. Teens use "just" when they want you to think whatever they did isn't so bad, and "like" when they want to mean that nothing is ever really anything. Suddenly there is almost no meaning in the communication. While these two words may seem innocuous, pay attention when your teen's use of them is primarily to manipulate or minimize.

Sexual Promiscuity

It is more common for parents to notice and be concerned about a daughter's sexual activity and promiscuity than a son's, but we all know that both teenage boys and girls engage in sexual activity and promiscuity. HIV is not gender-specific, nor are most other sexually transmitted diseases. Drugs, alcohol, and sex very often go together. Teens who are high or drunk are less likely to remember (or think it important) to use a condom.

The reasons teens become sexually promiscuous and the psychological and emotional havoc it wreaks upon them are about the same for boys as for girls. Most of what you read above about drugs is equally applicable to sexual promiscuity. Kids lie about it and brag about it; they use it to seem cool, grown up, and to be self-destructive.

It is unlikely your teen will tell you about what he or she does sexually. If your teen thinks you will condemn her for her sexual activity, there is little chance she will come to you for advice and help. It is impossible for you to "make your teen stop" by imposing restrictions on his activities or the people he sees. Like drug and alcohol use, sexual promiscuity is not an isolated act. It does not bespeak a teen who feels good about herself and her relationships. Teens often feel or pretend to feel grown up because they have had sex, and surely that message is delivered often enough in adolescent culture. Some teens, especially younger ones, just want to get it over with, so they agree to lose their virginity at frighteningly young ages. Kids get teased if they don't have sex, but ostracized if they become promiscuous.

Promiscuous sex can be a way for teens to try to control others, seem more grown up, and, oddly, to keep an emotional distance. It is often an expression of loneliness, lack of connection with others, and a deeply self-destructive attitude. Promiscuous sexual activity implies a lack of self-respect as well as a lack of belief in one's future. For teens for whom the rush is a continuing goal, sex can provide it. For teens for whom a momentary pleasure is all they choose to think about, sex can meet their needs. For kids for whom self-hatred is a way of life, sexual promiscuity is a way to perpetuate that way of living. Even teens who don't seem to be hanging out with other kids may be sexually promiscuous by means of the Internet, pornography on TV or on the telephone, or any of the many other types of pornography that are available.

Alienation and loneliness, feeling like a failure, and boredom with life in everyday reality may bring teens—boys as well as girls—to seek connection by means of sex. For many, having sex is a rush, but having wild sex is more of a rush; having sex with many partners is still more of a rush. Having everyone know you have lots of sex is a status symbol—but that type of status changes quickly. (I have never met the girl who really liked being called a "ho.") Underneath it all, most teens who find themselves caught in a type and level of sexual activity they don't understand and cannot manage—no matter their protestations to the contrary—use promiscuity as an expression of self-disrespect, self-destruction, and fear of caring about themselves and life. As a professional, I often find the kids who have been sexually promiscuous to be the unhappiest of all.

The Process of Change

Just eliminating these outward behaviors will not "cure" your child nor restore your family, but addressing change at a more profound level can. It is important to understand that change is a process, not an event. Real, deep, emotional, and psychological change occurs as the intangible product of many events. Each event helps to prepare you for the next, but there is no "right" order in which the events should happen, and you may experience some of the events concurrently. Likewise, some of the events will happen over and over again, each time offering you increased understanding and insight.

You cannot expect change to happen without changing. You cannot be both the same and different. Similarly, you cannot change without going through a process. You cannot expect your life, your family's life, and your teen's life to change without really changing yourself.

Central to your process of change will be clarifying your picture of your teen, his or her situation, the family situation, and who you are and how you feel about what is going on around you. To enter a process of change you must give up your illusions. At the same time, being in the process of change will help you to give up those illusions.

Remember: Just beyond change is freedom. Just beyond change is excitement. Just beyond change is joy. Sure, you can settle for one or two easy answers that might make things seem better for now, but why settle for bronze when you can have gold?

Oftentimes change seems frightening, but if you contrast change with the turmoil you live with now, it will become easier to take the risks involved in changing.

Both you and your teen will need to go through a change process. Neither you nor anyone else can force your teen to change. However, as you continue through your own process, it will become increasingly difficult for your teen not to change, too. Your new perspective will improve your confidence in your ability to be a parent again. The process of change has no specific end. Once you begin, you will probably always continue to meet the future and change with it.

When you cannot be manipulated or lied to, when you no longer rescue or excuse, when you don't lie to yourself, when you demonstrate self-respect and live your moral and ethical values, then your child will probably find that his or her one-person chaos show is no longer a viable alternative. But there are no guarantees. Your changing may not catalyze change in your teen. But, as one mother told me, "No matter what the outcome, I will always know that I have acted with dignity, integrity, and love. I can always look myself in the mirror."

Right now you are where the buck stops. Right now *you* are the first agent of change—for yourself and, by means of your change, for your teen and the whole family. The processes may be similar, but they will not be the same. They may or may not move at the same rate and in a similar rhythm. During the process you will rediscover yourselves and each other. It can be an exciting and wonderful time, but you cannot know that until you do it. Your belief that you can do it will energize you over and over again.

Events in the Process of Change

As you look through the list that follows, you will notice that the first eight events are familiar from the chapters you have just read. Now that they are familiar to you, you will begin to notice as you experience them and to integrate them into your life. The last eight events you will learn about in the chapters to come.

No matter where your teen is on the continuum of behavior—beginning to test limits or out-of-control and dangerous—this process will be invaluable to you as a parent and as an individual. Please keep in mind that no one can hurry a process as profound as this one, but that at the same time, you have no time to waste.

In the next days, weeks, and months you will find that you:

1. Burst your bubble of denial, lift your shroud of resignation, and begin to understand your adolescent's self-imposed image;
2. Stop being afraid of your teen;
3. No longer allow yourself to be manipulated and lied to;
4. Give up the blind hope that there is a "quick fix";
5. Acknowledge that your child didn't grow up in a bubble;
6. Decide you will no longer be either a passive or active party to chaos;

7. Recognize that the buck just stopped (you must be the first, but *only* the first, agent of change);

8. Believe in the possibility that life doesn't have to be the way it is now and that you can handle what comes your way;

9. Stop rationalizing, excusing, justifying, and rescuing;

10. Get rid of your guilt;

11. Rediscover yourself as an individual, not as just your teen's parent;

12. Reclaim your life—rediscover your passion, focus your ambition, and reenter the other relationships in your life;

13. Reclaim your emotional honesty and authenticity;

14. Let your child grow up in an age-appropriate manner;

15. Know you will carry through the process, no matter what;

16. Experience an inner shift.

Beginning Your Process of Change

You probably know already that you have experienced one, two, or perhaps more of the events in the list above. Record your thoughts, questions, and observations in a journal so that you can refer to them later. This journal may one day be a cherished part of your family's history, or something you will be able to share with another parent who is worried about her child. If you have not yet acquired a talisman for yourself, as explained in the Prologue, now is a good time to do so.

Here are two exercises most parents I work with find very freeing and therefore very empowering.

Exercise 1: Let Go of What You Hate Most

In your journal, let out what you have been keeping inside. Say it. Finally. Write down the five things you hate most about the way your son or daughter is living these days. Review the list of behavior-attitudes on page 19 if it would be helpful. Is it her language? Is it the way he dresses? Is it the secrecy? The intimidation? The lies? Drugs? His girlfriend? The depression?

This is the time for you to stop the rationalizing and excusing altogether. What do you hate most? Write it down and consider hanging this piece of paper on your mirror. It will remind you that you do not have to accept language, behavior, or attitudes that are loathsome to you. *You also have the right to a life.*

Exercise 2: Getting Rid of Your Guilt

Guilt debilitates. Guilt hurts. Guilt blurs your vision. Guilt hinders your judgment. Guilt makes you unhappy. Guilt doesn't bring anything very positive.

Do you ever wonder why you spend so much energy feeling guilty, even protecting your guilt as though it were your most prized possession?

It is easier to cleanse your soul of guilt than you may have thought. You can leave your guilt behind, not only because at least some of it is imagined, but also because feeling guilty will only sap your energy, suffocate your love, and help you waste your life.

Write all the reasons *you* feel guilty for what your child is doing now. Keep the list with you for a short time—thirty seconds to a few days. Share it with someone you trust if that makes sense for you. Then get rid of it. Flush it down the toilet, throw it in the fire, toss it into the ocean.

Allow it to be released from your being.

PART II

Learning from Other
Families

Chapter 4 ✿

Rescue Me! Ryan's Story

We all know the old adage about how much easier it is to see things in others than in ourselves. In this and subsequent chapters in Part II, you will find stories of families that will be at once familiar and foreign. Of course, none of them is exactly like your family but in watching, these families will help you clarify the picture you have begun to make of your teen, yourself, and your family. In each of these stories, you will see pieces of yourself, your teen, and what it's like living with a teen in turmoil. Putting those new insights together with what you learned in Part I will help you get a clearer picture of your feelings, your interactions with your teen, mistakes you make—and don't—and, most of all, show you new approaches and solutions to your problems.

At the first ring, Jill grabbed the phone. "Hello?"

"Hi, Mom!" Ryan's voice was deep and vibrant, just like always. Immediately she knew he was okay. Thank God he was safe! The visions of accidents, kidnapping, and murder that had been racing through her mind these last 30 hours disappeared.

"Are you all right? Where are you?" she asked. Released from her tension, she could feel her anger welling up. *Why is he doing this to me? He has no right!*

"Hey, Steve! Where are we?" She heard Steve laughing in the background. "Looks like Tennessee." Jill imagined the smile on Ryan's face, the smile that could make anyone think whatever he said was okay. She loved that smile. That smile was Ryan.

"What do you mean, 'looks like Tennessee'? What are you doing in Tennessee?"

"Steve wants you to call his parents for him."

"Do you realize all the things that might have happened to you? We didn't know whether to call the police or not." She wanted to keep him on the line; it was the only comfort she had had in two days—and she wanted him to know how hard this was for her. She thought that might bring him home immediately, but Ryan wasn't overly concerned about his parents being worried because that happened all the time for no reason anyway, and he wasn't planning to go home yet. He did not want to be picked up by the police.

"Did you?" he asked.

"No. I would have and so would Steve's mother, but your fathers said we should wait because you would be home before the weekend was out. But we still might," she threatened.

Careful not to betray his concern, Ryan said, "Naw, don't do that. You didn't have to worry. How come you got so worried? You know me, Mom, I can take care of myself. Anyway, I got my buddy here."

"Ryan, where are you? Tennessee is a big place." She wanted him to tell her, so his father could go get him. Her mind was racing with schemes.

"Well, I don't exactly know," he drawled. "A truck stop, by the looks of it. Mom, we're fine, only we're a little short of money. Do you think you could deposit some into my account, so I could use my ATM card? A couple hundred."

"If I send you the money, are you going to come home?"

"Just put it in my account, then we'll be fine. Okay?" He winked at Steve. "And we're going to need it. We're getting pretty hungry! I'll call you sometime tomorrow."

"What do you mean? Ryan?" Suddenly here voice was again panicked and shrill. "Do you mean you're not eating? Ryan! Are you out of money? I could wire some right now if you would just tell me where you are."

Ryan hated when she panicked, and he saw through her double motive. "Naw, it's okay. We still got two candy bars each. Ma, I gotta go." He hung up, and there wasn't anything she could do about it.

Jill was crying, but relieved. He was safe, and she knew approximately where he was. None of her worst fears had come true. They were just out having a prank, and he sounded okay, even more than okay; he sounded happy and excited. He was enjoying himself. Russ had been right.

She called Steve's house as they all had promised to do if either family heard anything.

Susan recognized Jill's voice immediately, and from her tone knew the boys were safe. Her relief quickly changed to anger. "Tennessee? What the hell are they doing in Tennessee? They're sixteen years old! I hope you told them to get their sweet little asses back here right now."

"Well, yes, but not in that way. I don't think they would have listened to me if I had said that. I don't think they plan to come home quite yet. I was afraid if I let Ryan know we're angry, then he would stay away longer. They sounded good, like they're having a good time. I heard Steve in the background; he sounded fine. I'm putting some money into Ryan's account to cover their expenses."

"I wouldn't send them money. They'll come home a lot sooner if they get hungry."

"It's fine for you to talk that way, but you know you've been just as worried as I have been. You just hide it better. You know perfectly well you would have agreed to give them money too."

It was true, and Susan knew it. "Well, maybe. But it isn't right."

"We can deal with that when we have them back. We don't really have much choice. I won't let my son starve!"

"I doubt they're starving."

"Maybe they have enough for a meal, but I bet they slept in the car—that would be two nights without a bed. What else could I do?" Jill pleaded.

They agreed to stay in close touch until the boys returned home safely.

It was on Friday night after the basketball game that Ryan had come up with the idea to take a trip. They were in Ryan's car, a dark blue 1992 Saab, driving around town trying to figure out what to do. "We got next week off from school, right?" Ryan said. "I got a full tank here. Let's just take off. Say drive south."

"What? Are you kidding?" Steve objected. "We don't have any clothes or anything. I've only got about fifty dollars." But Ryan quickly convinced him with an airtight argument. "If we ask our parents, they'll say no, but if we just take off and call them when we need money, what are they going to do?"

Without any particular destination in mind except Florida because they had heard about Daytona at spring break, they headed south. They drove through part of the night, then pulled into a truck stop to get something to eat. They felt a little intimidated, like guilty and naughty little boys. They wanted to order beers, but even though Ryan had a fake ID, they were afraid they would be questioned, so they ordered Cokes instead. They slept in the car and awoke late the next morning. Ryan felt powerful and free as he accelerated onto the interstate. "Yes!" he shouted.

"Hey, Ryan, what are we going to do when we run out of money?" Steve asked. "You got a credit card or an ATM card?"

"Yeah, I have a cash card, but I don't know how much I can get out. I wish I had a credit card. My dad is getting me one next year when I'm a senior. When we need more money, we just call our parents and tell them to send us some."

"What if they won't?"

"They will. My mother will. Don't worry. I got things under control," he said, passing a truck at 85 mph.

"You think they're worried about us?" Steve asked.

"Naw, not really."

"Yeah, my dad's cool. He'll understand. He used to do things like this when he was young. So, how far south are we going to go? Florida? Mexico? Colombia?"

Ryan laughed. "You know, we could change our minds and head out West. I think you can drive ninety or something in Nevada."

"You mean like to California? Yes!"

"We'll sleep on the beach, surf. . . .You heard of Venice Beach? Man, you can get whatever you want there. What do you say?"

Steve was quiet for a minute. His parents were more strict than Ryan's, but *What can they really do?* he asked himself. *Ground me for a million years? Whatever. I'll deal, and I will have been to California.*

Giving his buddy a fist in the arm, he said, "I say, let's go for it!"

"We'll stop at the next place to get some cash. I can probably get a hundred dollars, maybe more." At the cash machine, they found Ryan had only $50 available, but their spirits weren't daunted. Ryan knew he could get his mother to supply him with money. Steve wasn't so sure, but then he figured his parents would never really let him be stranded in the middle of nowhere. They discussed at length if they should tell their parents where they really were and where they were heading. They decided it would be safer to surprise them later because they didn't want their parents calling the cops.

Ryan had been his parents' darling from the day he was born. He was a beautiful little boy, with large dark eyes and blond hair. Even at two he could charm anyone into giving him what he wanted or forgiving him his mistakes. He just smiled, and if ever that didn't suffice, Jill or Russ was always there to rescue him. They excused his selfishness and laziness, rationalized his mediocre grades and how he never did his chores, and admired his athletic talent and his gorgeous smile. Middle school presented Ryan with the first problems in his life that he could not solve just by smiling or being sorry. Neither algebra nor Spanish could be learned by charming the teacher, but Ryan did not know any other way. He told his parents the work was too difficult. Jill and Russ spoke with his teachers, and together they decided he would do better if they took him out of his honors classes and put him in the regular ones, figuring the stress was too much for him. Jill began to sit down with him for an hour every evening while he did his homework, helping him when he had questions, typing out his papers if he had to go to bed or wanted to watch TV. Ryan's grades improved in the regular classes, and he and his parents were satisfied. "With his charm and good looks and that personality, he'll do just fine," they said.

In eighth grade, Ryan developed a sudden passion for whipped cream, the kind in the aerosol can, and Jill bought all he wanted, never thinking twice about it. But soon he lost his interest in "whippets" because he began smoking marijuana and even tried LSD and mushrooms a couple of times. He knew his parents had no idea what he was doing. "So long as I just keep up appearances, they don't hassle me," he boasted to his friends. "You know one of the best things you can do to keep your parents thinking you're clean? Go to church with them sometimes and take part in the youth group." He was right. When Jill found a bong in Ryan's room, he easily convinced her that a friend had given it to him to get rid of because he, Ryan, had persuaded the friend that using drugs was dangerous and wrong. Jill was proud of him and boasted of it to her friends.

In ninth grade Ryan cut a few classes and was suspended. Russ hurried to school and met with Ryan's counselor and managed to get the suspension lifted. Ryan promised not to cut classes anymore and to work harder— and Russ was persuasive. Jill felt it was really her fault, because she had not been doing enough for and with Ryan. She began to check in regularly with the teachers in order to help Ryan keep track of his assignments.

Ryan had always been a talented athlete, and in tenth grade he made the varsity baseball team. He also developed a passion for Gatorade. Jill could not believe the gallons he drank, but, like the whipped cream before, she bought him what he wanted without question. When Ryan failed a drug test for the baseball team and was told he couldn't play anymore, Russ and Jill blamed the coach and the testing. Russ hurried to Ryan's defense and managed to convince the coach that there must have been an error. Russ asked Ryan for a pledge that he didn't and wouldn't do drugs. Ryan played it cool, gave his word, and his parents never suspected how frightened he had been.

That summer Ryan started hanging with some guys he didn't know very well; they were older, and they had cars and wild reputations. They didn't do a lot of drugs, but they pretty much always had beer and hard liquor around, and they hung out in clubs. A few times Ryan came home drunk, but his parents were asleep, and they didn't notice that he was hungover the next morning. When he complained of a headache, Jill worried he was "coming down with something."

Jill and Russ had remained unaware of, or simply excused, most of what their son had been doing for the past few years, but they both realized they would have to deal with Ryan when he returned from this prank. Grounding him didn't seem useful, and although they wouldn't admit it, they knew they would never really carry through with it. It would be too inconvenient to take away his car. They talked of making him repay the money they had deposited for them, but then they felt Steve should be involved in that too. They decided to speak with Steve's parents before the boys returned.

By Friday, when the boys had been gone a week, Susan, Tom and Russ had lost their patience. Since she was speaking to Ryan regularly, Jill, who had been the most panicked at the beginning, was feeling the calmest. They agreed to meet for dinner to discuss the situation. Even Jill had no idea when the boys planned to return. Susan and Tom and Russ wanted to know how much money Jill had given them.

"I thought of depositing a thousand dollars all at once, you know, to make them budget it a little, but then I was afraid if I did that, they might not call, so I just put in a little bit every day, maybe a hundred fifty or two hundred dollars. I don't want them broke. That would be dangerous. I just make sure they have enough for gas and a motel and food," Jill explained.

"And drugs," Susan added.

"What? Are you crazy? Our boys do drugs? Well, at least I can tell you Ryan does not do drugs. He can't, you know, being on the baseball team. What about Steve? Isn't he running track? They can't be doing drugs. Anyway, they are too responsible."

"Oh, I forgot our sons were such perfectly behaved kids," Russ said sarcastically.

"I don't think they're bad boys," Jill said. "They just wanted some adventure." The cell phone she had bought to keep in contact with Ryan rang from her purse. "Hello? Ryan, dear!"

"Hi, Mom. Can I speak to Dad?"

"Sure, dear. He's right here. We're out to dinner with Steve's parents. There isn't anything wrong, is there, dear? You sound upset."

"Can I have Dad please."

Jill handed Russ the phone. "Hello?" Russ said. "I can hear Steve in the background," he whispered to the others. Trying to sound stern and businesslike, but still fatherly, Russ asked, "What's up?"

"Hi, Dad. Well, not much. It's just that, well, the car has sort of broken down."

"What happened?" The others were looking at him questioningly, but he remained matter-of-fact. He mouthed, "The car has broken down."

"The mechanic here says it would cost a few hundred to fix it. The engine is kind of shot."

"I see. How did that happen? Where are you?" Russ could hear Ryan whispering something in the background.

"Uh, well, we're, uh, in, well, we're in L.A."

"In L.A.?" Russ shouted, then looked around the restaurant, hoping no one had heard him. A few heads had turned, so Russ smiled and nodded a sort of apology.

"Yeah, we were just joking about all the places we said we were in. You know, just kidding."

"Oh. So. You're in Los Angeles with a broken down car, and—let me guess—no money?" Russ summarized so the others would know what was going on.

"Yeah. Kind of. I mean . . . Yeah. We were thinking, I mean," Ryan took a deep breath. He hated having to ask his dad for help. "Do you think you could maybe buy us plane tickets back?"

"And what about the car?"

"Well, leave it here, I guess. I mean, I don't know what else we could do."

Russ, by profession a problem solver, thought quickly and began putting the solution together. "I think it might make more sense if I fly out there tonight; then tomorrow we'll see if there is anything to do about the car. Then we'll see about getting you guys home for school. I'll drive the car back myself, once it's fixed."

"Wow, Dad! Thanks. That's great. You'd do that?"

"I don't have too many other choices, do I? Give me a phone number where I can reach you in a half hour or so to let you know when I'm arriving."

"We don't exactly have one," Ryan answered. "We're at a pay phone, by the garage."

"All right. Get Steve to go in there and get me the phone number, so I can call them to tell them I'll be there tomorrow to see about the car. They'll be more likely to be up front with me than with you. Then you two get out to the airport. Have you got enough cash to manage that? By the time you get there, I will have booked a room at the Airport Hyatt. Got that? The Hyatt. You check in there and wait for me. I'll give them my credit card. Get yourselves some dinner and sign for it."

"Man, that is so cool. Dad, you are the greatest. I mean, wow! You're not mad?"

"Not irrevocably. We'll sort this out."

"Dad, you are just the best!"

"I wonder if we should be saving their little asses, after this kind of prank," Tom asked as Russ made arrangements with the mechanic and for the hotel, his flight, and a rental car.

"Maybe not, but I don't want them running around L.A. with no money. That is one dangerous town," Russ answered. "We can talk about what they did when they're safely back home."

Russ caught the last plane out of Chicago. The first thing he saw as he walked toward the door of the hotel room was a room service cart outside the door piled high with dishes. Ryan and Steve were watching a movie when he came in. They were overflowing with stories about their trip. Their exuberance was contagious, and Russ was soon enmeshed in their excitement.

The next morning when they arrived at the garage, it was quickly obvious that to put more money into the car and then have the trouble of driving it back to Chicago did not make sense. "Yeah," the mechanic told him, "if they had just checked the oil, it might have been okay. They burned out the engine, you know." Russ sold him the Saab for $325.

Russ asked Ryan why he hadn't checked the oil, but Ryan told him they had, so he couldn't figure out what had happened. Russ remembered he had been planning to take the car in for a check-up for a month before they left and somehow had never managed to find a time when Ryan could spare the car. They called Jill and Steve's parents to say they would arrive in Chicago the next afternoon. In the meantime, it seemed a pity not to enjoy California, so Russ took the boys to Malibu beach and then out to dinner.

On the plane home Ryan broached the subject of a new car to his dad. "Look, I mean, I know I have no right to ask, but you know, I can't really live without a car."

"I know. I've already been thinking of that. I think I'll give you my Jeep and lease something new. It'll take a few days to get it worked out, but I think we should have it under control in less than two weeks."

Do You Want Your Son to Grow Up to Be a Boy or a Man?

Most parents who have read Ryan's story have told me they were furious at Russ and Jill. No parents could excuse and rescue like they did! One mother told me she kept expostulating aloud, "How can they do that? Don't they understand?" Then all of a sudden a light went on for her, and she had to say, "I used to be just that way."

Boys like Ryan are charming and charismatic. They usually approach me in therapy sessions the same way they approach everyone else: flashing a winning smile in an attempt to keep me at a comfortable, apparently friendly emotional distance. I don't really blame them; after all, the method has worked for them before. But as soon as they discover they cannot manipulate me with the smile and slightly flirtatious air, they tend to get angry. Somehow everything becomes my fault. But that makes sense to them, too, because that is the interaction they are used to with their mothers. Boys like Ryan are very good at getting somebody else to be responsible for them, and Ryan was definitely an expert at that maneuver. Unfortunately, like so many parents, Jill and Russ had not thought through to the long-term consequences of their reactions to Ryan's behavior and attitudes.

I first met Jill and Russ Kennedy about four months after Ryan returned from California. They came to see me because Ryan had not passed enough courses to become a senior. They assumed something was wrong—perhaps he had ADD or a learning disability, and they thought a therapist could take care of it. They told me they were ready to consider medication if it would work.

The first thing I had to tell them was that therapists couldn't solve anyone's problems. The best they can offer is guidance to help individuals or families find their own solutions. I also told them that I could not, and would not, prescribe any medications. I explained that I would not want to diminish Ryan's symptoms because then he or they might be fooled into thinking he was back on track without requiring him to change for real. I would not become another person in Ryan's life ready to give yet another easy answer; I would not take away his responsibility for the mess he had gotten himself into.

I asked Jill and Russ to recount to me some of Ryan's story. What was interesting was how they told it. Listening, I had the feeling they were telling me about an exciting, romantic movie they had seen. They spoke of their son as if he were some sort of fascinating hero who had simply gotten himself into a few too many scrapes. They saw each incident as an isolated event, never allowing themselves to observe the pattern which would have helped them to derive meaning from Ryan's actions. They seemed to be in awe of their son, quite taken by his wild nature. As they spoke I was already thinking how important it would be for Ryan to focus and redirect that wild nature into something more productive than driving to California on a whim and needing to be rescued by his parents.

Boys like Ryan are interesting and exciting; their spirits are volatile, but they can be too easily extinguished if they are quashed by therapy that is not also respectful of their so-called wild side. After all, it is that passionate spirit that has inspired people to climb Everest, to write extraordinary books, to invent things that change the world. It is precious—and also potentially very dangerous. For Ryan at this point, it was mainly dangerous.

As we talked further, I realized that Jill and Ryan probably did not know much of what their son really had been doing for the last few years. For me the story about failing the drug test was crucial. Although they still did not want to believe it, I felt certain Ryan was using drugs.

Russ—and the coach—had absolved Ryan of important personal responsibility, not only by ignoring that he had failed a drug test, but also by ignoring the greater issue of having let his team down. That was, however, a pattern his parents had established, even when he was a little kid. I wondered how Ryan had really felt about that.

My work with families is always about interactions; I realized that everyone in this family needed to do some changing, some growing up, some separating, and some redistributing of responsibilities. Fortunately, Russ and Jill were not looking to find a culprit; they wanted help for their son. Of course, that meant help for themselves and for the family.

When Ryan returned from California, he felt invincible, that wonderful feeling only adolescents and egomaniacs can have. He had done exactly as he pleased, and, although they could ill afford it, his parents had financed it. In the end, he had been rewarded with a newer and more expensive car. Jill was proud to tell me how apologetic Ryan was about the worry he had caused her. But in less than a month the worrying had begun anew: Ryan was kicked off the baseball team. He failed another drug test, and his grades had gone below the standard needed to remain on the team.

Russ and Jill were confused. The picture they had of their son just did not match the one of the boy they had to deal with now. They almost began to doubt some of Ryan's stories. Nothing quite made sense. The one thing they were certain of was that things were not okay with their son.

Jill and Russ were good, nice, hard-working, honest people. They didn't want Ryan to be sad or have problems, which is okay, except that when parents act on those feelings, they tend to make their children uncertain about whether they can deal with the world and themselves on their own, because they have so little practice. The result is that kids try to show they are grown up and independent, but too often they are just reckless and foolish, and, like Ryan, need to be rescued again. It becomes a vicious circle that can too often lead to a dangerous downward spiral.

When I work with parents like Russ and Jill, I begin by helping them to recognize that they routinely excuse unacceptable behavior. Even if you think you are very different from Jill and Russ and that you would never act as they did, take a few minutes to work through this questionnaire.

12 Excuses Parents Often Make for Their Children

Which of the following statements have you made in the last week?

- "She has so much homework; let's not ask her to help. She needs to focus on her own work." (But when you go upstairs, you find her talking on the phone.)
- "He's not as bad as . . ." (name a teen whom you don't like).

- "She's dealing with her issues." Or, "He has a lot of anger to work out."
- "You can't expect her to be able to have fun and keep up with her friends on twenty-five dollars a week." Or, "Here's the credit card (an extra twenty dollars); just don't tell your father (mother)." Or, "I must have spent that twenty dollars somewhere."
- "It's only a little past her curfew."
- "The only reason he yelled at me is because it's safe to take it out on me. Everyone always takes it out on those they love most."
- "It's okay as long as he doesn't smoke in the house."
- "But at least he came home." Or, "At least she told me about it."
- "Yes, but . . ." (Add the excuse of your choice—"It's only the first time." "He's immature for his age." "We moved around so much." "The divorce was so hard.")
- "All the other kids do it." Or, "I don't want my child to be the outcast."
- "They think he has an attention problem." Or, "I think he has a learning disability."
- "That stepmother . . . !"

Reevaluating Their Son

Jill was the office manager for a local pediatrician. Her efficiency was as prized as were her patience with, and kindness to, the children, parents, and her colleagues. Russ worked for a national consulting firm. His job was to solve accounting problems in some of the more important businesses in Chicago. Jill and Russ were what most people would call happily married, but what they shared primarily was being Ryan's parents. To their son's detriment, they centered their whole lives on him, teaching him he was the center of the world. Therapy would have to show Ryan that he was not. If he could not learn that lesson in therapy, then he would have to learn it in the world, and it might end up being a hard, hard lesson—the kind that sends kids right back into their old behavior patterns.

To help Russ and Jill put their relationship with Ryan into the context of their whole lives, I wanted to show them there was no one else in the world whom they would let manipulate and control them the way they let their son. Jill understood that if she was not on top of things in the office, children would not get the attention they needed, a prescription might get misplaced, and insurance forms might not get filled out. One of her main jobs was to delegate work and authority, something she would never think of doing at home with her son.

Russ was a sharp businessman; things didn't get by him, and he surely did not excuse laziness and stupidity. In his professional life he was used to hearing, but not accepting, excuses, rationalizations, or lies, and his company valued him especially for that. However, in the face of his son, he became putty.

"Since you wouldn't let anyone in your professional lives treat you this way," I told them, "do your son the favor of treating him with the same respect."

Russ looked at me skeptically.

"You don't give your son a chance to understand what respect is when you don't hold him to the same kind of standards of integrity you expect from everyone else in your life, including yourself. How can he learn to be respectable, much less respect himself, when you don't require that from him?"

"I never thought of it that way," Russ said. "But he's my son. I don't want to treat him like a colleague; he's a kid."

"True enough," I answered, "but that doesn't change the fact that you are subtly teaching him that he can get away with things, that you will make whatever he does okay, that he doesn't have to be honest and responsible. How do you think that makes him feel about himself? On the one hand he's probably glad because it makes things easy. But on the other hand, there's probably a little voice inside him that keeps saying he really couldn't manage anything without you. How can he imagine himself as an adult? He wants to be a man, but he feels like a boy, so he acts like a boy. You couldn't function in your professional life if you didn't have expectations, standards of conduct, honesty and integrity. Do your son a favor and hold him to much higher standards."

Russ grimaced. "I love that kid so much; I can't even describe it. He's my heart and soul. I never thought about it that way!"

"Of course you didn't. You're not an evil man with malicious motives, and this surely isn't about blame. It's about how to change things—for your son's benefit and for yours, too. Stop to think where this might all go if no one steps in to make Ryan meet the kinds of standards you have for yourself and others."

"Do you think my love for Ryan is bad?" Russ asked.

"No! Of course not! It's not like that. You have to reframe your picture. He wants to grow up and have respect—your respect—but he keeps on needing you to save his derriere. If you start with the concept of respect as a component of love, then tell me, do you respect your son?"

"Respect? I don't know," Russ responded. "I mean I haven't thought of it like that. He's a kid."

I told Russ he had to stop using the excuse "He's a kid." Then I added, "Okay, answer this: Do you think well of him for having let down the other guys on the baseball team?"

"Well, no. But that's a loaded question. Of course I don't. But that isn't what he did. At least it isn't what he meant to do."

"There I suppose I agree with you," I responded. "But that's the point. It never occurred to Ryan that others could be involved in his mess, that others could suffer because he didn't take care of himself, that you wouldn't be able to make everything better, to undo his foolishness. You're like that wonderful key on the computer keyboard labeled 'undo.' That's at least partially how your son thinks of you: as his 'undo' key. But how do you suppose that makes him feel about himself?"

"You know," Russ ventured, "Andy, his older brother, said something like that to me once, but I just put it down to jealousy. Andy's just not as . . . I don't know, not as charismatic. He's a hard worker, and I respect that. I love him, too." Russ stopped. He noticed he had used the world "respect" to describe his feeling about his elder son, and he felt a moment's surprise. He gave me a knowing look. "But there is something about Ryan that goes beyond love. I always have the feeling he needs me so much—he always has. And I like that. I can't help it, and I don't deny it. People need to be needed. It isn't bad."

"No, of course not, but the ramifications need to be examined. How has that affected your son's life?"

Jill had been crying quietly, listening attentively to her husband. "You don't think he's a bad boy, do you?" she asked me.

Although it seemed to be a non sequitur, I answered Jill directly because I could tell this was the burning question for her now. "Heavens, no! And I don't think you are bad parents. This isn't about finding a 'bad guy,' a 'fall guy.' It's about figuring out how the interactions work and what they mean. My clinical diagnosis of your son is 'Spoiled Brat,' but that hardly makes him or you evil or bad. There is nothing to stop him from changing and getting his life back together. That is, nothing except laziness and being a wimp, but that can change. However it won't happen if you keep taking all the responsibility for everything he does and thinks—and does wrong or doesn't take care of.

"Look, I haven't met him, but I imagine he is hardly stupid. I'll bet he doesn't like himself very much, although he probably hides it pretty well. I feel pretty sure he doesn't trust himself. You know, he's the kind of kid whom you can find charming, but whom you can't really like."

"What do you mean? Not like Ryan? Everyone always likes Ryan," Jill protested.

"Maybe. But how many close friends does he have? Can you really say you know your son? Think of it this way: Kids like Ryan really do believe they are the center of the world, but that makes the world a strange place because kids like Ryan also feel incompetent. Teens who see themselves this way understand people only as they can use others to make their world go round, as others relate to them. When others are not relating to these self-centered kids, it's as though they don't exist until later, when they reenter the teen's world. How can Ryan make sense out of a world like that? How can you have a relationship with someone like Ryan who hardly even knows you're there except to meet his needs?"

"But isn't that what parents are supposed to do, meet their child's needs?"

"Yes, but the point is not if you meet your child's needs, but how. It must be age appropriate. Does your son Andy need you to meet his needs in the same sorts of ways? Is that how your parents raised you?"

"You really think Ryan's that way?" Russ asked.

"Narcissistic? Self-centered? Selfish and entitled? Well, I've never met him, but, yes, I imagine so. I think I've met a few like him. Shall I describe him to you? He's good looking (but you told me that, so it doesn't count), he has a gorgeous smile which, frankly, he uses as a defensive weapon; he could charm the spots off a leopard, and he gets really angry if his charm doesn't get what he wants. He's always looking for the easy answer, the quick fix. He's nervous and demoralized, but he covers it with his charm. He's restless, and he tries to keep a lot going on in his life because he needs to be amused or he might start to think—and he might not like what he would have to think. You know what else? He manipulates you up and down the block!"

"Not Ryan! He doesn't," Jill almost whined.

"Tell me if I'm wrong. I thought you told me that instead of making him pay back the enormous sum of money his little jaunt out to California cost, you gave him a new car. Not to speak of the fact that he kept you just worried enough while he was gone for you to supply him with money all the way. And he called just often enough so that you felt you knew where he was and what was going on, but in fact you didn't. You aren't even sure he's doing drugs, although he has failed two drug tests."

"That's not manipulation. That's just the way Ryan operates."

"No kidding! Do you really think it's respectable? How do you suppose Ryan feels about Ryan?"

"No, but wait," Jill broke in. "How else was he going to be safe and get home if I didn't send him money?"

"How about the same way he left?"

"But the car broke down."

"True enough, but do you see how you are excusing him and rescuing him, over and over again? What about the drug tests? What about the fact that he failed three of his classes? What about getting kicked off the base-ball team? I know it's hard to accept, but Ryan's life is a mess. It's possible he's done that sort of 'on purpose.' He may be—not exactly consciously— trying to find out just what your bottom line is. He may just be trying to see when you'll say, 'Ryan that goes too far.' He needs you to oblige him to take responsibility and grow up. He has to do for himself, but you have to make him start."

After a moment's silence, Russ said quietly, "Jill, I'm afraid the lady may have a point. I don't think I like this."

"But . . ." Jill couldn't finish her sentence. I suspected she was frightened for Ryan, but years of practice excusing him made it difficult for her to admit what was really going on.

"I understand this is a lot to throw at you all at once," I said. "You have so many years of experience which you have understood differently, but you need to know that this kid may be heading for big trouble. Perhaps I shouldn't tell you this story, but I think it's relevant. About three years ago I started to work with a family that reminds me of yours. Sarah and Joe— those were the parents—just couldn't say no to their son; no matter what happened, Sarah or Joe was always there to bail out Chas. He was like Ryan, good-looking, charismatic, smart, an athlete—basketball, I think it was. Well, anyway, they were just getting ready to think about intervening seriously with Chas, but they wanted to let him have one last chance before they decided for sure. He had never gotten into any really serious trouble, at least not that they knew about. But that night Chas got drunk, really drunk, and tried to drive home. Instead he drove into the rocks in the canyon near his house."

Russ and Jill sat in silence. I had the feeling I had reached them, and I was glad because I was frightened for Ryan. My instinct told me he was doing a lot more drugs than his parents thought, and I wondered where he was getting the money. I guessed he was sneaking out at night to hang out with friends, and I was concerned about the kinds of kids he might be hang-ing out with. They could be a lot tougher than Ryan, and that, combined with his recklessness, well . . . I hoped I was wrong, but experience didn't let me think so.

"Have you had any money missing or anything like that?" I asked.

"What?" I had caught them off-guard.

Then Jill answered, "No; I mean, well, I let Ryan use my ATM card a couple of times, and I was kind of surprised how much he took out."

"I thought he had his own ATM card."

"Yes, but he can only get so much at any one time, you know."

"Jill, Russ. You need to wake up. Your son wants you to intervene. Why else did he create this turmoil—get himself thrown off the baseball team and fail three courses so he can't be a senior next year? This kid knows—without quite knowing it—that he's out of control. He is trying to get your attention. In his own unaware sort of way, he knows he is in trouble way over his head. Don't wait until he does something so rash, so risky, so wild that he really endangers his life! He doesn't have to be another Chas, you know."

Jill and Russ looked at each other. I had stunned them. I had wanted to.

"What should we do?" Russ asked.

"Well, it's not so simple as 'do this, do that.' It's going to be a process. A lot will hinge on you both and on each of you." I wanted to emphasize that they had to act together, but also as separate individuals. "You will have to make as many changes as Ryan will. It isn't that you are to blame, but that you are a part of the whole, and the whole must change. There are a couple of things I would suggest for you to do now. First, just start by being aware of each time you excuse Ryan or do things for him he really can and should do for himself. And, of course, I haven't met Ryan. I would like to meet with him alone—without you two."

"Okay," Russ said. "We'll do that. What about an appointment for Ryan?"

"You tell him you have seen me and that you require he call me for an appointment. Don't threaten him, just tell him he needs to do it."

"You think that will work?"

"Let's find out. At any rate, I don't think much would come of you bringing him here under duress. The other thing I want you to do is to set your alarm for 2:30 or 3:00 tomorrow morning and check to see if Ryan is in his bed. If he is, then do it another night or two, just to see."

"See what? Of course he'll be there," Russ stated emphatically. "What are you talking about?"

"My instinct tells me that he sneaks out at night. I think he's doing a lot of things you don't know about. He is playing that adolescent 'I'm invincible' game, and you know what? He isn't invincible. If I'm wrong, then I will be more than glad to admit it, and I will reevaluate my treatment thoughts."

"Okay," Russ agreed. "We'll do that, but I really think you are wrong."

"Let's hope so. But here is a parting question for you to think about at home: Do you want your son to grow up to be a boy or a man?"

When Jill and Russ left, I could tell they were feeling unsettled. I hoped they would check to see if Ryan was sneaking out. I hoped they would think about my question.

I wasn't sure if I would hear from Ryan, and I didn't hear from him the next day. But the following day he called. He was furious with me because I had guessed right: His parents had found he was not in his bed the night before. I think he was planning to set me straight about things when he made the appointment, but when he arrived, he was as charming as could be. As I had expected, he flashed me his best Hollywood smile. I expected that beneath his charm he was angry, so I thought it would be best not to mince words. He wasn't planning on trusting me anyway, so I had little to lose. The best I could do was to show him I don't like to waste time. I knew he would resent confrontation from someone he didn't know, but I felt I had to take a chance. I had to be tough with my words, gentle with my voice and manner.

"So where were you the other night?"

He stared at me. "Whatever."

"Right." I couldn't help but smile. He was giving me lots of silent messages. I think I received them all, but I chose to ignore them. Instead, I asked, "You do drugs?"

Ryan didn't answer. More silent messages. He wasn't used to being asked direct, uncomfortable questions. He wasn't sure whether to play the tough guy or the naive, innocent guy. It didn't really matter to me because neither was going to work.

"Look, obviously I know you were out somewhere where you shouldn't have been the other night; otherwise you wouldn't have to sneak out your window. And I know you do drugs, although I don't know which drugs or how much. But all that hardly counts, really. What counts is how you feel about yourself." Although I was confronting him, I kept my voice tone gentle, and my eyes intense. "And I suppose you 'know' that underneath all the charm and the cool haircut and the great clothes, you are worthless. That's what *you* think. You even think you have lots of good evidence to support that point of view. Now, as it turns out, I doubt I would agree with you, but it doesn't much matter what *I* think. What matters is what *you* think."

From his face I could see I had touched something in Ryan; he looked down at his feet.

I went on. "You must be feeling pretty bad about yourself. You've been failing at just about everything these days. School, baseball, fooling your parents. I don't suppose you are very good at fooling yourself; most kids aren't. That's the best thing you've got going for you now. You are smart enough and aware enough to know your life is not going well. I could be wrong, but I'm guessing that underneath your smile is a pretty depressed guy. You know it doesn't have to keep on being this way. It only takes some courage and perseverance. You could make your life better. You could start doing things 'the right way' and just see how it works out. I mean, if nothing else, your way hasn't been working too well lately." I stopped because it was time for Ryan to say something. I waited.

"What makes you say all that?" he asked.

I didn't answer at first, but I kept my gaze straight to his eyes. He looked away, as I had known he would. Then I said, "Anyway, it gets boring fooling parents as easy to fool as yours are."

"Look, you don't even know me."

"True enough. But was what I said really all that wrong?"

It took nearly two full minutes for Ryan to answer. "Sort of. I mean some of it. Not really. Can I smoke?"

"Not here. Hey, Ryan." I looked him directly in the eyes. "Are you happy? Do you think your life is in order? Is this the way you pitch a no-hitter?"

Suddenly the bluster was gone. Ryan became like a little boy, and tears welled up in his eyes. Both Ryan and I knew that nothing was working in his life. The veneer had begun to crumble. I knew we had a long road ahead, but I could see the possibilities. Ryan knew he was going to have to start doing things differently, but he had no idea what or how. But that wasn't really a problem—in many ways that was what the next several months of therapy or possibly an emotional growth high school would help him discover. First, he would have to admit, and then have the courage to feel, how "bad" he had been. He had to move beyond his past. That would take many weeks, but if he could do it, then he could close the failure chapter of his adolescence and begin the success one.

The first thing I knew I had to work on with Ryan was his honesty. Nothing really happens in therapy until a kid becomes honest. I knew that would not be easy for him, but I knew it was possible and essential and that it would take time. It would be important for Jill and Russ to stop believing Ryan and also to stop covering for him. There were no contracts to be made, then broken, then rationalized; rather, there were attitudes to be changed. Ryan had to gain the confidence to be able to be honest. At first he would find it almost impossible, but he could get the hang of it, and then he would discover how easy life becomes when you don't have to worry about which story you told to whom when.

Jill and Russ had to take Ryan off center stage in their lives. Then Ryan could stop the dishonesty of having to be the perfect boy, and he would be freed of "having to lie" to remain the star of their show. None of them had realized the stress that had caused for Ryan. Ryan also had to start thinking of himself as one member of a whole family, a team, a community. He had to realize his parents were individuals beyond just his parents. All that would take time.

For their part, Jill and Russ had to start relating to each other as Russ and Jill, not just Ryan's mom and Ryan's dad. They had to rebuild a life of doing things together, going places, and above all, making that inner shift which would allow them to trust their son enough to let him make mistakes and find his own way out of situations. They and Ryan had to accept that Ryan was not fragile, did not need to be rescued, and that he was not perfect. Ryan didn't really need them to find answers for him, fix his plans, give him extra money, "help" him with his homework. More important, Ryan had to stop setting up his parents to have to rescue him. Perhaps he had been testing them to see if they would keep on loving him, to see if they really could make everything turn out fine, if they would ever step in to say, "STOP!"

As Ryan begins to restore his future, he will need good friends he can talk to from his heart, friends who will be able to be there for him at an emotional level. Perhaps his friendship with Steve can develop into that. And he will need to get to know his parents as more than just Mom and Dad. Russ and Jill have to let—even require—that to happen, too.

For months, if not years, Ryan had been calling out for someone to stop him. I suspected that the best idea for Jill, Russ, and most of all for Ryan would be for Ryan to go away for a while to an emotional growth program. I had a feeling distance would make it easier for Jill and Russ to let go of him and begin to trust him enough to let him take care of himself and to begin to rediscover each other. In the meantime, while he tried to make up the credits he needed to be a senior, Ryan and I arranged to meet twice a week and once more every third week with his parents. I thought Ryan might have had quite a scare when his parents found he was sneaking out. Maybe now the whole family was scared enough to stop the "Happy Family" act and do the work to become one.

The next story about Courtney's family looks at a situation before it has reached the near-crisis proportions of Ryan's family. It is important to keep in mind that often, but not always, when parents decide to change their own behavior and their attitudes toward their children, toward themselves, and toward life in general, they can avoid a situation where circumstances spin out of control.

Chapter 5 ✺

Intimidated No More:
Courtney's Story

Courtney was fourteen, in her freshman year at high school. From her first day in school, Courtney was terrified that she could not succeed academically. Even worse, the other kids in school seemed so sure of themselves—they all seemed to have friends, and she felt lonely, lost, and very young. She took what seemed to her the first, best option. Psychologically and emotionally, she turned tail and ran, convincing her mother, Eleanore, that her educational needs could not be met in a normal school. Courtney told her mother she could not learn in a classroom with other students and that she needed the one-on-one attention of a tutor.

Eleanore had her tested, and although the tests showed nothing conclusive, she decided that Courtney's special kind of intelligence and artistic talent needed something more than her school could offer. Eleanore wanted Courtney to attend a private day school, but Courtney's tantrums convinced her that home schooling would have to be an acceptable compromise.

Courtney was testing her mother, and, unfortunately, in her effort to be understanding, Eleanore failed the tests, lowering her expectations for Courtney again and again. Confused and increasingly bitter as she saw her life—and her daughter—slipping away, Eleanore began therapy with Dr. Richardson. But, like many parents in similar situations, Eleanore did not feel this therapist understood what she was dealing with every day. In addition, Eleanore was having trouble differentiating her problems from Courtney's. Although Eleanore knew she needed help and continued to go to therapy, she felt she was not getting the kind of help she needed.

*   *   *

"I don't know why I come here every week," Eleanore said, looking idly at the now-familiar photos hung on Dr. Richardson's walls. "This isn't about me, but I don't know what else to do, so I come here. At least I feel like I'm doing something."

"I understand you feel frustrated," Dr. Richardson said.

Eleanore exploded. "Frustrated? I used to be frustrated—three months ago I was frustrated. If I'm *frustrated* it's because my life is hell, and I can't do anything about it. I don't have a life any more. I don't think you really know what I'm talking about. I don't think you listen. I doubt you care! Jesus!" she expostulated, then stopped herself short. "I sound just like Courtney."

Dr. Richardson honed in on Eleanore's outburst. "How does that make you feel? Understanding your daughter works better than judging her. We've discussed strategies you can use to calm yourself when you feel so overwhelmed. Take a time-out."

"I don't need a 'time-out.' Or, yeah, I do. I need about a five-year time-out until Courtney grows up! Do you think a five-minute 'time-out' is going to change anything in my life? My fourteen-year-old daughter has changed herself into some sort of alternative geek. I don't even know her anymore. In the last couple of months she has taken to wearing black clothes and dyed her hair black. She's a redhead, a beautiful redhead." She laughed bitterly. "If I don't laugh, I'm going to cry. I thought we just weren't understanding each other, so we tried family therapy. It didn't bring us anything. When she agreed to speak at all, she told the most unbelievable stories about me, and the therapist took her seriously. That wasn't going to bring us anything!"

"Courtney must be reacting to something in her home life," Dr. Richardson suggested. "Your relationship with Peter, for example. She might also be suffering from a chemical imbalance. She may harbor feelings of abandonment. You cannot blame her for something that is not within her control. Perhaps medication could help her."

It seemed to Eleanore that Dr. Richardson believed the life she described every session to be merely a figment of her imagination, and it made her angry. "What are we talking about? I live in the midst of daily turmoil my daughter creates for I don't know what reason. If I knew *why*, then maybe I could *do* something about it. Why has she suddenly changed from the girl I knew? I'm starting not to care, and that scares me. I just want life to be the way it used to be."

Suddenly sick of "working on her issues," and realizing that she was making sense only to herself, she decided to vent. Maybe then she would feel better; it seemed to work for Courtney. *How nasty I'm being,* she thought. *How childish, and about my own daughter.* She felt a sudden rush of something akin to dislike for her daughter but squelched it as fast as she could. She hoped it had not shown on her face because she didn't want anyone—even her therapist—to know that she had begun to wonder if she even liked her daughter anymore. Moreover, she didn't like herself when she let her anger take over.

"She plays this horrible, dark, creepy music, and if I ask her to turn it down, she tells me I don't even want to understand her, and then she puts on her headphones and gives me this wonderfully martyred, resentful look. Whoops, that was mean, and I just promised myself I wouldn't be mean anymore. So, fine; it gets quieter in the rest of the house, but that's only until you go into her room because she has it blasting so loud from her headphones, you can still hear it. Last month she and her friend Boris painted her room dark silver, and she bought some deep purple curtains and dark posters. Then they erected some sort of shrine. And I paid for it all." She laughed bitterly. "I used to hate her teeny bop posters, but I hate this more. I hate going into her room, so I don't."

"Do you ever speak to her about this new image?"

"What? Speak to her? Sure, I try, but she looks at me as though I have the wit of a chimpanzee. She has a whole new set of friends, and frankly, they are about the only people who could make her seem less alternative! I asked Courtney once why they all dressed that way, and she just looked at me and said, 'Eleanore, that is so banal.' I was supposed to feel rebuked, I think."

"She calls you 'Eleanore'?"

"Not with my permission. She just does, especially when she wants to show she is wiser and more mature than I—or to show off in front of her new friends. I don't like it, but with all the other things we find to fight about, this seems like one I can ignore. I don't ignore it, though, when she calls me 'bitch.'"

"How does your daughter's way of speaking to you make you feel?"

"Angry, sick, and tired. Like giving up. But that's not the point. The point is . . . I don't know what the point is. . . ." She stopped and became quieter. "Except for the times I feel, and I do sometimes, that maybe I have earned it. Maybe I haven't really comprehended what she experienced when her father died in the car accident she survived. Probably I haven't." Eleanore paused. She knew she was contradicting herself, but contradiction described her feelings most accurately. Her feelings of love for her daughter, combined with her dislike of the new lifestyle, were at the center of her inner contradiction, and she knew it but did not know what to do about it.

"That's an important insight, Eleanore. How do you feel about that?"

Pissed off, Eleanore thought and wondered why Dr. Richardson always asked her the same question. Instead she said, "Nothing. No, of course not nothing. Just going through my usual 'Whom shall we blame and curse this time?' routine. Sorry, I shouldn't be so bitter, but it's how I feel. I had a perfect family. I used to marvel at that. I never forgot to be grateful, so this can't be a punishment from God that I wasn't grateful because I was. Then, in a moment, it was gone. Nick and Courtney went out to buy some ice cream, and Nick had a heart attack; he lost control of the car, and he died. Thank God, Courtney didn't. Then, later, I met Peter, and he is wonderful. Courtney loved him. . . ." her voice trailed off. "This is all so new, so unexpected. I don't know what to do anymore."

"Turning all your anger back on yourself is not likely to help you," Dr. Richardson responded. "At the same time, just being angry at Courtney isn't going to be helpful, either."

"I really don't know what to do anymore." Eleanore sounded angry and resigned at once.

"Perhaps Courtney is looking for a little bit more direction from you. Not control—direction."

"I don't think I know what you mean."

"Courtney is apparently trying to find an identity that is her own. That's fine. But it sounds as though you are concerned about what sort of identity she is finding and how she is doing it. It sounds as though you experience her search as your prison."

"Yes, fine, but I still don't know what to do about it," Eleanore despaired. "What you don't understand is that when I leave here, I get to go home and deal with Courtney not having done her work for the home-schooling tutor. Now that should be fun because the last time it happened I was told that the next time it happens, Courtney is out of the program, which means she has to go back to school, which she won't do. I live my whole life in between a rock and a hard place. And that's on a good day."

Dr. Richardson did not confront Eleanore's bitterness. "You see, Eleanore, this is where the problem is about you. You seem to have lost confidence in yourself as her mother. I wonder if you haven't even begun to lose confidence in yourself as a person. Perhaps Courtney mainly needs you to take charge again."

As she walked to her car, Eleanore thought through the last few months. *We had such a nice life going until recently. Then Courtney changed. She didn't want to go to school. She found new friends. She started on her alter-native diet and began wearing those ridiculous costumes. When I walk in the door of my own house I feel as though it isn't my home anymore. Chaos reigns because Courtney's in charge.* For the first time, Eleanore could articulate the core of the problem, but solutions eluded her completely. *I just want the chaos to stop. I just want to go back to the way life was a few months ago.*

On her way home she stopped to do errands. She knew she was taking as long as possible because she didn't want to face Courtney. *If only she would just return to the old Courtney.* That thought passed through her mind a hundred times a day. At first she had thought it was just a stage that Courtney was going through, but instead of leaving it behind, lately Court-ney seemed to be embracing it more and more. First she stopped playing soccer, then she quit piano lessons. She had dropped her old friends—the girls she had grown up with—and saw only Boris and her other new friends. She had once been interested in school; now she was being home schooled. At one time she had a warm and loving relationship with her stepfather. Now she would barely speak to him, and if she did, it was with the complete disdain with which she treated everyone except Boris. Eleanore wondered if Courtney was heading for real trouble.

As she walked into the house, Eleanore smelled the odor she had come to despise: a combination of boiled seaweed, pumpkin seeds, and whatever else Courtney put into her "health" stews, together with the sickly sweet in-cense she burned while she cooked. She saw Courtney's pans piled in the sink, and barley and quinoa spilled on the floor, but she chose to ignore the mess. Revolted by the smell which she now associated with her daughter, and even more revolted because she felt revolted, she walked through the kitchen as quickly as she could. One thing had just come upon another, and each little thing hadn't seemed so radical until Eleanore looked at the whole lifestyle Courtney had created for herself. *I could have dealt with any one or two parts of it, even this stench,* she thought. *It's this whole crazy life she has put together that is intolerable.* She noticed she was wringing her hands—her newest habit—and almost shuddered as she put down her things, preparing to go to talk to Courtney.

As Courtney had constructed her alternative lifestyle, she had taken over the house and every aspect of their lives. Eleanore rarely cooked anymore; they ate cold deli food or takeout because she couldn't stand to listen to Courtney's diatribes about how unhealthy the food was and how disgusting everything else was. Eleanore and Peter hardly ever went out because they didn't trust Courtney in the house alone. They never really talked either because Eleanore—and Peter, too—was too tense to have a conversation; they had lost track of almost everything that had drawn them together. Whatever they began to talk about always ended up being about Courtney and somehow turned into an argument, although they each knew they agreed completely about the problems in their house. Eleanore's whole life seemed consumed by her daughter, but not really by her daughter so much as by the "Dark Force," as Peter had come to call it, which had overtaken their lives.

Eleanore walked up the stairs to Courtney's room and knocked on the door. She thought she heard the okay to enter, so she opened it. Courtney and Boris were sitting on the bed. Courtney was cuddling Polly, the cat she had adored since she was three. The bed was a mess, but what was new about that? *It doesn't mean anything,* Eleanore assured herself.

"Hello, Courtney. Hello, Boris." She attempted to be pleasant.

Courtney glared at her mother. "Eleanore, when you knock, aren't you supposed to wait for someone to say 'come in' before you open the door? You know, I think you are the one who used to tell *me* that." Her voice was quiet, but the tone was cold and caustic. It put Eleanore immediately on the defensive.

"I thought . . . sorry. I thought I heard you say . . ." She felt herself becoming flustered and defensive. She hated that she felt frightened to speak to her own daughter. Forcing herself to regain her composure, Eleanore said, "We need to talk, now or later, but after Boris has left."

"What makes you think Boris is leaving?"

Eleanore had no answer to that provocation, and she knew it showed on her face. "I made an assumption. Since Boris does not live here, I assume he will leave at some point." She hated the caustic tone she always used with her daughter nowadays.

"Or not," Courtney shot back.

"No, not 'or not.' Not only does Boris not live here, he is not welcome to live in my house."

"Our house. We are my father's joint heirs."

"And you are still a minor."

"And I can go to the executor of the will and tell him you are threatening me."

Eleanore noticed how Boris smiled at Courtney and squeezed her hand. That infuriated her even more. "You won't be doing that before tomorrow at the earliest, so until then, Boris does not live here. And if he did, I wouldn't. Boris, I think it is time for you to leave."

"Eleanore," Boris began, but Eleanore interrupted him.

"To you I am Mrs. Stone. It's bad enough when Courtney calls me that."

He rolled his eyes. "Eleanore, I was invited here by Courtney, and I will leave when she and I decide I should." Somehow his arrogance still shocked her.

"When Boris leaves, which will be within the next hour," she said to Courtney, enunciating each syllable, "we need to talk about your schoolwork. Apparently you didn't do it again."

Courtney gave her a bored sort of look. "Whatever. You are really making me angry! Would you please leave my room now? Boris and I were meditating."

Eleanore stood and considered for a few seconds, wondering how and why she kept getting caught up in these arguments. As she walked down the stairs she thought she heard Boris encouraging Courtney to teach "that bitch" a lesson.

Letting her anger and frustration overtake her, she walked into the living room and kicked the couch. Then she kicked it again, and sat down, too furious to move. *This is really it,* she said to herself over and over again. *I've had it. She is going to boarding school or to the hospital or to . . . God! I don't care where she goes. I can't stand her. I can't, I won't live this way any longer,* she vowed to herself for the thousandth time, knowing she wouldn't really do anything but rage inside herself.

Lost in thought, she didn't even notice it had gotten dark. She was roused by the sounds of Peter coming home. She heard his exasperated sigh as he walked though the door; he had seen Boris's van parked outside.

"Hi," she greeted him.

He looked startled. "Hi. What are you doing sitting there in the dark? Are you okay? You're not going gothic like Courtney, are you?" He smiled, trying to joke.

"No. And I'm not okay. How could I be with Boris upstairs!"

He went up to her and, for the first time in months, tried to kiss her. She stiffened and he moved away. "Sorry," he said coldly. As he left the room he asked, "Do you want me to put a light on?" She heard him going into the kitchen. Suddenly he was bellowing, "Courtney. Goddamn it, get into this kitchen now! Courtney!"

Upstairs a door opened. Eleanore could hear Boris's voice, but Peter's yelling drowned it out. "Courtney get down here this minute! Your mother may be willing to take this shit from you, but I'm not. What the hell is going on here? This kitchen is disgusting!"

"Don't worry, Boris," Courtney said. "I'll be okay. He just acts this way sometimes. You know," she said meaningfully.

"Courtney, it's time you declared your independence from these people," Boris proclaimed with decision. "They don't understand you at all."

"I know. Don't worry. It'll be okay. I'll call later. I can handle him."

"What the hell?" Peter was standing at the bottom of the stairs. He snapped on the light. There were Courtney and Boris, dressed in almost identical black costumes with long, blackened hair. They looked like ghoulish twins. "Boris," Peter bellowed, "you have just been declared persona non grata—you know what that means? No, I don't suppose you do since you don't believe in going to school. It means you are no longer welcome in this house. Get out!"

Even Boris was intimidated by Peter's intensity, and, squeezing Courtney's hand, he hurried down the stairs and out the door. Eleanore was overwhelmed with gratitude and elation. She felt like cheering. Smiling, she got up to go to Peter to thank him. She hardly recognized him; she had never seen him this way. "Eleanore, why don't you go back to the living room, please," he said. "I need to speak to Courtney."

"You have no right," Courtney screamed. "In the first place, this is my house."

"On which I pay the mortgage, young lady."

"And in the second place," she continued, ignoring Peter, "Boris is my friend, and he will come here whenever *I* choose. This is *my* house! You don't run my life. You have no legal rights over me. You have no rights over me at all. You aren't my father." She turned her back on him grandly and started to return to her room.

"You have one hell of an attitude, not to speak of a mess to clean up in the kitchen. Get down to the kitchen. Now. It's about time you accepted some responsibility in this house. You make a mess; you clean it up."

"Don't you touch me," she shrieked. "Mother, don't you let him touch me! I'll report him for child abuse! How can you let him do this to me?" she yelled.

Eleanore hurried back to the stairs. She could not imagine Peter would strike Courtney; it wasn't possible, but yet she felt frozen with terror.

"I have no intention of touching you," Peter said. "What makes you think someone needs to be violent to be decisive? Nevertheless, I expect you to walk down these stairs and go clean up the kitchen. Now. We can talk about your attitude later. It's simple, Courtney. You are no longer in charge here."

Eleanore saw Courtney fighting back her tears, trying to remain defiant. "She'll go clean it up, Peter. Give her a few minutes to calm down," Eleanore said. She felt torn between the two people she loved most in the world. She knew Peter was right; she had heard his outburst with excitement, but she had become too terrified of Courtney to imagine taking such resolute action.

Without a word, Peter walked into the bedroom.

"Thank you, Mother. I thought he was really going to hurt me. He's gone crazy, I think; you know, paranoid schizophrenic. That's what Boris was saying, and he knows a lot about those kinds of things."

"I'll bet," Eleanore said. "Go clean up the kitchen. Peter is right. It's gross." She wanted to add that Courtney knew very well that Peter would never hurt her, but something held her back.

"I'm going. I only forgot because you came up and yelled at me about school and Boris being here. . . ." Courtney was crying, but walking down the stairs toward the kitchen.

Eleanore followed Peter into their bedroom. Before she could begin to thank him for what he had done, he said, "Eleanore, I just can't stand to watch you be manipulated and lied to and intimidated by a fourteen-year-old and her scruffy friend. That is not the woman I married. I don't know where that woman has gone."

Eleanore took a deep breath. Something inside shifted. It was like the sky suddenly clearing after days of rain. "You're right. I would not have had the courage to do what you just did. I would have cleaned it up myself, getting more and more angry every moment. You are completely right. Maybe that's what Dr. Richardson was saying to me today. I can't go on being the way I have been. Suddenly I get it: I have to change if Courtney is going to change. Thank you, Peter."

They talked for an hour or more, hearing no sound from Courtney. Eleanore realized how much she needed Peter's love, support, and strength. They agreed they would no longer allow Courtney to orchestrate their family life. They agreed that chaos could not reign any longer and, most of all, that Eleanore would stand up to Courtney.

They went downstairs together and found her finishing up in the kitchen. It was spotless. She had done more than just clean up her own mess; she had wiped off all the cupboards and washed the floor.

"So, does that suit you?" she asked scornfully. Courtney looked at them with what looked like real hatred in her eyes.

"Please, Courtney, spare us the Cinderella show," Eleanore said. "If you are going to cook your own meals, you will have to use your own money for the food and clean up immediately. Peter and I will no longer support your alternative lifestyle. We have also decided it is time for you to get back into school. Home schooling was a bad idea in the first place, and since you have not kept to your part of the deal, it's over. We will be finding a school for you in the next few days."

"You can't do that. My life is my own!" Courtney screamed. "My father never would have allowed this! I will do whatever I like. I am fourteen years old and capable of making my own decisions. I will go to court if I have to. Boris's parents will help me."

Eleanore ignored her threats. "Let's be completely clear: You are the child; we are your parents. You've lost your right to make your own choices because you weren't making very good ones. I cannot allow that any longer. It's not right."

Courtney threw them a devastating look and walked as magnificently and with as much dignity as she could muster up the stairs and into her room. She made sure to slam the door.

Eleanore put her arms around Peter's neck. "Thank you. I couldn't have done that without you. Thank you."

"We can do this, Eleanore. How does it feel to be stronger than your daughter?"

"Great. Like myself again. I can't believe how I have been letting this child run our lives."

A Wake-Up Call

Courtney's story is hopeful. For some parents this story may serve as a "wake-up call," the example they need to realize it is possible to retake the control in their family and in their own lives. For others it will seem too easy, too pat because they know (or believe) their situation is worse than this one. But even if that is true, the idea that parents can and should retake control of the family and their lives is central to changing their status quo. It may not be as easy as it was for Eleanore and Peter, but then again, it might be. Most important, while professionals (therapists, counselors, psychiatrists, etc.) can often be helpful to teens and their parents, sometimes the professionals do not understand the situation and are not helpful. When parents feel that is the case, it makes sense to seek help from someone else, or to handle the situation without the aid of a professional. It is, happily, often the case that parents can help their adolescent, themselves, and their family to change a bad situation on their own.

Like many parents who suddenly decide to stand up to their teen, Eleanore was surprised to find that it was easier than she had ever imagined. She was thrilled to see how quickly life began to change in her family. She realized that Courtney would test her again and that it would be vital for her to maintain the stance she had assumed with Peter's support. Life felt better in many ways: She did not feel as constantly angry and depressed, and she even fancied she looked better. For the first time in almost a year, she and Peter were really enjoying each other.

About two months after the confrontation between Peter and Courtney, Eleanore and Peter found themselves explaining their experience to their friends, Melanie and Brian, who were also facing some difficult times with their son, Mark. It was the first time they had spoken openly about what had happened in their family.

"I understand what you are going through," Eleanore empathized. "You know, Courtney had me so bamboozled that I had actually agreed to take her out of school and try home schooling. Now I see it was her way of getting me to lower my expectations so she wouldn't have to face what she could and could not do. And I was scared of being the 'bad' parent who 'doesn't understand.' I went to therapy, but it didn't change things because I couldn't—or wouldn't—see what was going on in front of my face. I couldn't differentiate what were her problems and what were my problems, so I used therapy as a place to vent my anger."

"Mark just spends hours in front of the TV or the computer," Brian said. "I remind him and remind him to do his homework, but he always tells me it's done. Then I ask to see it, then we fight. . . ."

"Then *we* fight," Melanie added.

"Oh, I know," Eleanore sighed. "Been there; done that. Sounds like Peter and me before we figured things out. What is different now is that I don't wait for Courtney to establish the rules. She still gets angry, but her homework has to be done in the room where I am sitting. I don't look it over, but I have let her know that I will not trust her until *she* regains my trust. She doesn't really like it, but she doesn't scream and yell about it. Somehow we have just changed the ground rules, I guess. And Peter and I don't fight. That's worth a lot!"

"I'm beginning to worry that Mark might have something really wrong with him. He was never this way . . ." Melanie said, her voice trailing off. She shook her head. "I begin to feel so . . . I don't even know the word exactly. I feel so . . ."

"Manipulated? Intimidated? Angry? Powerless?" Eleanore asked. "That's how I felt, but I had begun to believe that was just how it was meant to be. I figured, you know, the tumultuous teen years . . . and I wondered a lot what I had done wrong. I mean I figured it had to be someone's fault, so I blamed myself. It was easier than not being manipulated. Or at least I thought so."

"The worst of it was," Peter said, "that we lost our whole way of communicating. But, well, I do want to say that Courtney isn't a bad kid. She never was. She hit some bumps in her road, and we didn't understand what to do about it. It was as though she wanted to be instantly grown-up and run the house, all the while being a scared little girl. It was like a misfire in her growing up."

"We try to give Mark room to grow up," Brian said, "but then he gets himself into trouble, so what can I do besides jump in to fix it? I can't just stand by and watch him ruin all his chances for college. I have to help him keep his options open."

"Been there; done that, too!" Eleanore said again. "I never realized how common all this is. Me? I never exactly rescued Courtney, *per se*. It was more that I didn't even let her get into trouble first. I was the 'advance rescue party.'"

Melanie nodded. She knew exactly what Eleanore meant. "Sometimes I think Mark is just afraid of growing up, but that seems so trite, too simple. Sometimes I think Brian is even more afraid of Mark growing up than Mark is.

"I don't think it's trite or simple," Peter corrected her.

"Let's just not talk about it any more," Brian sighed.

"Brian," Peter said, "that's not a good plan. That's what we tried, and it nearly led us to break up—not to mention what Courtney was doing to herself. Don't be embarrassed. Don't be ashamed, and most of all, don't play ostrich! These things happen nowadays, you know. Don't let your own fear and hurt send you running to hide from the world."

Eleanore nodded. "Been there; done that. Again," she said softly.

"We had definitely become afraid of Courtney growing up because she seemed destined to do it the wrong way," Peter said. "I have to say, I still don't know why she started acting the way she did, but it doesn't matter. We can't dwell on that. What we have to do is help her get over or beyond her bumps. What happened to us is that we bumped along with her. We began to believe her fears for herself, and we reacted to them. We got caught in her world and her ideas about herself."

"I never thought about it like that," Melanie said, "but it kind of makes sense. Brian, what do you think? Do we do that?"

Brian was silent. "I don't know. I mean, I just wish it didn't have to be this way. I don't even feel comfortable sitting here because I never know what he might be up to in our house."

"This sounds just like what had happened to us," Peter said. "I mean, I can't tell you what to do, but I know that as soon as we declared ourselves back in control, life started getting better. I don't know if that would work for you. . . ."

Brian and Melanie exchanged glances. Peter and Eleanore could see they were wondering if they could retake the control in their family.

"Looking back at the worst of it," Eleanore said, "I realize I had stopped being myself. Trying to deal with Courtney on her terms made me angry, and I became bitter and sarcastic, which made me ineffectual as her mother.

I was a wreck, but it was from that really weakened place that I was trying to glue Courtney's life together. Obviously, it couldn't work! It frightens me to think how lost I had become."

"I think I saw what was happening to Eleanore before she did," Peter said, "but I didn't act decisively enough, soon enough. I could have spared Eleanore and Courtney—and myself—some grief."

"I spend half my time and most of my energy trying to figure out how not to fight with Mark," Brian said. Melanie nodded as Brian continued, "But we fight anyway until I give in about whatever the issue is, but then when his way doesn't work out, I race in to rescue him. I don't know. This is too confusing!"

"I remember that," Eleanore said. "It was because I had to be confused in order to let that turmoil continue in my own home. Listen, one thing I learned is that confusion is confusing, and then you can't see clearly enough to help your child. I ended up helping Courtney sabotage herself because I wouldn't stand up for what I knew to be right and better. I'm not proud of that—and I have absolutely changed it. I can't say that Courtney is totally ecstatic about it all, but at least I know I have done what I should."

"She probably will be in a few years," Peter said.

"It's really that simple, Eleanore?" Melanie asked.

"Yes and no. I mean when you start to stand up to your teen it isn't easy, but after the first couple of times, it gets easier. What had happened was that Courtney learned she just had to wait me out, and she always did, or she hammered down my resolve so she got what she wanted, but not necessarily what was best for her. I still don't like the fights, but I prefer them to the old way, to letting her be in charge. And, in fact, we don't fight nearly as much now. What I used to think was that if I fought for a little while, then got worn down, I had 'made my point,' so I could give in. That was completely wrong!

"For me it's mainly about remembering I am her mother." Eleanore stopped and thought for a moment. "I mean, after all, how can you expect a fourteen-year-old to have the wisdom to know everything she should do? I know it sounds corny, but you know what? I do know some things she doesn't know!"

"That makes me think," Melanie said. "I get into these long discussions with Mark, and it feels as though I don't know anything. I never know how they turn out to be the way they turn out to be. Somehow . . . I don't know, it feels as though the world isn't quite recognizable. Last week we started out with me reminding him (for the twelfth time) to mow the lawn. The next thing, he said he didn't know how to use the lawn mower! Brian, we have to do something. Peter and Eleanore are right."

Eleanore nodded. "For us the important thing is to make sure we don't lose track of what we have learned for ourselves and for Courtney. I have to keep reminding myself that I had let my life begin to spin out of control, and it was bad for all of us. I don't intend to live that way ever again!"

The How, Not the What

If or when your teen begins to challenge you and the basis of your family life, it is easy to question whether a safe, secure, loving atmosphere and time will be enough to take your child through adolescence. Although it probably doesn't seem like it to you any more than it did to Eleanore, your home should provide a significant contrast to the adolescent worldview. You aren't out of touch or hopelessly old if you question if the "rush"—the intense experience of excitement and risk that adolescents crave—is the only viable goal. Nor are you wrong to question your teen's image, language, grades, and friends.

Parents' standards of integrity and dignity are what provide the contrast between adolescent culture and adult responsibility. It is easy to be convinced—not only by your teen, but often by the school, by a counselor, by a therapist, and by the culture around you—that lowering your expectations for your child and for yourself will make him feel safe and secure. In the end, that is more likely to substantiate your teen's own questions about and for himself, the future, and his search for meaning in his life.

For many parents, retaking the control in their family is as easy as doing it. Courtney is neither violent nor yet seriously self-destructive. She is mainly a girl seeking an identity, but one who has very little idea how to go about it. Keep in mind that it is not the seeking of a separate and distinct identity that is the problem, but rather the self-sabotaging methods some teens use.

If Courtney had been allowed to remain in control of her family, the situation might have become drastic. Peter might well have decided he was not able to stay with Eleanore. Had Peter not intervened as he did, Courtney could easily have moved beyond her search for an identity into a serious self-destructive pattern. She had already intimidated her mother enough to convince her she should opt out of the challenges of school.

In my work, I have found that teens who choose the "alternative" path, as did Courtney and her friend Boris, tend to be mainly reactive: reacting to their parents and to society, trying to establish their identity mainly by saying "NO!" (And yes, this behavior is slightly reminiscent of the terrible twos.) Being alternative may also serve as a marker of how much these teens are afraid they will not be able to compete in the world, afraid they will not be able to find individuality within a "normal" context. But as your teen reacts to what she believes she cannot manage and as you react to her, chaos takes over in the family. The only motivators, then, are reactions *against* something or someone, instead of positive action in support of standards and integrity.

In Courtney's family, the future looks brighter since Peter discovered that Courtney's control of the family was really tenuous, and since he and Eleanore returned control to themselves, the parents. If he and Eleanore remain consistent with Courtney and with their decision not to let her parent herself, there is a good chance she will rediscover herself.

Manipulation and Intimidation

Like the parents in this story, most parents accept varying degrees of manipulation and intimidation from their kids. As we saw in Chapter 2, manipulation and intimidation are part of a pattern of behavior teens use in order to try to gain control, however misguided, of their lives. In order to break the pattern and stop it from happening, first you have to be aware it is happening. Then you have to make the commitment to stop letting it happen.

Pay close attention to your reaction as you read the following, probably all-too-familiar, questions and statements. If you realize you hear these lines frequently but you have become accustomed to them, it indicates that your teen is manipulating and/or intimidating you and is doing such a good job you hardly even blink when it happens.

How do you feel as you read through these lines? Have your journal handy to note down your responses. If you find yourself getting angry, demoralized, or embarrassed, take note. There is meaning in your reaction. Does your teen:

- Repeat your question back to you, rephrase your question or statement, and/or lengthen it by asking what you mean?
- Give you a thoroughly blank look so that you begin to explain and rephrase and minimize or change what you have just said or asked?
- Turn on the tears, the pouting face, the droopy-eyed look?
- Misquote the school, the therapist, the other parent?

How often does your teen say something like:

- "I don't know what you want me to say."
- "Couldn't you please, just this once, bring me . . ."

- "What do you mean? Don't you trust me?"
- "You're the one making a big deal of this!"
- "You just changed what you said. That's not what my curfew was last weekend!"
- "You just don't understand!"
- "All the other kids get to . . ."
- "I was just going to. I'll do it in a minute; don't rush me."
- "I can't believe you would invade my privacy!"
- "I'm going to get angry."
- "Do you think I'm lying to you?"
- "My teacher is so stupid (my teacher doesn't understand me; my teacher doesn't like me)."
- "Nobody could be expected to do this much work."
- "I just don't understand this grade. I handed in all the work; she was just too lazy to grade it."
- "You don't want me to have fun."
- "My therapist believes me."
- "I'm going to go live with my father . . . my mother (whichever parent the child doesn't currently live with)."
- "I'll report you for child abuse."
- "You don't think I'm an alcoholic, do you?"
- "Please don't tell Mom (Dad), I don't want to hurt her (his) feelings!"
- "Why can't I have a key to the car?"
- "I know, I know. You're right. I'm going to work harder. I really am. I know this isn't okay. I'll do much better this term."
- "Just get me a beeper (or cell phone), and you'll know where I am."
- "Look, if you are going to make my curfew be so ridiculously early, you can't really expect me to keep it!"
- "It would be so rude if you called his parents. It would sound like you don't trust them."

Still Another Way Teens Manipulate: Lowered Expectations

Once your child is accustomed to manipulating you successfully, you are but a few short steps away from lowering your expectations. Without realizing it, adolescents often believe that lowered expectations make their lives easier. With less expected of them, they can do what they want, and they don't have to face the increasing challenges school and society bring them. But the other side of that coin is that they begin to doubt themselves because they don't ever really test their own mettle. The more you lower your expectations, the more you justify your teen's self-doubt and need for immediate gratification of simple but ongoing wants.

Lowering expectations usually happens so slowly that, like Eleanore, you may not notice a change until all of a sudden you realize you have stopped expecting your daughter or son to be responsible, to remember things, to complete chores, or even just to be kind and caring. Some parents even give up expecting their teen to be able to finish high school, must less go on to college. Soon everyone in the family thinks the adolescent can't do much of anything, and no doubt he believes it by then, too. That leaves him with no responsibilities and, very important, with very low self-esteem.
Have you begun to think:

- It's not even worth the fight.
- He only needs to sit with us until he finishes eating (when you are at a family gathering).
- Maybe my child really isn't all that bright.
- All the kids look that way nowadays.
- Most kids talk to their parents that way.
- I want my son home, but I can't stand to be around him.
- All kids experiment with drugs nowadays.
- Most teens don't show affection; I guess I shouldn't expect mine to either.
- You can't expect a fifteen-year-old to be able to manage money very well.
- I'll be happy if she just gets a GED.
- I just hope he lives!

Notice when you:

- Gradually stop expecting to have conversations or to know anything about his or her life.
- Stop expecting your home to be a place that feels like home.
- Stop feeling because you feel you don't dare.
- Stop dreaming, not only in relation to the child, but to yourself as well.
- Put the rest of life "on hold."
- Begin to have tunnel vision: you stop noticing that your child

doesn't shower every day, his clothes aren't very clean, or she just looks dirty.

- Know you treat your child more like a nonpaying boarder than a member of the family.
- No longer dare to hope your child might treat you with even common respect or even acknowledge your presence.
- No longer dare to hope your child might buy you a birthday card or send you flowers for Mother's Day.

Your teen may be succeeding in failing, and by allowing yourself to be manipulated and lowering your expectations, you are helping him or her in that project. You expect nothing, but then your child does even less. It is not the kind of success you want to foster.

How Much Control Can a Parent Really Exert?

How much can a parent really control his or her teen outside the home? The answer is not really very much. Your control is in your home and it comes from the stance of a parent who actively chooses not to be manipulated and lied to and who refuses to lower standards for herself or her teen.

You would probably prefer that I tell you three ways to be able to control your teen's behavior outside the home. I cannot do that—nor can anyone else. It just doesn't work that way. In fact, you cannot keep your teen from sneaking out, even if you put bars on the bedroom window—and just think what that would do to you and to the whole tenor of your family life! Teens who want to sneak out, do. Kids who want to see the friends you don't approve of will manage to do so.

There also isn't much you can do about the clothes your child wears. I have known many kids who simply changed clothes when they got where they were going. In fact, you cannot even force your teen to go to school. I know a mother who drove her daughter to school every day, watched her go in the front door, but had no clue that her daughter walked right back out the side door.

So what do you do? Give up? The temptation can be momentarily great, but it is only momentary. You know things have to change. You have already begun the process. The more you allow yourself to give up your illusions and your denial, the closer you will be to seeing a clear picture of your situation and the more you will be able to act instead of react.

Behavior is a manifestation of attitude; therefore, behavior won't change until attitude changes. *You* cannot change your teen's attitude, but you can set and maintain standards that are incompatible with your teen's behavior and attitudes. Home is where you have always set the standards by which your child can learn how to behave when she or he is away from home. By being honest, caring, open, and honorable, you taught your child what is right and what isn't. The testing that teens do is often to make sure you really believe in your own standards. Letting your teen make inroads into those deeply held beliefs may seem momentarily convenient, but the cost can be very high indeed. Deciding you will no longer accept either behavior or attitudes that are unacceptable, you oblige your teen to reexamine his world from a different point of view.

Other kids (read: peer pressure) and commercial adolescent culture are all saying one thing, giving one undifferentiated message: Buy, have fun, instant gratification is fine, being responsible is boring, and tomorrow is just another chance to buy things and have more fun. Your teen is depending upon you to question that message, even though he or she will probably not like to hear that you don't accept those standards. But think about this: If you do not challenge that message, you are tacitly approving of it. Most kids still know the "good stuff" you taught them as kids, but when they are worried about peer pressure, those ideals become harder to live by.

Reclaiming Your Role of Parent

As you begin to internalize the events in the process of change, all of a sudden you will notice that something feels different. As you break through your denial, decide you will no longer be manipulated and lied to, and raise your expectations for your teen to a reasonable level, you will begin to regain control in the family and in your own life.

You can be like a brick wall that withstands all manipulation, lies, rationalizations, and excuses. You can be strong enough that nothing shakes your resolve, nothing gets around, over, under, or through the standards you set. In his or her heart, your child expects you to have standards different from those of his or her peers. Your teen absolutely needs that from you.

For many families, like Courtney's, the downward spiral started as the parents tried harder and harder to be "understanding" of their child. But beware: Being understanding is so often a euphemism for giving in to your child, a way to rationalize to yourself or to someone else when you know you have been intimidated or manipulated. When you are overly "understanding," too often you are rationalizing for your teen, justifying behavior and attitudes that cannot be justified. It can become a way of convincing yourself that it is okay to lower your standards and to depart from your most deeply held convictions. It can become a way of life.

There is no foolproof way to tell whether a teen is just searching for an identity or heading for big trouble. I tell parents to refer to the rule of thumb spelled out earlier: If your teen makes mistakes but learns from them, the problems are probably not too serious. If, however, your teen keeps on making the same and bigger and more important mistakes over and over, probably that teen is heading for trouble. Never mistake outward compliance for real learning and changing. Do not make the mistake of wanting things to be better more quickly than they can be. Remember: You do know your child. If, at any point, you feel your teen is no longer that familiar person, take that as a serious warning sign.

Chapter 6 ✿

A Divided House: Adam's Story

It is not uncommon for teens to be adept at dividing and conquering the adults in their lives. Although divorced parents often present the easiest target for teens who seek to get what they want and do what they want by means of dividing and conquering, it would be a mistake for parents who have remained married to imagine that their teen could not or would not use that strategy on them, too. Teens who are bent on living by the divide and conquer strategy will use it in all their relationships.

In the story that follows we see a classic case of parents teaching by their own bad example. Bob and Laurel have been divorced for some years, but their animosity has not waned. Their thirteen-year-old son, Adam, perfects his own divide and conquer strategies, keeping his parents locked in an angry relationship, unaware they have become mere pawns in their son's intricate family chess game.

Bob Heller had been back in the country only a couple of hours when he placed a call to his ex-wife, Laurel. He dreaded the call, but it was the only way to get in touch with his son.

She's just as warm and friendly as ever, he thought to himself when she asked him in a cold voice why he was calling. "I might have thought that was obvious: I want to see my son," he said.

"Why?"

"Why?" How quickly it turned into the old-style argument, though he had promised himself he would not let it happen. "Because he's my son, and it's been a long time since I saw him—and since he saw me." Bob heard the antagonism in his tone.

"He's doing very well without you."

"I'm glad he's doing well. My work may take me to some strange places, but he is never 'without me.' I can always be reached for my son."

"Fortunately, mine doesn't," Laurel replied. "He needs one parent who can always be there."

Bob ignored the provocation. "Now that I'm back, I need to see him, and he needs to see me. When would be convenient?"

"Don't pressure me! Call me next week."

"Just tell me when he will be home, and I'll call and make arrangements with Adam. You don't even have to be involved."

"I just don't know how Adam is going to feel about this. Kids can be very sensitive, you know. You have been gone for more than a year, and Adam is doing very well. Let's just let sleeping dogs lie."

"I am not a sleeping dog in Adam's life; I'm his father."

"You represent a very painful part of his life."

"I don't *represent* anything. I'm his father, and I love him!"

"He can't understand why he hasn't heard from you."

"He has, unless you have intervened. Relief work in Central Africa isn't exactly conducive to lots of phone calls, but there have been about a hundred letters. He might even be proud of his father—unless his mother or his grandmother here propagandized him."

"I don't have to listen to this. You deserted your son and me. If you choose to do that kind of work instead of being with your son, well, that's *your* business, but you can't just pop in and out of his life whenever it's convenient for you. He doesn't really talk about you, and I surely don't bring you up."

I wonder, he thought. Trying to change the tenor of the conversation, he asked, "How is he? How's he doing? School, hockey, friends?"

"He's fine" she answered. "It's been hard for him, and it's taken a lot of therapy, but he's doing better now."

"What are you talking about? Did something happen or are these just your feelings? What kinds of things do you say to him?"

"We don't talk about it. He talks about it with his therapist."

"That must be fun! Why does he need to see a therapist?" Though his tone was derisive, he felt concern. Had he abandoned his son? "Is something wrong with him?"

"He's got some issues to work out."

"Oh. *Issues.* Then I'm not worried. This conversation is going nowhere.

When can I speak to Adam to make plans to see him? I'm not sure how long I'm going to be here."

"Well, I don't want you to upset him. If you're just going to leave again, it would be better not to see him. I'll let his therapist know you're back and that you want to see him. Then we'll decide. Call me in a week, and I'll let you know."

"I'm not waiting for you to badmouth me to him for a solid week and discuss me with his therapist and decide I am going to upset him too much—as though you don't do that anyway. I am his father; I'm not evil, and I am going to see him."

"Don't threaten me, Bob. You've been gone a long time. It was your idea to walk out of the marriage and your parenting responsibilities."

"Don't threaten *me,* Laurel. I have always wanted to be—*and have been*—Adam's father. I'll call tonight about nine. I expect to be able to speak to my son. If he does not want to talk to me, *he* can tell me that, and I will respect it."

"You can't expect a child to say something like that."

"He's not a child. He's thirteen. I'll call at nine."

So much for trying to do it the normal way most divorced parents deal with each other, he thought. *No wonder I divorced her. The wonder is that I ever married her!* He could feel himself getting ready to go off on her just like he did in the last years of their marriage and just after the divorce. *No,* he told himself. *This is about my son. The rest doesn't matter.* Still, he was angry, and he wanted to get the best of her. He wanted her to know that the divorce was her fault. *She* had caused her own misery *and deprived him* of the chance to watch his son grow up on an everyday basis.

He made himself stop to think about the work he had been doing, about the real pain and anguish that he had seen every day for the last year and had helped to ease. He felt calmer. He had arranged to have dinner with an old friend whom he hadn't seen since he went to Africa. He was looking forward to it. He needed to talk to someone who would understand. Tom had been through his own difficult divorce and hardly ever saw his kids either.

As soon as he and Tom had greeted each other, Bob began complaining about his conversation with Laurel. "Part of the reason I took that job in Africa was to get away from this. I hate to see what she is doing to that boy. I can't wait until the day he tells her to 'fuck off.'"

"Whoa!" said Tom. "I thought you told me the work in Africa had changed you completely. You have to leave the divorce behind; it's been five years now."

"The divorce? Yes, but I am not leaving my son to his mother's and his grandmother's smotherings—then he *would* need a therapist! He's a great kid, or at least he would be if his mother would give him half a chance to be."

"So, are you going to take another assignment like this one?" Tom said to change the subject.

"I've been asked to go to Cambodia, but I don't think I'm going to take it. That one is probably too dangerous even for me. There's work in Kosovo clearing land mines, and I could take Adam—let him see life without every comfort, life when it's just about life. Like his mother would let that happen! 'What if he couldn't see his therapist?'" He mimicked Laurel's tone and accent.

"Bob, that is not a good route to go," Tom counseled.

"I know, I know. I'm thinking of taking a job here in New York. It would be a stretch financially, but I think it might be worth it. I don't like being a sometimes-Dad."

Tom smiled. "Yeah. I know." He paused, thinking of his own situation. "So, are you going to call Adam tonight?"

"Of course. I don't suppose I'll manage to talk to him, though. I doubt she'll let me. I really don't want to go through lawyers to see my son. It's so destructive to him—and me. And she always wins. Do you realize I have already given her just about every penny I ever had or will ever have? It isn't as though she doesn't have money anyway."

"Calm down, Bob. You're too involved in fighting. Forget how you feel about her. You're just back from Africa where you did some amazing work. You will have a chance to see your son and tell him about it—let him get to know his father. He's old enough now. Give your fight with Laurel a rest."

"I know. You're right. I won't get sucked into any more useless arguments. Scout's honor." He paused thoughtfully. "Maybe I should settle here for a while, just to be with him."

Tom handed Bob his cell phone. "Make your call, right now, with me sitting here to support you and to bust your balls if you start to argue with her."

"Thanks," Bob said. "Hi, Laurel. It's Bob. May I speak with Adam, please."

"I told you that it's going to take a few days to get Adam ready to talk to you. He's not ready. It's too sudden," Laurel greeted him.

Bob thought he heard Adam in the background asking who was on the phone. He would be reasonable, no matter what. "Yes, Laurel, you did, and I told you I would call him tonight. This is not a good thing we're doing. I . . ."

She cut him off with, "You deserted him when he was eight when you ran off with that woman. Then you deserted him again when you went to

Africa. You come back and you want him to jump for joy because you happen to remember he's alive. That is not *my* idea of being a father."

Bob held the phone a few inches from his ear, shaking his head and clenching his teeth. He wondered if Adam was hearing his mother. "No, Laurel, that's not how it was. Just let me speak to him without having to go through lawyers. You don't do him any good by that tactic—or the therapist one. You can't deny him the right to have a father."

"I don't need advice from *you*. I've arranged for you to call him at his therapist's on Thursday at 4:30, then she can be there to help him."

"What? He needs help because his dad telephones him? No, Laurel. Either I speak to him now or later this evening or we are back in court. Which, come to think of it, is probably what you want because it gives you something to do." Tom's look reprimanded him, and he tried to calm down, even though he felt she was provoking him. "I do not accept speaking to him with his therapist in the room. It's bad enough to know that you're going to be there coaching him. Stop trying to make me into the bad guy." He knew he had either said too much and ended all chances of speaking with Adam until he had a court order, or he had intimidated her enough that, indulging in her victim role, she would let him speak to Adam.

There was silence on Laurel's end. Then she whispered, "Call back in two hours. I have to think about this."

Bob looked at Tom and knew he empathized completely. It made him feel better. "God! How I hate that woman! To think she is the mother of my son! She's probably going to call the therapist for an emergency session." He wanted to vent his anger, but Tom stopped him, and Bob knew Tom was right.

Laurel collapsed into a chair, her mother standing over her. "I can't take any more of this. Things just quiet down, Adam gets back on track, then *he* comes back and upsets everything."

"Shhh. You don't want Adam to hear."

"Oh, yes I do. It's about time. He has to know the truth about his father. I have protected him enough! He is going to have to learn the truth."

"I know, dear. I know what a good mother you have always been to him."

"What am I going to do about him speaking to Adam? I can't allow it. It's going to upset him so much, and he doesn't see Marcia until Thursday. He's got an English paper due on Wednesday."

"Well, dear, if you are there when his father calls, you know, then he'll know he doesn't have to worry about being abandoned, that there is real stability and security in his life, someone to take care of him."

"Okay. I have to be strong. I'll tell Adam he only has to speak to his father for a few minutes *if he wants to* and that he doesn't have to see him. I'll stay in the room with him, just in case."

Laurel went to prepare Adam. He was at his computer. "Are you doing your work, dear? You're not just playing games or anything, are you? Let me see."

"Ma, leave it. It's fine. I finished my work."

"Are you sure? Everything? What about your history assignment? Do you need me to correct it for you? I could just proofread it for you."

"It's okay, Ma. Never mind."

"I have something to tell you, dear. I know it's going to be upsetting."

Adam's concentration on the computer screen didn't waver, and he made sure his mother didn't see what he was doing there. "Yeah, what?"

"Your father called." She waited for his reaction, ready to comfort him.

"Yeah?" Adam was elated. "That's cool. I thought that was who was on the phone. How come I didn't get to talk to him?"

"I didn't know if you would feel up to it. You've hardly heard from him for years. Only those couple of phone calls and the letters. He has been out of your life for so long, leaving us like he did. I didn't want to upset you. I knew how you would feel."

Adam kept his eyes focused on the computer screen. He was used to ignoring his mother. "I feel fine. When's he calling back? Did he leave a number? I'll call him."

"I told him you needed to talk this through with Marcia before you spoke to him."

Adam turned away from the computer and gave his mother a withering look. "No, Ma. I don't need to 'work this through with Marcia.'" He imitated her tone, a tactic he knew infuriated her. "I don't need Marcia at all. Maybe you do, I don't. I hate going to therapy. It's bullshit. Marcia's bullshit. Maybe I'll stop going altogether. You can have my appointments."

Marcia had warned her that Adam might react violently if his father returned. "I just don't want you to feel your life is a mess when you're older because you have all sorts of issues you didn't work through. Having a father leave you isn't easy to overcome. I've read enough books on the subject, so I know."

"Hey, Ma, have you ever thought of becoming a therapist?"

She did not register his sarcastic tone. "Yes, I have. Do you feel up to speaking with your father tonight, or would you rather I have him call you at Marcia's on Thursday? That way she would be right there to help you through it. You don't have to talk to him at all, if you don't want to."

"Ma, maybe you need 'help through this,' but I don't. Yes, I would like to speak with my dad when he calls back. Is that clear enough for you?" His attention returned to the computer. "Now leave me alone. I'm busy."

"He's calling a little after nine. I would like to be there when you talk to him, so he doesn't fill your mind with lies about me and your grandparents." Adam ignored her.

The phone rang at 9:15. "Dad?" Adam grabbed the phone and hurried out of the room to his bedroom. "Hold on a sec, Dad. Shut up, Ma. Just let me talk. No, I don't want you with me. Leave me alone, for Christ's sake! Sorry, Dad. Yeah, I'm fine. Wow! Well, yeah, she's being a pain in the butt for a change." Adam said, making sure his mother heard him.

"Sorry to hear that," Bob said. "It's nothing new. Wow! I missed you so much! How's life? What are you doing?"

"Life's okay, except for Ma. She's always worrying about me and sending me to therapists. I have so much to tell you. Where are you? Are you in New York? When can I see you? How was Africa?"

"New York. Yes. How about from Friday to Sunday night? We'll go to the Rangers game and maybe go eat some thick steaks. I'll tell you about Africa. It's amazing!"

"Cool. Yeah."

"I've missed you so much! What time can you get a train? You still playing hockey?"

"No, Ma made me quit. She said it was too dangerous, and it interfered with seeing my therapist." Adam's tone was sarcastic, and Bob felt elated his son was making snide comments to him about his mother; it was a sort of bonding.

"What, your mother made you quit hockey to see a therapist? Maybe she's the one who needs a therapist."

"Tonight I told her she should become a therapist. It would save money!" They both laughed. Laurel had come back into the room motioning to Adam he should get off the phone. She was suspicious of the laughter; she suspected it was about her. He waved her vehemently out of the room. "Yeah, so will you tell me all about Africa? I would love to go to Africa. Look, I gotta go. Ma's on my case. You know how she gets."

"I sure do. I used to have to live with her, too! I was the living expert on your mother's crazies at one time." They both laughed again. "I'll call you on Thursday to finalize plans. I'll call you tomorrow just to talk. I love you, Adam."

"'Bye, Dad."

Laurel had been pacing the living room smoking while Adam was on the phone with his father. "He's such a terrible influence on Adam," she said to her mother, making sure Adam would hear. "He doesn't understand love and responsibility and a child's need for security. He has a lot of issues, you know, but he won't work on them."

Adam took his cue. "I'm going to the city to see Dad this weekend. We're going to do all sorts of cool stuff. My dad's so cool."

The weekend was wonderful for Bob and for Adam. Each felt they had really connected. Bob decided to take the job in New York. Although he worried he might not find a desk job to his liking, spending time with Adam as he grew up was worth it to him. When he mentioned it to Adam, his son was thrilled. "Then I could see you all the time!"

"Yeah, that's the main idea behind it."

Laurel was not pleased with Bob's decision to stay in New York. She was terrified Bob would teach Adam to be wild and adventurous like he was, and in the ensuing months she did her utmost to make home especially comfy and secure. Bob was afraid Laurel would turn Adam into a wuss, so he thought up as many wild and exciting adventures as he could. They were competing for Adam's love, attention, and approval. They knew it and carried on the competition with a vengeance.

Adam carefully fed each just enough information about the other, much of it false or embellished, to keep the other always angry, mistrusting, and unsure who was winning the competition. It became a game to him, a deadly serious game, and he got a rush out of it. Adam continued to see Marcia because he could feed his mother ideas through her without anyone realizing it and use her to keep his father thinking that he was being manipulated by his mother.

When, at fourteen, Adam began to smoke, Laurel blamed Bob and Bob blamed Laurel. When his grades went down, Bob blamed Marcia, Laurel blamed the divorce, and Marcia blamed ADD. When Adam stopped coming to his appointments regularly and on time, Marcia and Laurel blamed Bob. When Adam came in late, Laurel blamed Bob. When he didn't want to jog for an hour, Bob blamed Laurel and Marcia. When Adam had a "new look" and began to wear new clothes and an expensive gold bracelet, everyone blamed everyone else and believed his stories that the other parent had given him the money.

In his freshman year, Adam began to complain bitterly about his inability to concentrate. Marcia suggested testing him for ADD; Laurel agreed, and he was prescribed Ritalin. At first Bob didn't know anything about it, but one Friday Laurel called him unexpectedly to warn him that Adam needed to be reminded to take his medication on schedule. Bob was skeptical, which made Laurel hysterical, which made Bob more skeptical. He decided it would be best to speak to Adam about the Ritalin. Adam was mainly evasive, and Bob did not pursue the topic. He figured it was just Laurel trying to be in control, and Adam said nothing to dissuade him from that idea.

When Bob first noticed unexplained 900 number calls on his phone bills, he asked Adam about it, but Adam denied any knowledge of the calls. Bob believed him, and they decided it was a computer glitch. When Laurel also discovered unexplained 900 numbers on her phone bill and questioned Adam, he said his father had told him to make the calls from his mother's phone. She was appalled, but not surprised. She considered speaking to Bob about it, but decided it was just more of his aberrant behavior, and she could use it to deny him weekends with Adam. Neither ever spoke to the other about it, so Adam was free to carry on placing bets on sports events and investigating telephone sex.

Lost in their battle with each other, neither of Adam's parents realized the intricate and dangerous game their son had been playing. Neither was aware that Adam had begun to gamble, funding his habit by selling the Ritalin he had been prescribed. Only Adam knew how much trouble he was in, and he was busy trying to figure out how to pay his gambling debts without either of his parents finding out about it and losing his power over them.

No Winners in This Game

Many parents have reacted to this story rather like they did to Ryan's: "Get real! No parents could be that vengeful, that ridiculous!" Unfortunately, sometimes parents do become involved enough in their own resentment, anger, hurt, and desire for revenge that their teen can manipulate them up and down the block. Even parents who live together can find themselves at each other's throat, brought there by a teen trying to get what he wants. What seems so obvious from the luxury of distance can take on quite a different hue when one is in the midst of it.

As you read this story, you may have imagined that the stories Adam told one parent about the other would be too obviously false to have been believed. Of course you are right, but that never occurs to either Laurel or Bob because, choosing to remain lost in their own animosities, neither understands what turmoil Adam is creating. One warning I give parents is that when they cannot make sense of a story or stories, it is because the story in fact *doesn't* make sense. The main reason a story doesn't make sense is because it's full of lies.

When I met with Laurel and suggested her son might be lying, her answer was, "My son would never lie to me. I trust him implicitly." She did not want to see that the confusion Adam was creating gave him a wide field for manipulating—and self-destructing. Because Laurel did not want to see her situation clearly, she helped her son sabotage himself, his future, and their relationship. It is more common than I would wish, but parents too often think that protecting their child means accepting their lies. Bob, also being enthralled by his hatred for his ex-wife, fell into exactly the same trap.

"The more you believe Adam's lies," I told Bob and Laurel when we all met in my office, "the more confusion there will be. The more confusion there is, the more Adam can—and will—get himself into trouble. He thinks he's a big shot, but he's a kid overwhelmed by his own grandiosity. Unfortunately, you each buy into and feed that very grandiosity. I rather imagine that he is already involved way over his fourteen-year-old head. The rest of the world is not going to be so easy to fool as you two choose to be. Adam's lies will continue to get bigger as you believe them—as does his own hubris, which, by definition, must overtake him. You are teaching your son that he can be a sort of god who makes the world move by his design. It isn't so, and he will, someday, pay a huge price. So will each of you—in real guilt.

"Each of you prefers to ignore what is really going on. Each of you believes Adam to be honest with you and dishonest with the other. Each of you believes you have a fine relationship with him, much better than his relationship with the other. Adam uses that to foster distrust, competition, rancor, and jealousy in each of you. He keeps you enraged with each other. You keep fighting, and this kid is totally in charge, potentially wrecking his life, not to speak of yours."

I find it is often productive, even if uncomfortable, to ask parents and teens what they "get out of" the situation they are passively or actively creating. I asked Laurel and Bob what each felt she or he was getting out of perpetuating the anger and bitterness in their lives. "What is this doing to your lives? *To your own futures?*" I asked. I knew these were questions Bob and Laurel would have to think about for a while.

I wanted to make them aware of one more thing before they left my office. "I'm sure neither of you realizes that by keeping the two of you always fighting, Adam *keeps you in a relationship.* You declared yourselves separate years ago, but he's got you together—on his terms. Is that what you want? Does that make sense? Adam won't stop until you make him stop!"

The Circle of Blame

Parents, whether divorced or married, can be easily brought to blaming the other for the teen's problems as well as for the general turmoil in the family. Blame isn't useful. Blame is easy. Blame goes in a circle that repeats and repeats like an old-fashioned broken record. Although blame can seem satisfying for the moment, there are dangers to the circle of blame. It keeps you angry. It keeps you from self-reflection. Blame keeps you locked in history, and there is no way to change history. Blame goes backward, and your direction must be forward.

The In-Control Teen's Favorite Game: Divide and Conquer

Divide and conquer is the way some teens perpetuate living by the credo, "I want what I want when I want it, and I should get it because I want it." But the game is insidious because it also helps to keep the crazies going in the family and provides something in life at which a teen caught in his own turmoil can always succeed: getting others fighting. Until you decide you will no longer be manipulated into disagreeing and arguing with your spouse (and/or ex-spouse), your teen will be able to control the family.

Like Adam, kids of divorced parents are usually the champions of the divide and conquer game, and so stepparents also need to be especially wary of falling prey. Kids sometimes try to divide one or both sets of parents/stepparents with the dream of reuniting their biological parents in the end. (You may assume that statement couldn't apply to you, but don't be too sure.)

Realizing that dividing and conquering can work in many different parts of the teen's world is important. When you suddenly notice yourself feeling in coalition with your daughter against someone, anyone, you have probably been divided and conquered. The result is that your daughter can easily escape responsibility for her actions because you and she are united in thinking that someone else is responsible for whatever it is that happened. Forming coalitions with your child can help her to play the role of victim.

When, for example, your daughter tells you that her English teacher is unfair or stupid, or your son says it's only because of the coach that he can't play soccer any more, that is divide and conquer in action. If her technique is successful, then instead of asking your daughter if she has been going to class and doing her homework or if she has been mouthing off to the teacher, you are more likely to feel suspicious of the teacher and ready to jump to defend your child. (Of course, it is always possible that the English teacher *is* unfair or stupid, and if you have never heard such a statement from your daughter before, it may make sense to check out her claims.) Instead of wondering what your son did to get himself kicked off the soccer team, there you are thinking that he has been wronged yet again. It becomes you and your child against the world, and there you are, excusing, rationalizing, hiding from what you do know about your child. You have been divided and conquered once again.

Anyone in the teen's world can be brought into the divide and conquer scenario. The person from whom you are being divided does not even need to be present. Adopted kids often separate themselves from their parents or their parents from each other (also teachers, counselors, and others who may be involved) by referring to their biological parents. ("My *real* mother never would have . . .") Teens whose parent has died may begin to idolize him or her, always using that parent as an emotional reference point, forming an emotional coalition with a dead person. ("My father cared what I did, but you don't.")

When you play into divide and conquer, it keeps your child in control of the family and of you because on a deeper level, it controls everyone's emotions. When you have been successfully divided and conquered, you will find yourself feeling angry, frustrated, and distrusting. And you will be feeling those feelings in relation to the person or institution from whom your teen has divided you: your spouse, the stepparent, your own parents, your other children or stepchildren, the school, the police, anyone.

It isn't that your teen sits up nights plotting how to get you and your spouse arguing, or conniving to hurt you with comments about his father's new wife, although some kids do consciously plot when they are planning a divide and conquer campaign that relates to school, it's that it becomes a useful modus operandi. Often it's a tactic kids first try out when they are young. If you have let such behavior go by in the past, or even laughed at it because it was "so cute," it's no wonder it has become a part of the family tradition. That is a tradition you need to end!

Divorce and Being a Parent

Divorce is rarely painless, and no matter what the laws may be in any state, few experience divorce as a "no-fault" occurrence. No matter who initiated it or why, everyone experiences some pain, anger, loneliness, and guilt. It is especially sad when parents become so caught up in their own concerns that they forget that their *children's* welfare needs to be the *pri-*

mary concern of all custody decisions. Woe to the parents who forget or ignore that point. That disregard is far too likely to catch up with them.

Even years after the divorce, either "ex" can still feel bitter and vengeful, guilty and regretful, victimized or unable to let go. I have worked with ex-husbands as well as ex-wives who were not divorced in their hearts even years after the final decrees had been granted. Divorced adults usually need to process their feelings, but there is one hard and fast rule: Your child is *never* the one with whom to do that. Never. Equally important, the children will need to process their parents' divorce (possibly, but not necessarily, with a therapist), but doing it with either parent is risky because of the parent's own feelings. Parents can only help their children process feelings from a position of no blame, no guilt, no revenge, no bitterness. If you cannot do that, you should not be the one to help the child process his or her feelings. The same rules apply to grandparents, other relatives, and friends.

Kids of any age will want to know why their parents are no longer together. That does not mean they will ask directly. Each parent must offer an honest answer from the heart, avoiding revenge and bitterness. It is not honest for you to pretend you are not hurt, lonely, or guilty—whatever you feel—but that does not give you license to take out those feelings on your children or to expect or even require your children to share them. It is not okay to try to turn your child against your ex. Don't forget how easily that becomes a two-way street, leading the child to play even more vicious games of divide and conquer, as does Adam. All too often one parent is, or at least feels, the less guilty and uses that position to control the child's feelings about the other parent. That tactic is fraught with peril.

I do not believe divorce is inherently problematic for children, but it can be and often is made so. Be wary of family members, friends, and professionals who rather automatically assume your child is in terrible shape because of his parents' divorce. Kids are resilient and able to cope with all sorts of emotions—until or unless someone tells them they can't. If parents and all the other adults around the child are open, honest, refrain from blaming others, and listen with respect to the feelings the child is expressing, many kids will get through their parents' divorce with little or no emotional scarring. However, if parents choose to use their children as artillery on the divorce battlefield, they must expect to reap what they have sown.

Far too often, one of my first interventions with children of divorced parents has been to teach the child one hard and fast rule: She must not be the go-between, the passer of information (real or fake), the therapist, the lawyer, the confessor, or the mediator. Kids often argue with me when I tell them they have to enforce that rule. They say it isn't possible. As a parent, please remember that *you* don't have to make it "impossible." Quite the contrary: You must not try to manipulate your child into breaking that rule. Your child should never have to listen to one parent bad-mouth the other. Allow your child to be the *child*. Whatever caused you and your ex-spouse to divorce should not impact your child.

The "Wicked" Stepmother (or Stepfather) Who Sees All Too Clearly

I have known more than a few "wicked stepparents" who, because they were less emotionally involved with the teen, were much quicker to identify the problems, to call a spade a spade, and to recognize who was taking the money, "borrowing" the car, and keeping everyone fighting. Like Peter in Courtney's story, that parent is often more ready to try to change the situation than the more involved parent who refuses to see the true picture. And like Peter, you must trust your otherwise good relationship with your spouse in order to be able to demonstrate that there are problems and that the problems are not just normal adolescence—and that your view of them is not resting only on the fact that the child is not yours.

The possibilities for being labeled the "wicked stepmother" (or stepfather) are many and varied. The potential conflicts in your heart if you have children of your own, or if you and your new spouse have children together, are enormous. It may well be true that you love your own children more than your stepchildren. That does not make you bad. The problem comes in treating them in an equal fashion. Hard as that may be, it must be your goal. Beware, because divide and conquer can be played particularly effectively between stepparent and biological (or adoptive) parent. Don't speak ill of the child's other parent no matter what you think, but don't be disingenuous and say complimentary things you don't mean. Silence can be golden. Don't let jealousy or envy cloud your vision. If you experience the common conflict about, "But I am allowed to . . . at my mother's house," explain as simply and as dispassionately as you can that you have different rules in your home.

It is important to realize that if the rules are stricter at one house than at the other, many teens will simply choose to spend more time in the house where the rules are more lenient. The best answer, of course, is for rules to be as consistent as possible between the two households. Since that is usually not very possible, the only real choice either family has is to maintain its own rules without criticizing those of the other household—until or unless they are blatantly damaging to the child, such as the use of illegal substances, alcohol abuse, or violence.

Parent and stepparent must decide together who has what authority over the child. Rarely is it useful for the stepparent to have no authority over the stepchild, but if there is authority, it must be clear and should not be given and withdrawn erratically. On the other side of the coin, it is not helpful to try to "buy" the teen's friendship with leniency, gifts, use of the credit card, or unhealthy coalitions.

It is easy to become angered and embittered at a stepchild who is using up far more than his or her fair share of the family funds. No matter if it is therapy or what is sometimes jokingly called "retail therapy" (extra spending money from a guilt-ridden parent), it is risky to try to force, or even suggest to the parent not to spend money on his or her child. It is not useful to make it seem as though the best way for a child to get what she wants is by acting out, but at the same time you don't ever want to seem to be taking sides against your stepchild.

So many divorced parents with whom I have worked acknowledge that they made their need to have the child in their lives supercede good judgment. "I would do anything if I could take back the arrangements my ex and I made," one mother said. "We were mainly thinking of ourselves when we decided that Sean should shuttle back and forth between our homes twice a week. We each wanted to be involved in his growing up, but we didn't think how distressing it would be for him." She couldn't change the past, and neither can you, but you can decide to remember in all the decisions you make concerning custody, visitation, school, child support, vacations, etc., that your child's welfare is paramount.

Avoiding the Divide and Conquer Game: Some Easy-to-Follow Rules for Divorced Parents

Spend some time thinking about how the elements of divide and conquer may be being played out in your life. How many of these things can you say you do now? (Remember, you don't have to be divorced to fall prey to divide and conquer.)

- Don't use your children as pawns in a game with your ex or your spouse.
- Don't use your kids as part of the divorce settlement.
- Don't use your children to try to assuage your guilt or mitigate your loneliness. If you do, you will pay that emotional bill later, and it will be much higher than you can now fathom.

- Don't be selfish.
- Create a living situation that provides stability. Moving from one parent to the other on a twice-weekly basis (or even a weekly basis) is not a stable living situation.
- Don't try to turn your child against his/her other parent, even though you are enraged by your ex.
- Don't wash your dirty emotional laundry with your kids.
- Don't talk about each other to the children.
- Don't use the children to get information about your ex.
- Do manage to be on the same page with your ex in relation to your children. You don't have to give your adolescent an engraved invitation to divide and conquer!
- Do find a way to communicate civilly with your ex about your child—no matter what.

Chapter 7 ✿

A Lost Parent Can't Really Help:
Caroline's Story

Thank God for sunglasses, Diane Hammil thought, peering secretly around the commuter van. *At least no one can see I've been crying.* Sniffling as quietly as she could, she coached herself: *It's a misunderstanding. There must be a good reason Caroline didn't come home last night. I have to trust my daughter. Anyway, it isn't that serious. Teenage girls do things like that.* She sighed deeply.

It's only that I didn't sleep all night. Everything will be okay. She's just being a normal teenager. Still, Diane recognized the dull, anxious feeling of dread that had become familiar in the last few months. She wondered if she had forgotten to take her anxiety medication. She bit her lip, thinking about last night and how the hours had dragged by, and still Caroline hadn't come in. She had tried not to panic, telling herself she wasn't worried, that she was sleeping instead of watching the clock and listening for the sound of the car.

Her stomach tightened as she remembered some of the scenes she had imagined—the police at the door, a hospital calling, never hearing Caroline's dear voice again. Finally, overcome with love and terror, hoping to find some sort of clue to where her child might be, she had gone into Caroline's room.

She cringed as she remembered how she had stood there looking around, aghast at the piles of clothes on the chair and the bed, a package of condoms on the floor next to her own Gucci loafers. *But it's normal for girls to have condoms nowadays,* she had reassured herself. *What does she need condoms for anyway? She's sixteen! I didn't even know she had a boyfriend. Maybe they're just to show off,* she had tried to comfort herself. She had wanted to look in the package to see if any were gone but had recoiled. *It's none of my business.*

Shocked and confused by what she saw, she had wondered if she really might be dreaming. *Where was Caroline getting all those clothes? And why? How was she paying for them? How long has it been since I was last in here? How did my diamond tennis bracelet end up there next to an ashtray full of cigarette butts? She isn't allowed to smoke in the house.*

She remembered how she had rummaged through the things strewn about the dresser, unable to decide whether to take back her bracelet and shoes or leave them to use as evidence when she spoke to her daughter. *Evidence? I don't need "evidence." I'm her mother. But still, I don't have the right to look through her things, do I?* One thought had contradicted the next. Feeling completely distracted, she had returned to bed.

Finally, at 4 A.M., she had heard Caroline drive in. She had just lain there, unsure what to say to Caroline. When Caroline had tapped lightly on the door, she hadn't answered, and she had heard Caroline walk softly to her own room. She knew it was a test, to see if she was awake and realized how late it was. Even now it made her angry and frustrated. Even now, she did not know what she should have done. She hated that they had ended up screaming at each other as she was leaving for work, when she had been so worried and so glad Caroline was safe.

Feeling ashamed and guilty, Diane knowingly indulged in self-pity. *It must be my fault. I shouldn't have tried to keep up my career all those years when she was younger, but I had to earn a living. Maybe I work too many late nights, but I always call. We shouldn't have moved here after the divorce. We should have stayed where her friends were, nearer to her father, but I couldn't turn down this offer. I never should have had that relationship with Tim. It hurt Caroline, made her afraid of losing me like she had lost her father. What is going on? Everything is just going to hell. I don't even know my own daughter any more! I hate this!*

Diane looked out the window of the van and realized it was time to gather her things and her spirits to walk into the office. For a moment she wasn't sure she had the strength. *I can do this,* she coached herself, but Caroline's screaming, tearful condemnation rang in her ears: "You don't trust me. *You* stay out all night. You don't even love me." One part was justified. *I have stayed out all night, but never without making arrangements for Caroline, until she decided she was old enough to take care of herself. I've probably let her be too "independent" because it has been convenient. But then she had that party when I went away for the weekend with Tim, and the house got trashed. I did what I had to. I broke off my relationship with Tim because it was compromising my relationship with Caroline, preventing me from being the mother Caroline deserved.*

Knowingly using self-deprecation to feed her self-pity, Diane carried on. *Maybe Caroline is right. I am overprotective. And I spend too much time and energy—no, it's attention—on my work. I broke up with Tim in order to have more time and attention for Caroline, but then I spend it all at work.* Her self-pity metamorphosed into anger. *I do try to spend time with her on the weekends, but then she wants to be with her friends, so I work. She's always with her friends. I hate her friends. I don't even know if I know her friends!*

Suddenly Diane realized she was in the elevator on the way up to her office. *Thank God for automatic pilot.* She wondered how she looked and, with a deep breath, composed her face. *At least I have my work!* In her work, she felt competent and in control of herself and her world.

The elevator door opened. The receptionist smiled at her as she stepped out of the elevator. Diane sighed audibly.

"Good morning. Are you okay, Ms. Hammil?" the receptionist asked.

Diane smiled, hoping to erase the tension from her face. "I'm fine," she said. "Thanks for asking. Any messages?"

She started down the corridor to her office, sorting through the messages, smiling hello as she walked by her colleagues. For a moment she felt she could handle things. *I must look okay, or maybe everyone is just too polite to say anything.*

I wish I could talk to someone. The thought had crossed her mind several times, but she believed she had no real options and no one she would dare to talk to except her therapist, so the decision was made: Keep it to herself and hope things would get better.

I hate what I saw in Caroline's room last night. I hate that I had that second cognac while I was waiting up for her. I'm beginning to hate myself. How am I going to ask her about it? She'll just tell me I don't have any right to be in her room. She's right, I don't, but where did she get all that clothing and the jewelry?

Taking off her coat, Diane looked at her desk piled high with letters, files, and assorted papers, and she felt calmer. She could handle this part of her life very well.

The telephone rang, and Diane quickly used the opportunity of working with a client whose problems she could solve to put her fears and self-pity out of her mind even if only temporarily. She gladly lost herself in her work.

She was engrossed in a meeting when her assistant Jake interrupted her with a call from Caroline's school. Diane felt the now-familiar rock in the pit of her stomach as she picked up the phone. She smiled wanly and turned her chair away from her client and looked out the window at the mountains as she listened simultaneously to Mrs. Price and to her inner monologue. It was not as bad as it might have been. Caroline was only suspended. She had not gone to school. *What is the point of having her in that school anyway? She never goes.*

"What am I supposed to do?" Diane asked Mrs. Price, not expecting an answer. She wanted to ask her about Caroline and the clothes, the jewelry, and the condoms, about her staying out all night, but it didn't seem appropriate, and she didn't want the school to know everything anyway. She realized she sounded helpless, but it was how she felt. She who had answers for everyone had no more answers for herself.

She swiveled her chair around to face her client again, clearing her face as best she could of the shame and anxiety she felt. "Sorry. The school . . . my daughter." She laughed as casually as she could and raised her eyebrows.

Her client, Dick, an oil company executive, tensed visibly. "You too? I don't know what to do about my son. He . . . I suppose they're just teenagers. Is that her?" he asked, nodding at the photos on the desk.

Diane nodded.

"She's a beauty."

"I know," Diane said softly. Their eyes met; Diane shrugged her shoulders. "Yeah. Teens will be teens." She knew it was a weak response. Each looked back at their papers, and they went on with their meeting. It was easier.

At one o'clock, just as she was leaving for her lunch appointment, Caroline called.

"Hi, Mama. I'm sorry about this morning. I didn't mean to get mad at you. I was just, you know, upset, and then it hurt me when you attacked me. I hate when you yell at me. Don't you trust me? I hurried home the minute I realized what had happened, and then you attacked me."

"I didn't attack you." A defensive response had become automatic. She heard Caroline take a breath to answer her, so she changed tactics, ignoring the question of trust. "But, thanks for saying that. I probably overreacted. I just wish you would let me know if you change your plans. You know, you shouldn't be staying out so late on school nights. And . . ." She could feel tension and her fear of her daughter taking over. She wanted explanations for everything, but at the same time, she didn't. Most of all, she didn't want to argue, not now.

Caroline interrupted her. "I wasn't really *out*. I was just at Julia's. We were studying chemistry, then we fell asleep. As soon as I woke up, I drove home. You know how hard chemistry is for me."

Caroline's voice had that whiny tone Diane hated, but she didn't let herself react. She knew there was more she should say, but she shied from saying it because she knew Caroline would get angry again, and it was nicer not to be fighting. The hopeless feeling welled up once more. "Okay, we'll talk about it tonight. I'll be home about eight. No, say seven. We'll have dinner and talk. Okay?"

"Did you put any money into my account?"

Diane wanted to reply, "If you were in school, all you would need is lunch money," but she didn't. "I put seventy-five dollars in for you last week. What do you need it for?" She started to add up how much she had given Caroline recently, and thought fleetingly about the cash she had missed from her wallet, but she made herself stop. *I can't do this to myself. I have an important meeting. I can't work with these sorts of pressures.*

"I found some boots I really like. I could just get them after school."

Diane knew she should confront her daughter on the panoply of lies, but she didn't. She told herself it was because her assistant was in her office and because she had to leave for her lunch meeting. "I'll try to get to the bank, dear, but I can't promise." She knew she was placating her daughter. "Why don't you wait on the boots? Or use your Discover Card." She couldn't believe she had said that. "I have to run. Bye, dear. I love you."

"Is there any cash in your jewelry box? Just a twenty or two?" Caroline persisted.

Diane didn't want to think about her jewelry box or why Caroline needed cash. "I don't know. We'll figure that out later. I *must* go now, sweetheart." She wanted to say, "Don't touch my jewelry box," but she couldn't start that conversation on the phone. Not now.

Caroline had heard the undertones in her mother's voice, but she wasn't worried. Her mother was manageable. She walked into the kitchen, undecided if she would binge. She hated to eat, but at the same time, she loved it. She knew it was better to have a cigarette, so she opened the window to let out the smoke. She resented that she wasn't allowed to smoke in the house, but it was easier to be sneaky than to fight it out with her mother—even though she knew she could win that battle too. Being sneaky had become a way of life, and she found not getting caught exhilarating and enticing. She stared at the photo of herself and her mother in London. She felt a pang, as she noticed again how stunningly beautiful her mother was, and how gawky she felt she looked in comparison.

She exhaled smoke and watched herself in the window. She liked the way she looked smoking. *My hair needs cutting.* She took a handful and checked it for split ends. She examined her face and found no blemishes. *I wish I had more interesting eyes. Not just brown, but some sort of interesting color. I should get contacts to change the color. Deep lavender, and do my hair dark. Elizabeth Taylor. I need to lose weight.* She checked her stomach to see if it was flat. She felt a sense of revulsion. *I am so fat. God! I really have to lose at least ten pounds. Even my face is fat. My arms have no tone. I am so ugly.* She sucked in her stomach as much as she could; her ribs showed prominently, and she wondered if she could really ever be that thin. Caroline heard her phone ring and went to answer it, not caring that she had a cigarette in her hand. *Whatever. Sometimes my mother is such a pain in the ass,* she thought as she answered the phone.

"Hey, sexy! What's up?" Caroline's voice became deeper and her demeanor changed as she answered the phone. She imagined herself as Cindy Crawford. "No, everything's okay. She was just a little mad, but it's okay. You know how she is. Yeah, I'll manage to get out tonight, don't worry."

Diane returned from her lunch meeting feeling rejuvenated. She had done an excellent selling job and she knew it. Last night seemed almost like a dream. *Probably it isn't as bad as I thought. I didn't sleep all night. Maybe I was sort of dreaming.* She reached for the pile of mail her assistant had left on her desk. Picking up the phone to make a call, she opened her Discover Card bill. She screamed.

Jake ran in. "What happened, Diane? Are you okay?"

"No, I mean, yes. Thanks, Jake," Diane replied, making herself appear calm. "It's okay. No, I was just surprised. Don't worry. But thanks for checking." She knew she sounded breathless. She looked again. She could not believe what she saw. She had charges totaling more than $7000 on her bill. It had to be a mistake. Then she began to look at the charges. Now that she could explain where the clothes and jewelry were coming from, she wondered what she should do.

Circles That Go Nowhere

Perhaps you feel a bit like Diane, caught in concentric mental circles that go around and around and end up nowhere. Such mental circles are the result of becoming so involved in your teen's problems that you become lost—giving up your life and yourself in what will always be a vain attempt to "save" your child. Guilt and self-pity nurture the mental circles. You begin to dislike the person you are becoming, and you find yourself hiding behind a mask of the parent who must fix everything.

It may be some comfort to realize your distress makes sense. No one in your life can ever cause you pain or bring you joy like your child. No one can ever worry you or hurt you the way your children can. Through the whole spectrum of emotions and all the people you know, no one in your life can ever make you feel as intensely as your child makes you feel.

And so it is hardly extraordinary if you find yourself completely caught up in your son's or daughter's potential, impending tragedy—and intent upon avoiding it. But, as we have seen in Diane's life, the corollary to that is that when all of your emotional energy flows outward toward one child, there is little left for others in your life—and, equally important, for yourself. As you mentally go around in circles, you may realize, if only vaguely, that your own life seems elusive, more a memory than a reality, yet you are always able to justify to yourself that it must be so.

In order to help parents break out of that circle and rediscover themselves and their own feelings, I often ask them this unexpected question: "How's your sex life?" Obviously I don't ask it wanting details, but rather to help parents put into perspective just how much of themselves they have given up in a vain effort to rescue their teen. Searching for a meaningful answer to that question can catapult parents into seeing the depth and breadth of their intense involvement with their teen's problems.

In fact, parents often express a similar feeling when they tell me, "I just want my life back!" It is a justifiable wish, but one that many parents find hard to realize because they remain caught in the circle of overinvolvement with their teen. And, due to that overinvolvement, it is easy to think that you can only have your life back when your child has his back. But that is not true.

The real scenario is different. As you reestablish your life and your right to have your own life, you will find it easier to deal with your teen, no matter if he is just beginning to test your limits or already is engaging in out-of-control behavior. As you reclaim your own relationships, it becomes difficult, then impossible, for your child to be your only emotional tie. As you regain your life, it becomes increasingly possible to stand up for yourself and for your beliefs.

The Circle of Overinvolvement

Because you can see that some or much of what your teen is doing and thinking is not beneficial to her, you probably find yourself arguing with your teen more often and more intensely. But the more you argue and fight with your teen (and ultimately with your spouse or partner), the more angry, resentful, depressed, and frightened you begin to feel. One result is that it becomes harder to like yourself. Of course! It is hard to like the person you feel you are being forced to become. A sort of cascade effect begins: The fights, the worry, the unspoken lack of trust in your teen end up touching every part of your life, and you feel crabby, tense, even mean, cold, or bitter.

Has this happened to you? You finally decide to remind your teen to do something, and the answer you receive is, "Mom, don't nag me!" It hurts particularly because you know you aren't a nag. Still, it makes you angry because you both know he wasn't "just getting ready to . . ." You hate the very sound of your voice when you remind, but the other choice is just doing it yourself and stuffing your anger. Having no really good options, you choose one bad option or another. The fighting grows louder, and emotionally everyone is increasingly strained. Life really is maneuvering between the proverbial rock and the hard place.

In every relationship, there are layers and layers of interaction and meaning. But when parents like Diane or many others I have worked with join their teen on a downward spiral, they notice they are becoming someone they don't like. The next step, of course, is that other relationships become still less possible. The more often you look in the mirror and see how tired you look, the less it makes sense to you that anyone could find you appealing. It is so easy to start eating too much or too little, to try to hide behind more makeup than you really want to wear, even to give up on your appearance altogether.

Many parents, seeing their child heading for trouble, simply redouble the energy they put into doing, thinking, and feeling for their teen, trying again and again in different ways to eliminate the worst of the symptoms, to salvage some semblance of a future for their teen. The problem with that approach is that it doesn't work. You can't make someone else change to be the way you want him or her to be, no matter how right your intentions may be, nor do you have the emotional energy left to be effective. Like a run-down car battery that makes a little cranking noise when someone turns the key in the ignition but does not have enough power left to start the engine, you keep cranking anyway. You deplete yourself until the emotional and psychological boundaries between you and your teen are blurred beyond distinction. There you are, feeling his feelings for him, living his depression for him, excusing, rationalizing, reinterpreting.

If ever there were anything to make parents become overinvolved in their child's life, it is failure and sadness. Standing by watching your child close door after door of opportunity as he succumbs to peer pressure, irrationality, fear, and a generalized lack of belief in himself and the future creates excruciating emotional and psychological pain for everyone involved.

When you use all of your energy for one child, there cannot be any left for your other children or the other people in your life. Even worse, there isn't any left for you! Nevertheless, your adolescent will try to suck more and more energy from you because he or she needs fresh emotional energy. But the more you give without keeping something for yourself, the less worthwhile is your gift.

It feels wonderful to be the giver, and it is natural, I think, for us to want to give to our children. But when you give—not thinking about how your gift is received, not thinking about anything except whether the gift might somehow make your daughter finally smile or your son not be angry—your gift becomes one more thing he or she takes without having to give anything back. Two truly valuable lessons you can teach your child are those of gratitude and reciprocity. Those lessons will continue to be valuable throughout his or her lifetime. The one about taking won't.

Extricating Yourself from the Circle of Overinvolvement

You have the right and the duty to remain whole and have your own life. That does not make you selfish or self-centered. Quite the contrary: Narrowing your identity to that of parent-of-an-adolescent is tantamount to destroying the other relationships in your life and therefore defining your own life by the turmoil around you. It is not a good trade-off, and it won't help anyone. One of the most important things you can do for your teen is to rediscover your own life. One of the most important by-products of that decision will be that your teen will no longer be able to control you by means of negative attention.

Here are some hard questions you will need to ask yourself. Answering them can help you extricate yourself from your circle of overinvolvement. "What am *I* getting out of the turmoil in which I am living and which I am helping to perpetuate?" Am I seeking to control my teen? Is the turmoil a way to prolong my teen's childhood? What do I get emotionally out of rescuing my teen?

Although you tell yourself you are trying everything you can think of to help your child—to keep him from feeling so much pain and from noticing he is making a mess of his life—is that honest? Are you trying to spare *yourself* the deep pain of having to watch, powerless, as your child screws up his or her life?

Protecting yourself is not necessarily a bad motive, but facing your own answers to these questions will not only reveal the reality of your situation to you, but will guide you toward, and give you the energy for, reclaiming your own life. Being clear and honest with yourself will allow you to understand what you can do and how.

Eventually, your child will leave home and you will still have decades of your own life ahead of you. If you have allowed yourself to be emotionally drained, accustomed to living for your child in all sorts of ways, you are setting up your own failure—and that is as true for men as it is for women. The patterns in yourself wrought by your overinvolvement with your teen can become permanent—and they will not have helped your teen any more than they are helping Caroline.

You may be in trouble as much because you are losing track of yourself as because you have a difficult teen. The two are often intertwined—until you decide to reclaim your own life. Keep in mind: If you cannot get yourself together, there won't be anyone there to oblige your teen to change. If you aren't there for yourself, there won't be anyone there to notice when your teen changes. You have the right and the duty to remain emotionally intact. You have the right and duty to remain whole.

The Uselessness of the Circle of Guilt

In the story, we saw how Diane had turned her life into a sort of personal guilt crusade, expending enormous amounts of emotional and psychological energy which didn't help her daughter. But she made sure she always had lots of reasons to feel guilty. Her guilt crusade led her to self-pity, which is surely one of the most debilitating of all emotions. Caroline, without exactly realizing what she was doing, used her mother's guilt and self-pity to keep her mother from really recognizing what she, Caroline, was doing. As Diane began to navigate her way out of her mental circles, she told me, "I felt so sorry for Caroline as the child of divorce that I excused everything. I felt so sorry for myself that my closest relationship these many years has been with my self-pity. It was like self-pity became a person with whom I conversed all the time. It wasn't that I refused to get over the divorce and make a life with a family of two, it was that it didn't really occur to me to do that. I wouldn't give up my silly, live-happily-ever-after dreams. And because I wouldn't talk to anyone about it, I never noticed how my thoughts went in circles that went nowhere."

Diane felt desperate, and, like most parents, she did exactly the opposite of what would have been best for Caroline and for herself. She turned inward, blaming herself, feeling at once resigned and unable to give up. She excused and rationalized behavior and attitudes that she knew to be inexcusable and impossible to be rationalized. Instead of confronting Caroline on her jealousy and selfishness, Diane rewarded it by giving up a relationship with a man she loved.

Like so many parents, Diane did not realize how much her daughter was competing with her. Caroline knew she was not doing well in many ways, and it embarrassed her that her mother was not only successful but seemed more beautiful and, worst of all, thinner. Caroline couldn't let Diane or herself know that, and so she also used her mother's guilt and self-pity to keep her mother diverted from seeing that she felt herself to be not nearly good enough.

Guilt and self-pity are strange emotions because they hoodwink you into thinking they are real and meaningful, but usually they just keep you from feeling true remorse, sorrow, or deep, deep disappointment. Working with Diane and other parents like her, I must always ask this difficult and painful question: "Are you really doing this just for your child? Is this about you needing to appear to be the perfect parent of the perfect child? Are you looking for ways to assuage your guilt? To increase your guilt?"

Who Is Really at the Center?

Similar to her overinvolvement, Diane's selflessness had mutated into selfishness and her own type of self-centeredness. Diane's neverending monologue: *What have I done wrong? It's all my fault. If only I hadn't decided to divorce . . . or I should have . . .* is familiar enough to many parents. Diane believes herself to be the cause or motivator for everything Caroline is or does. She is wrong, and it is psychologically damaging to both of them.

It is always hard to say just when a psychological/emotional web becomes so tight it constricts. In fact, there never is a single moment, a single incident; rather, it is a continuum. The end result may be how you live now. Without realizing it, Diane's constant question to herself is: Can she, by the strength of her emotional bond with her child, "save" her from herself? My answer to her is simple: No.

Trying to be, and believing you are, the ultimate influence on your child can be what causes teens to rebel, just to get some emotional and psychological space. The more Caroline fails and seems to need rescuing, the more she tries (stupidly) to be independent, confusing independence with a façade of sophistication. The more Diane tries to hang on to the old parent-child relationship, the more Caroline rebels.

Carol Maxym's Old-fashioned Chocolate Chip Cookie Lecture

So many mothers I have worked with want to do kind things for their kids. When their children are unhappy, they bake cookies or do other types of special favors. And why not? Well, here is why not.

In the hands of an adolescent in turmoil, whether it's big trouble or small, cookies can take on a deeper, symbolic meaning. Homemade cookies and all the time it takes to make them are a symbol of a mother's love—and sometimes of her reluctance to require a "Thank you."

One mother I worked with made cookies and delivered sandwiches to her son's room when he returned from school (if that's where he had been). When he was angry with her, she fixed him his favorite dinner.

He asked, she produced; he asked, she gave. So he asked for more and more. He developed an insatiable appetite, not just for cookies but for having his way, for more of the family resources, for a car.

Fathers may or may not bake cookies, but they too often fail to expect reciprocity from their kids.

You expect reciprocity from other relationships in your life; why not expect reciprocity from your child? If you don't, you are teaching your child a false and dangerous lesson: that he or she can take and take and take, and never need to give back!

Breaking Out of the Circles

Like Diane, parents of teens nearing or already in turmoil find themselves closing inward, building a kind of emotional fortress, just like their teen has done. Because your life does matter and because you are more than your teen's parent, imagine yourself once again as *this man, this woman*. Take the time to think about yourself in relationship to others, to your other children, to your spouse or partner. To help yourself begin that process, consider these questions: Do you have conversations, discussions, even arguments with yourself the way Diane does? Who do you see when you look in the mirror? Do you like who you see? Can you see your feelings? Will you let yourself? Do you dare to be honest with yourself? Do you pretend the tension you see around your eyes is really about work, or that maybe it's just natural because you are getting older? Can you see a woman or do you see only someone's mother? Do you see a man or only someone's father? Is the person in the mirror the woman or the man you want to be now? Is she or he the person you want to be in five years? In ten years?

Whatever it is that you are giving up in your life because of your teen, it is important that you reevaluate your sacrifices. Martyrdom or even pseudo-martyrdom will never convince your teen she needs to change. It will never give you your life or your own self-respect back. Remember: This is not just about your teen! It's about you because you matter, too.

Giving Up the Mask of Perfection

Diane feels caught between two identities that she experiences as contradictory and impossible to unite. She feels competent in her job, but incompetent as a parent. She knows she has the training and skills to be successful in her career, but the mercurial nature of being a mother makes her always feel in just a bit over her head. Like Ryan's father, Russ, she fails to realize that if she applied the same quality of standards to Caroline that she does to herself as a professional and to the people with whom she works, she would be a better, more competent mother.

Instead, lost in her concentric mental circles and losing track of herself, she tries to be a "perfect" mother. But she tries in all the wrong ways: not confronting her daughter about her lies and attitude, not acknowledging the true situation with Caroline, thinking she is responsible for Caroline's behavior. Not letting anyone else know what is going on, Diane thinks she can at least look like the perfect mother to the rest of the world. The end result is that instead of being a "perfect" mother, she becomes an ineffectual one.

For many parents it is at first hard to give up the invincible and infallible parent guise. That mask provides an immediate (and psychologically safe) distance between you and your child, giving each of you an established role. However, when you do give it up, you will experience an immense freedom. You aren't infallible or invincible, and you don't have to pretend to be. Allowing your child to see you as a "normal" person, able to move with human dignity through emotional, psychological, and practical aspects of life, will ease both your teen's and your difficulties as she grows up. And if the process of leaving behind your aura of infallibility is gradual and natural but continuous, it won't feel like a betrayal to your child or to you.

When you present yourself as a "regular person," you also take away the need for your child to do it for you by cutting you down with constant criticism. Suddenly your teen doesn't have to tell you how stupid you are or how you don't understand anything because your guise of perfection is gone. It means that you can tell your child when you are worried or concerned, instead of always feeling you need to be stable and happy and feeling guilty and inadequate when you can't do your Laura Petry act or when you are not as wise as the dad on "Father Knows Best." Because as a parent you teach mainly by example, it is possible that if you show your child a more real version of what being an adult is about, he or she won't misinterpret adulthood, thinking it's either a time when people are simply "allowed to do whatever they want" or the opposite, "never having any fun."

There is still another negative aspect to remaining hidden behind the infallible parent mask. It automatically puts your child in the place of feeling inadequate because she is not infallible like her parents, and cannot imagine ever being so. When your daughter was younger, of course, the fact that she perceived you to be invincible and infallible provided much of the stability for her life. But now your teen knows you are not really infallible, although she feels she is still supposed to *believe* you are, and may really *want* you to be. Those conflicting emotions can easily become the source of defiance for a teen, borne of feeling betrayed by a suddenly imperfect world, or they can become the source of feelings of helplessness and hopelessness. Your ability to show regular human frailty is a potent message to your teen that you are not better than he or she is, only older and a bit wiser.

I remember one father who "wanted to spare his daughter the sorrow and pain" of dealing with the fact that he had been fired. Instead of allowing himself to get the support he needed from his daughter, he hid behind his infallible Dad mask, not only becoming ever more lonely, but denying her the right to offer the loving support she might have given (and grown and matured from having done so). Even more, by deed he taught her that showing feelings and asking for help from your family is something you just don't do.

If you give your child the chance to see you as the person you are, it demonstrates to him that adults have as wide a range of feelings as teens do. You can live as the differentiated human being you are. Your teen may not appreciate that gift right away, but in the long run, you will both discover it is not only the best but the only way to begin establishing an adult-to-adult relationship which is, after all, the only one available to you for a future.

Emotional Authenticity

There is another aspect of the parent-child relationship I have encountered many times therapeutically. If you are wearing the mask of the perfect parent, you are not being emotionally authentic with your child, and your child may become wary of your emotions. They are, after all, hidden and therefore unfamiliar and easily take on a mysterious character. Your teen, in reaction—usually without quite realizing it as such—may try to protect you from having to know how hard things are for him, how much, for example, he feels the outsider in his school. Your child protects you at the same time you are protecting him. It all becomes a messy, messy thing, with one emotion spilling over into another. It's like putting frosting into the vegetable soup and calling it nourishing and tasty.

Emotional authenticity is a simple concept. It says that you are in touch with your feelings and that you have the courage to live them. It is not the same thing as wallowing in your feelings, which is what happens when your emotions overwhelm you and you feel swept away in their tide (which may be how you have been feeling lately). It means instead that you do not hide feelings from your child in order to "spare" him or her something bad or painful, or even something joyful because you feel a need to keep a parental distance from your child.

Living your emotions authentically also means you cannot expect your child to pay your emotional bills. You may feel angry or cheated if, for example, your father was an alcoholic. But it is important for you to remember that although there is some evidence to support the idea that alcoholism may be an inherited trait, it does not mean your child, when he exhibits behavior and attitudes that upset you very much, is ready to become an alcoholic, too. It is important that you not expect your child to do all the things you wanted your father to do to stop being an alcoholic to prove to you he isn't one. Because your mother was controlling does not mean that you need to give your child free rein to do whatever she wants so you can be sure you are not controlling. Of course you have strong feelings associated with your own parents and childhood, but they cannot become the prime motivators which cause you to *react* to situations based solely upon those feelings. Most of all, you need to spend time and energy sorting out what are your leftovers from things you haven't figured out about yourself, and what are the fresh emotions which define and describe your life now.

As soon as you realize you don't have to do all sorts of emotional magic tricks with yourself to make yourself seem perfect or to shield yourself and your teen from how you really feel, you will find an enormous new energy stirring inside you. When you no longer scatter your emotional energy, you will find it will be easier for you to distinguish between who you know your child to be and the teen who is living in the house with you these days. You will realize you are not the only, or even the prime, motivator in your child's life—for the good things as well as for the bad things. Suddenly life will be better!

Emotional authenticity also means adopting a forthright attitude which shows more by deed than by word that a full range of emotions is valid. For example, an emotionally authentic person knows that being sad is as valid as being happy, that there are days or even weeks when a "normal" person feels depressed, that disappointment happens, and although it isn't fun, it isn't the end of the world. Acting from an emotionally authentic ground reminds you that neither you nor anyone is always happy, successful, or can fix everything.

Diane is an example of a mother who finds it difficult to be really open with her feelings, and my experience is that many parents share that difficulty. There are a number of reasons why. It may simply be lack of practice, since it does not make sense to share your feelings with a small child. It may also be that one spouse is protecting the other or another loved one. It may be that you just don't want to "rob" your child of that wonderful illusion that Mom or Dad knows everything and can fix anything. Some parents do not want to relinquish the one place in their lives where they can seem infallible and invincible. They use their children to give themselves identity or status. Other parents maintain an emotional distance from their child because that is what their parents did.

These thoughts can be frightening, possibly because they suggest something new and different, but even more than that, they whisper something you may already know: *Your child is growing up, and that means soon the only relationship available will be that of adult to adult.* If that has not turned out so well between you and your parents, the concept of having an adult-to-adult relationship with your child is likely to be uncomfortable and unfamiliar. Even more, as you look at your son dressed in his ridiculous imitation of the Grateful Dead or your daughter outfitted to look like the mother from *The Addams Family,* it is hard to think seriously about an adult-to-adult relationship. No one would expect you to be able to have an adult relationship with a teen spiraling out of control. Nevertheless, it is during the teenage years that your future relationship, your adult-to-adult relationship, begins to form. It can be one of the sweetest fruits of the process of change you have begun.

Once you can look through the list on page 136 and know you have internalized these feelings, you will feel lighter, younger, freer, and much happier. It won't happen overnight, but that doesn't matter. Give yourself the luxury of enough patience to take the time you need without sabotaging yourself by waiting to reach this new kind of freedom.

The Steps to Emotional Authenticity

- Realize you are not, and need not be, infallible or invincible.
- Accept that your child doesn't really need you to be anyway.
- You must not live, redo, interpret, or reinterpret your child's emotions.
- Take all the responsibility that is yours and none that isn't.
- Move beyond your own emotional history instead of using it to excuse how you are and/or how you treat your teen.
- Allow your child the luxury of not being perfect.
- Allow your child the luxury of being sad.
- Allow yourself the luxury of not being perfect.
- Allow yourself the luxury of being sad.
- Allow yourself to live with your emotions but not wallow in them.
- Let your child grow up.
- Keep yourself separate from your child, but don't ever think that means you stop loving him or her.
- Don't use your child to justify what you do or what you did or might do.
- Don't be held prisoner by your fears—use them to motivate you to act.
- Don't oblige your child to feel the way you do.
- Don't use your child as your therapist.
- Don't use your child as your parent.
- Don't use your child emotionally/psychologically as your spouse.

Chapter 8 ✿

A Master Manipulator Explodes:
Danny's Story

"I don't care what you say," Shelly said to her husband, Gordon. "Danny is not a bad kid. He got himself into some trouble, but even his counselor said he's a good kid. His grades are excellent. He lost control once. *Once,*" she repeated for emphasis.

"Fine." Gordon agreed grudgingly. "His grades are okay, but I don't care what you or his counselor say, this kid is out of control. This isn't the first time . . ."

"He made a big mistake today," Shelly interrupted, "but that does not make him out of control. Out of control means doing drugs, staying out all night, never going to school, getting picked up by the police. He's not doing those things."

"Okay, if Dan's not out of control, why were we in the principal's office today? You tell me when you expected to be in the principal's office trying to convince him not to expel your son. I didn't particularly enjoy my afternoon. I never expected . . ." His voice almost broke. "Okay, Dan is not a bad kid, but telling teachers to 'fuck off' and calling them 'pricks' because they question if some stupid song lyrics by some drugged ruffian are poetry is not acceptable behavior for my son."

"Okay, but . . ." Shelly began, but Gordon interrupted her.

"There are no more 'okay, buts.' Stop excusing him. Things are going to change. We are going to have rules, and we are going to enforce them. There will be no more 'understanding' and no more excusing or explaining for him."

"You excuse him as much as I do. Fine, it can be like boot camp; just tell me who is going to be the sergeant. You get home about eight most nights except the nights you're traveling. You'll enforce this by phone? Because I won't."

"You can just cut the sarcasm," Gordon retorted. "I really don't need that from you right now. This family has a problem, and one I know how to fix, with your help—or without. If you don't want to be on my team, that's okay; just don't be against me. I do not plan ever again to be called into another conference like the one we had today. I will never again plead for my son not to be expelled from school. Never."

"That's fine with me. Stop blaming me; I'm not the one who called you out of your deposition. You think that was my idea of how to spend a pleasant afternoon? It isn't like I haven't been trying to tell you there were problems—*and* trying to do something about them."

"So now it's my fault, is it? That's what I call parents working together," Gordon said as he turned and walked out of the room. He returned a few minutes later and apologized. "I'm sorry. I don't want to fight with you. This is our son. How can we be fighting about our son? We both love him and want what is best for him. We're just upset by what has happened. Let's not fight anymore. We love each other too much and have for too long."

Shelly nodded. "But don't take everything out on me. I've done everything I could to be a good mother."

"I know you have. And I have tried to be a good father." Gordon's voice broke. He thought of all the things he hadn't done, and suddenly he felt this was all his fault. He walked over to her and put his hands gently on her shoulders.

She put her hand over his. "I know you have. We need to be on the same page now. We haven't been lately. I try to talk to Danny, then you come in shouting. . . ."

Gordon pulled his hands from her shoulders and stepped away. "I have a lot of pressure in my life; sometimes it comes out in the wrong way. I'm sorry."

"Will you finally realize that my life isn't just a bed of roses either? Who do you think makes things happen here? You know, people depend on me, too, only I don't take my frustrations out on everyone else."

"Shelly, please let's not fight. I'm so tired, I just can't."

"So now it's my fault; I'm making us fight."

"No, it's not your fault. It's no one's fault. Or it's my fault. I don't care. Just please don't look at me that way. I hate it when your face gets like that."

"So now I'm ugly, too."

"Shelly. No." Gordon looked tired and beaten as he walked from the kitchen to the family room. He turned on the TV, but he wasn't watching.

Their fights had become so regular now they had developed a whole routine around them. When it was especially bad they wouldn't speak for a couple of days, but neither would have to acknowledge it because, with their busy lives, it was easy to pretend they just didn't get the chance. Then they would begin to speak again, usually in a stilted way, ignoring that they hadn't settled anything. They both hated it, but neither took the initiative to change the pattern. They did not recognize that most of their fights were about or caused by Danny. Shelly had begun to think about divorce. She wondered if Gordon had, too. Maybe he was seeing someone else? Someone younger, less complicated? She was upset, so she decided to take something to help her sleep.

Gordon sat in front of the TV, watching the same news stories over and over again. After an hour he decided to say good night to his daughters and speak with Danny.

Climbing the stairs, he heard Annie's soft voice talking on the phone. He knocked softly.

"Come in—hang on just a sec," she said into the phone as he opened the door. "Hey, Dad, what's up?" She saw he was tired and sad, but she didn't know what to do.

"Nothing, dear. Just saying good night." He blew her a kiss and closed the door quietly. Annie returned to her phone call. "That's so weird. He never comes in like that. He's upset about Daniel. It's so embarrassing to have your parents in school like that. Daniel's embarrassing; everyone but them knows what he's doing."

Gordon saw Katie's light was off, and he supposed she had gone to bed already. At least he didn't have to go to school meetings about his daughters. *Maybe it's just a phase boys have. . . . Danny will just grow out of it.*

He knocked on Dan's door and entered. They hadn't spoken since the principal's office. Dan had his headphones on and had not heard his father's knock. He looked at his father and continued listening to his music, bobbing his head. "Danny, I want to talk to you. Just for a few minutes, Son." Gordon spoke loudly to be heard over the music.

Dan wondered if he should take off his headphones. He decided to play it cool with his father. "Yeah, what, Dad?" He knew it would be best for him if he took the initiative. "Sorry about today, Dad. What I did was stupid."

"You can't speak to your teachers that way. We don't use language like that in our house. You are a bright boy, Dan, you know better. You must learn discretion."

"Yeah. But the thing about me doing drugs—I mean you know that's nothing, right? If you and Mom want, I'll go for a drug test. It's just when the school says it, you know, then it's different. I mean they don't have the right; it's an invasion of privacy, a presumption of guilt. But if you and Mom want, I'll go tomorrow. You trust me, don't you?" Dan's self-righteous tone worked its magic on his father.

"Thanks, Son, for saying that. I appreciate it. Of course we trust you. We don't need you to go for a drug test. We've always operated on an honor system in this family."

Dan was relieved, but he hid it well. "Just because I lost it with Shuler today doesn't mean I do drugs. That prick doesn't have the right to tell me what is poetry. I'm going to stand by that, Dad, just like you've always taught me—to stand up for what I believe. I know I didn't do it in a very constructive way," he said parroting his father's words from the principal's office. "It won't happen again. I promise."

Gordon winced at the language. He felt he was not in control of the conversation but didn't know why. Tensely he prepared his next statement. "We need to change some things around here, Son. Mom and I trust you," he said hoping to placate his son, "but we don't like all your friends."

His tactic backfired. Dan exploded, "That's bullshit, and you know it! Aaron, right? You're so hypocritical; you always taught me not to judge a person by how they look."

Gordon took a step back, "That's true, of course, Dan. It isn't that he has bleached hair . . . it's that he looks, well, disheveled, unkempt."

Danny strummed his electric cello. "So he doesn't care about his appearance. Inside he's a very special person. Really creative and musical and really spiritual. He writes poetry, which is more than Shuler does," Dan sneered.

"I find it hard to think of him as 'creative and spiritual' when he is neither polite nor clean," Gordon said. "I wish you would clean up, too, Son. You are such an attractive boy, but you look like . . ." Gordon's eyes scanned the room. He looked bewildered as he suddenly registered how it looked. "What are all these posters on the wall? And since when have you been . . . what is that, Dan? Have you been gouging the wall with a scalpel?"

"Nothing, that was just one day. I was pissed off."

"It's not nothing. Son: This room is disgusting. You need to clean it up." Gordon's face betrayed his pain, but he forged ahead with his plan. "There are going to be some changes in the way things work around here. This is unacceptable."

"I know, Dad. I agree," Dan looked around his room as though he, too, had no idea what a mess it was. "Yeah, it's sort of gotten out of hand here," he laughed. "I can clean it up this weekend. Maybe I can even do something about the wall." Dan yawned. "I'm really tired, and I have a history test tomorrow."

"We'll finish this conversation tomorrow."

"Good night, Dad. Thanks for being so understanding."

Gordon got up to leave the room. His eye fell on a pornographic magazine. "Dan, well, I understand you're a fifteen-year-old boy, but this just isn't a nice thing to have in the house with your mother and sisters. Where is your respect, Son?"

Dan blushed, but answered calmly, "Yeah. I understand, Dad."

"And, Dan, I will never again be called for a conference in the principal's office." Gordon wanted to sound decisive, but he sounded sad and tired.

"You won't. That's a promise, Dad. Really."

Gordon walked out of the room. He didn't want his son to see the tears in his eyes. He felt he was watching the dreams of his life evaporating before his eyes, but he didn't know exactly why or how. He felt old. *This is what I've worked for?* Gordon almost sobbed aloud, but instantly pulled himself together. He went into the room he and Shelly shared and noticed the care and taste with which she had redecorated it last year when life was still in order . . . or maybe it hadn't been, it had just seemed that way. He glanced at Shelly sleeping, apparently peacefully, unaware she had taken a sleeping pill, and shook his head.

He went to his study and wrote the list of rules. As he was printing it, he thought he must also give a copy to his daughters. They might be resentful, but he had always believed the rules and expectations for all his children should be the same. He hoped Shelly would agree. Each wanted the best for their children; it was the means to get there that caused problems.

Gordon left the house early the next morning. When he reached his office he called Shelly and invited her to lunch. He knew they needed to talk. They walked hand-in-hand to the restaurant.

Shelly expected an apology for the night before, so when Gordon produced his new family rules document for her approval, she was hurt, disappointed, and angry.

"Gordon, I won't live like this. I won't expect our children to live by a set of rules you set down one night when you were angry at Dan. It's insulting to the girls. This is going to make all the kids resentful, and I'm the one who is going to bear the brunt of it."

"I agree this is not necessary for Annie and Katie, but it isn't right to make different rules for the girls than for the boy."

"Katie and Annie are about as perfect children as anyone could want. It's our son who is a bit confused these days. He'll outgrow it if you don't insist on making him more angry and resentful. This will just cause problems!"

"Cause problems? Shelly, we *already have* problems. Have you forgotten where we were yesterday at this hour?"

"What are you trying to accomplish? This is just about your disappointment that your son isn't perfect."

Gordon flinched. "I would have thought you and I were trying to accomplish the same thing—namely, keeping our son on track. Have you been in Danny's room lately? Do you know what it looks like?"

"Yes, but I admit I don't go in more often than I have to."

"It's a pigsty full of pornographic magazines and posters, not to mention holes in the walls."

"Maybe if you went up there a little more often you wouldn't be so shocked."

"What is that supposed to mean?"

"Don't you think you're overreacting with your rules and regulations? Dan cursed out his teacher yesterday, but his grades are tops. Maybe Mr. Shuler deserved it. He is kind of pompous, you know. Look, I don't agree with you, but if you want to give your rules and regulations thing to Dan, go right ahead. But you enforce it. I am not going to become the family police force."

"That's how you see this? Then I'm not sure there is much we have to say to each other." Gordon was shocked by how global his statement was; he wondered if he meant it. He saw the shock in Shelly's eyes and moderated immediately, "I mean about Dan, only Dan. I love you. We can't let all this come between us."

Shelly took his words at face value. She forced herself to calm down. "Okay. You take charge of Dan; you deal with him—everything. Let's talk about something else."

When Shelly arrived home, Dan was already there. "What are you doing here?" she asked. "You have class until three." Shelly's heart began to beat wildly. She could not deal with a repeat of the day before. Her voice quivered, "You haven't been expelled or anything?"

"Yeah." He waited briefly for the effect, then said, "No, just kidding. Classes got canceled for a pep rally." He paused to see if she would question him further. Shelly wondered if she should believe him. His face looked honest, and she squelched her worry.

"Dad and I talked last night," he continued. "It was cool. He told me you guys trust me, and you know I'm not doing drugs or anything. He just asked me to clean up my room, and I was just going to."

When Gordon arrived home, he went directly to Dan's room. Dan was strumming his cello. The room had not been cleaned, but the magazine had been turned over. Gordon fought to control his temper. "Clean up your room!"

"Just getting started, Dad. I heard this one melody in my head, so I had to . . ."

"Bullshit! Put that thing down. Clean up this room, and don't come downstairs until you have finished! Then we will talk. Things are going to change around here, Son. I don't think you understand that yet." He stormed out of the room because he felt something foreign welling up in him. He was afraid he would strike his son, something he had solemnly vowed never to do. He felt Dan was throwing all his generosity and understanding in his face. The rage he felt welling up in him terrified him.

At dinner he was still seething. He made his feelings known by angry silence. As they finished eating, Gordon asked Dan if the room was cleaned up.

"Almost, Dad. Almost. Just a little more to do."

"Bullshit," Gordon exploded. "When it's done, come to my study." Gordon knew nothing had been done yet, that Dan was lying. He squeezed his napkin with all his strength to keep from striking his son. He suffered a painful revelation: Dan lied to him all the time!

Dan finally knocked on his father's door at 10:30, carrying his cello. Gordon had regained his self-control and was stern and reserved. "Put the cello down. Put it down!" he said again louder and more angrily when Dan sat down with the cello across his lap. "Here," he said, handing Dan the document he had prepared the night before. "These are the rules which will govern your life until you have proven to me that you are mature and responsible."

Dan took the paper from his father. He was completely taken aback. He had never seen his father quite like this, not even when he had stolen a bicycle from a store and had been forced to return it and apologize. He glanced up to check his father's face. It was expressionless. He did not know how to respond; he just sat there looking at the paper.

"Questions?" Gordon's voice was cold and distant. "I allow for no compromises."

"This is a joke. I mean, like here where it says my room is going to be inspected every day? By whom?" Dan's voice became shrill as it got louder. "My room is mine; you don't have the right . . . I won't allow it." Dan was already thinking how to make his room more disgusting if his father persisted with the inspection demand. "I can only go out once on the weekend *if* I have followed all the rules all week? That's such bullshit. Fuck you. No way.

No fucking way. This is such bullshit." Resentment and anger overwhelming him, his mind raced, and he felt himself ready to explode. He was the victim of his father's pride. His father could shove that. He started to leave the room. "You don't understand me at all. You don't even care. All you care about is that everyone thinks you have perfect children. You can shove this up your ass. Fuck off!" He screamed and threw the paper at his father.

"Son, you don't have choices. That incident in the principal's office will never be repeated. But more than that, it told me we have been too lenient with you." Gordon spoke quietly, using a voice Danny hated for its precision and coldness. Gordon debated if he should confront Dan on lying all the time and decided against it.

Dan quickly rethought his tactics. Outward compliance might bring him a better, easier deal. "Look, Dad, I already said I was sorry. It won't happen again, so why are you making these stupid, fucked-up rules?" He felt himself losing control but he didn't care. "Does Mom know about this? Does she agree? You can't do this without her, you know. She's my parent, too."

"Yes. No. It changes nothing."

"What about Katie and Annie? Do they have to obey this shit? They aren't as perfect as you think. You don't have any right to do this. I might call a lawyer—or child protective services. I can ruin your whole fucking career! You can't do this!" he screamed. He knew, in the end, he was not speaking in his own interest, but he couldn't stop himself. He was angrier than he could ever remember being. He had not felt so powerless for a long time, and it enraged him. "Fuck you! Fuck you! That prick Shuler had no right to tell me—me!—what is poetry. I *write* poetry, which is more than he or you will ever dream of. He's an asshole. Who is anyone to tell me? You're embarrassed because your son told some stupid fuck he's a stupid fuck. You should be proud of me. Katie and Annie don't embarrass you. What they do, they do secretly. That's what you want. It's all about whatever anyone can get away with. Just like what you do for criminals in court." Dan was screaming and crying.

Gordon looked at him over the top of his reading glasses. "Dan, don't push me."

Danny left the room, slamming the door. As he started up the stairs, he realized he had forgotten his cello; he felt foolish, but he wanted it, so he returned to get it, slamming the door even louder. He went to his room, put on his headphones, connected his cello to the amplifier, turned up the volume as high as it would go and started playing. He played for a few minutes, then took off the headphones and punched the wall. Then he kicked his closet door until it splintered. He took out his weed, rolled a joint, and opened the window. He had not even begun to clean his room, and he was glad. *I'm not cleaning my room for them. They can just fuck off, both of them! Hard!* How could his mother let his father treat him this way, make rules for him like he was a little boy? *All because I told that asswipe Shuler to fuck off. Fuck them. Fuck everybody!*

It was late when he appeared the next morning, and he was already high. He had no intention of staying home for the day or the evening or of cleaning up his room. Either they accepted his terms, or he was leaving. He didn't much care. He had decided to go to Mexico. He would take his father's car to teach him a lesson. He would call his father and tell him that if they called the police, he would tell his whole story to the newspapers to wreck his father's reputation. He would return only when his father agreed to let him do whatever he wanted.

"Where's Dad?" he greeted his mother.

"Good morning." Shelly detected something was wrong, and she wanted to smooth it over. "Dad's gone out for his jog. He said he would be back in an hour or so." She felt panicked, but she didn't know why.

Danny came right up to her, towering over her, intimidating her with his height. "Look, you tell Dad he can fuck off. He can take his paper and cram it up his ass. Hard. I'll be home later—or not. Understand one thing: I am not living by some fucked-up rules." He picked up two muffins and a banana and walked out of the room.

"Danny. Wait. What are you doing? Where are you going?" Shelly called after him. She was shaking.

He ran back into the room with his cello on his back like a guitar and stood over her shaking his fist and screaming. "I will not be treated this way. You will not make me your fucking prisoner. I will do what I want. It's my life! You and Dad and Shuler can all fuck off. Tell that to Dad for me." He stormed out. "And tell him to cram it up his fat ass, too," he yelled, slamming the front door.

What Is "Out Of Control"?

Danny's story, the most multifaceted of the five, touches on almost every issue common to parents of teens in turmoil. The story beings with a relatively "small misdemeanor" and escalates, apparently suddenly and almost inexplicably, into a crisis. It was Dan's loud but indistinct cry for help when he stole his father's car that catapulted Shelly and Gordon into the realization of just how serious the situation had become. They each realized there were problems, but neither wanted to admit it, and each half-secretly blamed the other. Nevertheless, they were two mature adults, living a loving marriage—except that they were brought by their teenage son to the brink of divorce. They both loved their son and wanted what was best for him.

Shelly and Gordon contacted me just after Danny had returned from Mexico. In our first session, they told me their story, and I realized quickly that my first goal would have to be to help them realize how completely their son had manipulated each of them. The result was that they reacted to Danny instead of acting from their own principles and beliefs. One moment Gordon was angry and Shelly excusing; the next it was Shelly who saw more clearly and Gordon who rationalized. Dan is a master manipulator, interspersing threats and compliance to remain in control of the family.

Gordon began our conversation by telling me, "Dan is bright, talented, musical. He used to be loving and sweet. . . . Now, well, Dan is a good boy who seems to be a little off-track right now."

I couldn't quite agree. "I'm sure Dan is a good boy," I said, "but he sounds more than just 'a little off-track right now.' Didn't you tell me you found drugs and drug paraphernalia in his room? Didn't he just steal your car? Didn't he essentially try to blackmail you? I think this boy is pretty much out of control. You won't do him any service by glossing over that."

Shelly sighed, "I don't think I really know my son anymore. Ever since that morning when he was standing over me yelling, I don't know . . ." her voice trailed off. "It was one of the worst days of my life," she whispered, tears welling up in her eyes.

"I suppose I feel the same way," Gordon said. "One day we have a family life, the next I am in the principal's office. Next thing I know I find pornography in my son's room. He sweet talks me into thinking I should trust him, then the next day I almost hit him. In between, of course, I tell my wife of twenty-four years I don't think we have anything in common any more. I'm sorry. Life just doesn't make sense." Gordon paused to collect himself. "And through it all I know my son to be a good kid. I'm sure that sounds silly to you."

"Not at all!" I responded. "Good kids lose their way and do things they never even really meant to do, dragging themselves and their families into a downward spiral that doesn't make much sense. It happens. I'm not here to judge. What I want to help you do is figure out what you two have to change in your home and how to do it." Shelly and Gordon nodded.

"I feel scared of my son—and scared for him," Shelly said quietly. "I don't know where this all might lead. I just want my son back. I just want my family back." Gordon nodded. They were both fighting back tears.

Shelly breathed deeply a couple of times to compose herself. "You know, Gordon, I never really knew if Dan would carry out his threats to go to the newspapers with his wild stories of abuse at our hands—your hands—but I do know that thinking up things like that terrifies me."

"I felt guilty; I still do," Gordon said. "I figured I had brought him to that point with my list of rules and regulations. It was my fault. I overreacted."

"No, you didn't," I said. "You may not have taken the most efficacious approach, but you were not and are not responsible for your son's actions. He is. Your motives were good. Don't take responsibility which is not yours! What Danny did, he did. Don't lose sight of that."

"I never thought he would threaten me the way he did the morning he ran away," Shelly said. "I didn't really know how far Dan would go."

"Not really that far. Not all that far," Gordon said.

"Who are you trying to convince, Gordon? Me, or yourself?" I asked. "I think Dan has demonstrated how far he will go. It looks to me as though Dan has been testing you for a long time to find just how far he could push you; he can push you pretty far. He pushes; you react. He pushes again; you react again but he has managed to change your expectations, your standards," I said. "And if you don't make some changes, he will continue to do so. That will not be good for anyone in the family."

Apparently trying to protect his own feelings of hurt by minimizing the problems, Gordon blustered, "He found out how far he could push us!"

I could empathize with his feelings, but I knew how dangerous his denial of the real situation was. "Yes, he did," I answered, and my voice made it clear that he and I found a different meaning in his words.

Shelly shook her head. Gordon and Shelly had switched roles, and now Shelly took on the role of realist. "I'm not so sure about that, Gordon. That's part of what I've been thinking about in the last few days. It goes deeper, I think. I know I protected Dan—I always knew it, but I never understood why. I think I'm beginning to figure it out. In a way I wasn't protecting him so much as I was protecting myself and the family and trying to preserve some semblance of peace and quiet—albeit false—in the house. So he pushed, and I gave in, usually without too much of a fight. He could always win me over with his air of trustworthiness. And it suited my purposes to do so because all I wanted was to believe we were one happy family.

"Gordon," she continued, hardly taking a breath, "I couldn't stand your battles with him. I had to agree with him; you were trying to control him. You did want him to be just like you, and he isn't. But that's not exactly it. It was that I always ended up being the one to have to fight your battles, but it wasn't my way of fighting. I couldn't enforce rules I didn't believe in, so it was easier to make you think things were better than they were." She paused and shook her head. "It was more than that. When Dan does something wrong, I cover for him so you won't attack me. You're afraid of him, too, Gordon, so half the time instead of dealing with Dan, you attack me. I know you don't really mean to, but it hurts me just the same." She looked at Gordon. He was staring out the window, the little muscle on the left side of his face pulsing with emotion.

"And, Gordon, I've never said this before, but I was also protecting you. I could see how Dan pushed you, and how angry you got. I was afraid you would end up hitting him, and I know how much it means to you that you never hit your children. And when he would get angry or provoke you in some way, then you would get angry. It always seemed to me the best idea was to try to keep everyone's anger below the boiling point."

"In other words," I summed up to home in on the psychological point, "Dan had complete control of the family by means of subtle and not so subtle intimidation. Dan intimidated you, Shelly, because he had learned that was the way to get you to protect him. Unfortunately, you protected Dan from having to face the consequences of his own attitudes and behavior— you protected him from having a real chance to mature emotionally. You may have wanted to foster his independence from his father, but instead you took over as his guardian angel. Your son has a conscience, I am sure, but you kept him from having to rely upon it on a daily basis. Think about the ramifications of that."

I paused to give Shelly and Gordon time to think about what I had said before I went on. "It's understandable that you wanted to keep the anger level down, Shelly," I said, "because kids like Danny can make your life *very unpleasant* if they choose to do the anger thing at you. They can make you act in ways you don't want to act. But it's important to keep in mind that anger is a manipulation at least as often as it is a thing unto itself. It is quite obvious that Danny used his anger to keep you each where he needed you to protect him, so he could do what he wanted.

"There are a couple of other things I think, Shelly, that you and Gordon need to look at," I continued. "I think this kid plays you both better than he plays his cello. Because you two mean to be good parents, agreeing all the time like everyone tells you parents should, Dan is able to intimidate you with that." I noticed their skeptical looks and went on to explain. "Think of it this way: it isn't realistic to imagine that parents always think the same thing about everything. From your own experience, you know that's true, but you think it isn't right, so you end up fighting because you each try to control what the other thinks and does, justifying that you always need to be in agreement. That's one of the ways Dan manipulates you. His game is to make sure you don't think of compromise with each other, or even wise disagreement, and because you each have expectations of how the other will act and react, you end up not really communicating about Dan. Conversations about Dan probably start with each of you ready to become defensive. At the deep level of your love and commitment to your son, you are together, but on everyday levels, Dan makes sure you lose track of that. He's subtle, but good at it. And everybody is losing. It is important for you to decide when and where you can disagree. Dan is smart enough to know you don't agree about everything, but that doesn't mean he should be able to use that as a weapon—a weapon that in the end, of course, is turned against himself." I waited for them to consider what I had said, then I asked, "Does Danny ever ask you if you trust him?"

Shelly and Gordon looked at each other and smiled ruefully. "Well, sure, he's asked me that," Gordon said.

"Come on, Gordon," Shelly said. "He plays that card all the time. And we each always fall for it!"

"That is the ultimate manipulation," I said.

The Meaning of Trust

No parent ever wants to face not being able to trust his child. Saying "I don't trust you" to your child is a final admission that things are not working in your relationship with your teen. It feels like standing before an abyss. In real despair, parents often ask me, "Where do I go now?"

Fortunately the answer is simpler and more hopeful than they imagine. You still trust your child at the deepest level—as the human being you used to know, as that kid who once ran around singing in the yard. What you do not trust are the actions and attitudes that now obscure that child from your view. Do not confuse distrusting what your child is doing right now with distrusting the person you know your child to be. It would make perfect sense to say, "I don't trust you, Dan, because you lie." But that does not mean Dan has become a bad person.

Gordon and Shelly need to understand that at this point they cannot trust their son to tell the truth about anything. That does not affect that they still trust in the soul he once was. The recognition of that trust is what will give them the courage to persevere in changing themselves in order to help Danny to change.

Teens in Turmoil Lie and Cover Their Lies

"Okay. We've accepted that he's been lying to us," Shelly said, pondering what I had said about trust. Looking at Gordon, she said, "After you found the marijuana in his room, and we saw how he had destroyed his room, we couldn't kid ourselves anymore." She noticed Gordon was ready to contradict her as they slid into opposite roles again. "Okay, *I* couldn't kid myself. What I'm worrying about now is that we don't really know how much he lies—or really what he's doing or thinking. I want to think he doesn't lie all that much, but how would we know?" She paused and shivered, as though trying to shake off a demon, then cleared her throat and began in a more matter-of-fact voice. "I somehow have a terrible feeling we would be the last to know."

"Teens," I began, "whether just beginning to test the limits or when they are already getting themselves into real trouble, have one thing in common. They lie. Then, to cover their lies, they lie even more. Most parents shy away from acknowledging that their kids lie. Sometimes parents minimize the meaning of dishonesty, downplaying the significance of a particular excuse or cover-up. But when you put one lie into the context of others, it takes on a different and important meaning."

Like Gordon and Shelly, every time you agree to accept a lie, you agree to be manipulated. You reinforce that lying and manipulating are acceptable means for living in the world. You imply that lying *is* good enough—just so long as you don't get caught. Here are a few of the more common lies parents hear:

- "Those aren't my drugs. I took them away from my friend."
- "I did wake you up when I came in last night. You just don't remember."
- "I would never steal money from my sisters or from you. It has to be the cleaning woman or my sister's friends."
- "Some of my friends drink, but I don't."
- "I worked as hard as I could."
- "That bastard! First he gives me permission to miss the class, then he goes and marks me truant."
- "I told you that last night. You already said it's okay. You just don't remember."
- "I should have higher grades than on that report card! I worked really hard. I know I did better."
- "You never told me I couldn't do that."

- Seeing a plant you suspect might be marijuana growing in your garden or in your teen's room: "It's an experiment for school."
- "If you don't believe me, just call my teacher."
- "You know I don't smoke. You just smell it because I was in a car with people who were smoking."
- "I didn't say that. You didn't hear me right."
- Look, I could tell you the whole story, but it's too complicated. But I will if you want."
- "I was there when you called, but they just couldn't find me."
- "Me? There? Are you kidding?"
- "Yes, her parents will be there."
- "I finished all my homework during detention."
- About the nasal congestion and sore throat that often accompany heavy cigarette and pot smoking: "I think I've got allergies."
- To cover up a hangover: "I think I'm coming down with something."
- "Of course I took my medication; you just didn't see me."
- "That therapist is crazy!"

After I finished reading this list, they both looked up at me with wide-opened eyes. Shelly smiled a half smile and cocked her head.

"A lot of these don't apply," Gordon objected.

"And a lot do," Shelly said, "even if not exactly. Now I understand all those 'colds' he had last winter. But are we supposed to confront him on every lie?"

"Do you really have a choice?" I asked. "Can you justify letting him go on this way?"

Gordon answered first. "No, of course not. We also have to consider how this affects our daughters."

"You know, they probably knew all about Dan long before you did," I said. Gordon was silent. I waited a moment, then I asked, "So where is Danny in school now?"

"That's a story unto itself," Gordon began, glad to change the subject. "Before he agreed to come back from Mexico, he gave us an ultimatum that he would choose his school or quit altogether. Now how could we argue with him?" He looked at me for confirmation. "We had to get him home, and he has to go to school. We agreed because we didn't really have a choice. When he got back, we sat down and made a contract. I think he acted reasonably and in good faith, and I am sure we did. We worked out that he had to be home by ten on school nights, do his homework, and maintain at least a C average. We reminded him that categorically we do not allow drugs in our house, but we agreed he could smoke cigarettes in his room or outside. Dan has to be home for dinner with the family twice a week. He promised to tone down his language and clean his room."

"Is he holding to it?" I asked.

"Well . . . he hasn't said 'fuck you' as often this week," Shelly began, then stopped. She knew she was getting ready to make excuses for Dan, and she did not want to do that any more. "I can't use my energy any more to excuse my son. I just can't do it."

"Then don't. Why should you?" I asked. "You do your son no service."

"I know," Shelly said. "In fact, the contract isn't really working. Dan's never *very* late for curfew, but the fact is, he's never really on time. I suppose his grades are okay, but I don't know because we haven't seen a report card yet. We haven't all had dinner together yet, but that's because he's been busy with his band. He mainly confines his smoking to his room and the patio. Oops, there I go," Shelly corrected herself.

I nodded in encouragement. "You have to see the meaning of that. He is challenging the terms of the contract at every turn."

"But, compared to most kids, he's okay," Shelly defended again. "I mean, he's not worse. Teens do things like this." But she knew her own daughters belied her statement, and the words seemed to stick in her throat. "I sound just like Dan, making excuses, don't I?" she said sheepishly. "Okay. I'm finished with this," she said. "I don't want to have to make excuses for my son any longer."

The False Promise of Contracts

It is my experience that, just as in Shelly and Gordon's case, almost all contracts parents make with teens are useless. There are several reasons why. Stop to think about when you might consider making a contract with your teen (or when he might even suggest one to you). Stop to think with which of your children you are making a contract. The answers are obvious and meaningful. You take the contract seriously, but your teen probably doesn't.

When things aren't working well in the family, parents, therapists, or counselors often suggest writing a contract between an adolescent and his or her parents. In reality, making contracts is what parents do when they realize their child is in control of the family, and they want to *limit* that control somewhat instead of taking the control back altogether. As in the contract Gordon and Shelly made with Dan, family contracts generally specify behavior that should be a given: respect for others and their belongings, not abusing siblings, not using vulgar language, cleaning up the room, coming in on time, being an active member of the family. When those things are not happening, it isn't because the teen doesn't know what is expected, but because he chooses to ignore your rules and instead make his own rules for living in (read: controlling) the family. Writing down what should be happening anyway degrades the sense of trust in the family.

Making contracts also inevitably raises the question of just what you will do if or when your teen breaks the contract—which, if you think about it, is likely. After all, you don't need to make contracts with the children who are keeping to the family rules, but rather with those who are not. If a teen is not keeping to the family rules in the first place, why would making a contract change that attitude? If your teen is already coming in late, and you make a contract that he will come in at curfew, what has anyone gained if he not only comes in late, but also breaches the contract? Contracts can be, and usually are, nickel and dimed out of meaning. And then, what have you, as a parent, taught your teen besides that his word doesn't count, but that it's sort of okay.

Families already have an unwritten and sacred contract anyway, and it is only when that contract no longer works that another one is suggested. The unwritten contract that exists between parents and their children is based on trust. "We trust you; you trust us. We are bound by love and respect." It is when that contract—which is the *only* contract that will ever really work in a family—isn't sufficient to prevent unacceptable behavior that parents decide to write a detailed, behavior-based contract with their teens.

Making a contract between you and your teen is a clear, if unspoken, admission of your impotence as a parent—that your teen is in control of the family and that you know you cannot trust your teen. If you need a contract, it is a sure sign that your moral authority has been successfully challenged. Contracts in families work only when parents and children know they can trust each other, in which case they probably don't need a written contract. Writing a contract to control behavior will never change attitudes. Feeling you need to oblige your teen to sign a contract tells you that deeper changes are needed.

Where to Go from Here

"I am not certain this is a kid we can keep at home," Gordon said when we finished discussing contracts.

"It is always hard to be sure," I said, "but I think it's worth a try. If it doesn't work, there are plenty of good programs. It depends more on you than on Dan right now. Remember, Dan is a good kid. Now that you two are communicating about Dan instead of arguing and reacting, it just might work to keep him at home. Can you manage not to be intimidated by him? Can you confront him, lie for lie? Do you have the courage to tear up the contract and tell him the only one you will make with him is that he may live at home so long as he is responsible and trustworthy, but that if chooses not to be, you will send him to a program? Can you stand firm when he throws his anger at you?

"If you can be certain you will act instead of reacting to provocation," I continued, "it's just possible the really difficult time might not last too long. Here are some specifics: Shelly, you must stop protecting everyone's feelings. Gordon, you must give up your bluster, expecting Shelly to be the enforcer of your rules. Try slowing down your reactions to Danny. For example, when either of you gets that uncomfortable feeling in your stomach that something isn't right, take the time to speak with the other, then confront him together. Think through your actions instead of just reacting to Dan's provocation," I concluded.

"We realize it might make sense for us to consider sending Dan to a program for a while," Shelly said. "We don't like the idea, but we realize it may be for the best."

I nodded in agreement. "Sometimes you have to send your kid away in order to get him back. It may be an option you will need to consider. It isn't the end of the world. Keep in mind, Dan is going to leave home at some time. The point is not if, but rather how and when. Once you have accepted that and know which programs you would be comfortable sending him to, you have all the 'insurance' you need. It is by no means an admission of your failure as parents or as human beings if you decide that will be best for him."

It is impossible to say exactly when "normal" teenage testing of the limits changes into something more serious. There is no precise line to demarcate a border between "normal" and potentially dangerous teenage behavior and attitudes. Parents who allow themselves to be aware not only of their teen's behavior and attitudes but also of their own feelings and reactions are in a position to understand how serious their situation is or is not.

Courtney's parents realized in time that her testing was crossing that line from normal to serious. Adam's parents, lost in their own anger and vengeance, not only ignored but actually encouraged their son's increasingly dangerous behavior. Ryan's and Dan's parents, each in their own way, decided not to understand the meaning of what they saw and experienced. Diane, aware her daughter was not okay, made a common mistake and became so lost in her supposed guilt for her daughter's troubles that she was unable to help the daughter she so loved. But none of these teens is lost. Each one can have the future he or she deserves. Changed parental attitudes are the key.

Reading these stories and the psychological explanations of what was happening and what needed to happen will help you to clarify your own thinking. Take time to think back over the stories, spending more time on those situations you find familiar. I think you will find you now have a clearer understanding of your teen and your family, and how you can become an agent of change.

In Part III, you will see how to put into practice what you have learned. You are ready to begin to find solutions to your own particular situation.

PART III ✺

Finding Your Own
Solutions

Chapter 9 ✦

Becoming an Agent of Change

You do have choices in how you act and react with your child. Teens test their parents—and generally all the adults in their lives, too. Although it may not seem like it, they do want you to pass the test. But just because you were manipulated yesterday doesn't mean you must choose to be manipulated today. Just because you chose to believe a lie last week, doesn't mean you must make the same choice this week. You can begin to do things differently. You can make real changes in how you feel. Once you do, you will find that affects everyone in your family in a positive way.

The stories in Part II gave you the opportunity to watch five families struggle with living with teens in turmoil. Now it will be useful for you to look at your own family, using the knowledge you have gleaned from what you have read and realized. Here is an exercise that will help you see your family situation from a new perspective.

Observing Your Family from a Safe Distance

One rather simple way of consolidating your new thoughts and focusing on the picture of your teenager and your family is a technique that will probably seem at once familiar and unfamiliar to you. It is a way of being able to peer into your own family life and see it as though it were a movie being acted by others. This exercise allows you to be a much more objective observer than you can be while involved in the turmoil of your everyday life. It grows out of the common knowledge that we are all much more adept at seeing what is wrong with someone else, understanding someone else's difficulties, and giving advice to others than to ourselves. It is my own somewhat simplified adaptation of Giorgi's phenomenological psychological research method. Similar to the realizations and insight you gained from reading the family stories in Chapters 4 through 8, this exercise takes you a step further and gives you the means to bring the picture of your situation into clear focus. It is easy to do, and the whole process should not take you more than a couple of well-spent hours.

Step 1

Write a description of your experience of one time you felt overwhelmed, threatened, or intimidated by your teen or a time when you just couldn't understand what happened. Perhaps you will want to describe something that happened this morning or last week that wasn't okay, that made you feel angry, hurt, or afraid. Maybe you will want to describe the scene or event that sent you to the bookstore in search of this book or whatever just happened that made you decide to open it today.

Don't analyze or interpret while you are describing (that step comes later). Be sure to describe your experience fully. If you find it hard to begin, start with a simple physical description of your son or daughter, or even of the place where the incident occurred. It will help to get you warmed up to the work. This is not a writing class, so you need not concern yourself about your style or even your spelling or punctuation. Remember, for now all you are doing is *describing your experience.* After the first few lines, the description will almost "write itself." The description should be as long as it needs to be to describe your experience, usually one to three pages.

Step 2

When you have finished, take a few minutes to wind down; go have a cup of coffee, take a short walk, wash the dishes, or work in the garden. When you are ready, look at your description again. Your goal is temporarily to depersonalize your story, to distance yourself from the action so you will be able to look at it with few prejudgments and preconceptions.

Now take the description and change all the first-person pronouns in it to a third-person form. Change "I" to "he" or "she" or think up a name to which you have no relationship and use that name for yourself. You can also choose to use nouns such as "the man" or "the woman," "the father," "the mother." Next, change your son's or daughter's name and anyone else who is in the description to another name to which you have no relationship, or use a noun such as "the teen" or "the coach" or a third-person pronoun.

The object of this step is to take yourself and your family out of the situation so that you will be able to see it without prejudgment and preconceptions. For the time being, let your story be someone else's story. Think of it as a story about someone else's troubles because you will be able to see and understand the situation better from the "distance" of a "casual" and "objective" observer.

Here is an example to help you get started:

Step 1: Description

After breakfast I went upstairs to get ready to go to work. I knew my son, Jake, wasn't awake, but I didn't wake him. I kept worrying with myself that he would be late for school, but I knew if I went into his room, he would yell at me. I decided to do it anyway because if he didn't make it to school, I would get a phone call later, and I had to be in court all day.

Step 2: First to Third Person "Distancing"

After breakfast she went upstairs to get ready to go to work. She knew her son, Brian, wasn't awake, but she didn't wake him. She kept worrying with herself that Brian would be late for school, but she knew if she went into his room, Brian would yell at her. She decided to do it anyway because if Brian didn't make it to school, she would get a phone call later, and she had to be in court all day.

Step 3

Read your revised story. Try reading it aloud to yourself or even to someone close to you. Read it as though it were about some "other" family, and let yourself see what you see. How did you react when it was "someone else's" family? How does that family look? How do they act? What do you know about them that you didn't know about your own family? Do you have any new ideas about how you could do things differently and better?

Having clarified your own understanding of what is going on in your family, you are now ready to begin to find *your* solutions to your family's problems. There is no guarantee your teen is going to demonstrate immediate joy that you are retaking control of the family and of your own life. You will have to remain courageous, so that with each choice you will be ready and able to remain consistent with the decisions you have made. Acting from the firm ground of emotional authenticity, the knowledge you do not need illusions, and your love for your child, you will find this an easier choice to make and to stick with than you could have imagined previously.

Following are six short scenarios, probably similar to ones you experience, which will give you an opportunity to try out some of your new thoughts. They are designed to help you understand how to see through a situation, a confrontation, a lie, a manipulation quickly and decisively. They are *not* designed to provide you with a script to use with your teen.

You will be able to feel how far you have come in your own process as you watch the following scenes unfold and realize how much more quickly you are able to see through the teens' manipulations, lies, and games than you were when you first picked up the book. You will also find that you notice nuances that would have escaped you had you not at least begun your own process of change.

It is not easy to recognize that the buck stops with you, but as you read through these stories, you will know that is just the way it is—and you will now be able and ready to do what you must. You may want to "test" yourself by reading the scenario, then asking yourself what would be the result or "fallout" for a parent who reacted to the teen in the way described. Think through the type of justification you would once have given in a similar situation. Your greater knowledge of your situation will make it easier for you to understand the consequences of such thoughts and actions, and you may well almost be able to do the Instant Replay yourself.

1. Controlled Stupidity—An Effective Way to Manipulate

You, Mom (or Dad), knock on Heather's door. Heather, a straight-A student, is sitting on her bed surrounded by catalogues. Her face is aglow with the excitement of twelve-year-old purchase power.

"Did you see the new J. Crew catalogue? Ohmigod, their stuff is soooo cool! It's like, you know, I mean, it's like toduhlly awesome! I neeeeeed so many things! Wanna see?"

"I thought you were cleaning up your room."

"I am, but just look at this really cool stuff I found. I mean, like I don't like really like the stuff in the L. L. Bean catalogue. I'm not going to buy anything from them."

"Would you please not say 'like' every other word! This room is kind of a mess, Heather."

"These cargo pants are like sooo awesome! They toduhlly go with my new blue sweater."

"I don't want to buy you anything else, if you won't take care of the things you already have."

"But Maaaahm, I neeeeed some things. I mean, like you can't like expect me to wear all those dorky things I have from elementary school. I'm in junior high now. Anyway, they don't fit me. But like there were some things in like the Gap that were like toduhlly awesome! We could go over there like right now. Wanna go?"

"Not now. I'm tired," Mom says, bending down to collect some of Heather's laundry. "Heather, I would really appreciate it if you would straighten up in here. Just a little."

"Look at this fleece. It's like sooo cool. You wouldn't have to buy me a winter coat."

"We just bought you a winter coat, remember? I really would appreciate it if you could just hang up your clothes."

"I don't know how to hang them up right. It like never works for me."

"I'll show you," Mom answers, beginning to hang up the pile of clothes. "See, this is how you do it."

"I try that all the time, but it never works."

"I'll do this for you, while you pick up your dirty clothes. You could straighten up the top of your dresser just by putting things in their places. It wouldn't even take you that long."

"I don't know where their places are."

"Well, you put the socks in your sock drawer and your underwear in your underwear drawer. Put all the desk things in your desk drawers. Throw out all the extra papers or whatever you don't need or want into the garbage."

"But like it's like sooooo hard. Just look at these two things I like best. They would look sooo cool with my new boots."

Heather remains engrossed in her shopping thoughts. "Where should I put my dirty clothes?"

"Right over there in your hamper. But not your sweater!"

"Huh?"

"Give it to me, and I'll take care of it."

"And what do I do with this? And with this? This is soooo hard!"

"If you'll work with me to clean up this room, then keep it neat for two weeks, I'll buy you those new cargo pants and the fleece."

FALLOUT

You teach Heather the power of controlled stupidity, the sort she can turn on and off as she finds useful. It helps her not to have to be responsible for her own things. Not only will you "help" her to clean her room now, you will probably "help" to keep it clean for the next two weeks, preferring not to have a daily argument about cleaning the room or about not buying Heather what she wants in two weeks. By doing all this, you keep your daughter in a little girl place, but sometimes or at some other time in the future, that may not be convenient.

YOUR JUSTIFICATION FOR YOUR RESPONSE

She's only twelve! She really didn't know how to clean up her room, and it was the right thing for me to teach her how. Now that she's in junior high, maintaining straight A's is not only hard work, but stressful. The right way to teach her is to give her an example of how she can get her needs met when she acts in an appropriate way.

CONSEQUENCES OF YOUR JUSTIFICATION

Because you fell for Heather's pretending she didn't understand something she obviously did understand, you taught her that playing stupid is a viable means to get her way. Heather hones her manipulation skills instead of learning to meet her responsibilities. Her sense of entitlement is validated. Meanwhile, you congratulate yourself for having dealt with the situation well, but unfortunately, you have allowed yourself to lower your expectations of your daughter.

INSTANT REPLAY

Mom knocks on Heather's door. Heather, a straight-A student, is sitting on her bed surrounded by catalogues. Her face is aglow with the excitement of twelve-year-old purchase power.

"Did you see the new J. Crew catalogue? Ohmigod, the stuff is soooo cool! It's like, you know, I mean, it's like toduhlly awesome! I neeeeeed so many things! Wanna see?"

"No, not now. It looks as though you haven't finished cleaning your room."

"Like, yeah, but, like I just had to like look through the catalogues first. I mean, like I don't really like like the stuff in the L. L. Bean catalogue. Like I'm not buying anything from them."

"You aren't going to be buying any stuff from anywhere until you clean your room and take care of the things you have."

"You can't expect me to do that every day!"

"Why not? I hang up my things everyday. It's not hard."

"I know, but you're a grown-up. Grown-ups have time. You know what to do."

"You know what to do, too. In the first place, it isn't difficult, and in the second place, you aren't stupid. In the third place, you are in junior high now. I really don't think this is more responsibility than you can handle."

"But it's soooooo hard! I neeeed your help! I don't know where anything goes, and I don't have any hangers!"

"There are plenty of hangers in the basement. Figure out where things should go, and that's where they will go."

"You're not doing anything, and I have hours and hours of homework."

"Then you had better get started!"

OUTCOME

Heather is held accountable for her own things. You do not offer rewards for meeting everyday responsibilities. You did not fall for Heather's "stupid-me" act, so you did not lower your expectations. You are clear and concise. Heather probably won't try this manipulation too many more times.

INDULGENCE

Parents usually tend to think of indulgence as material. And, of course, it's true. Many parents indulge their child's every material wish—and then they find that they have created an "I need it" monster (with the implied threat: I will make you unhappy if you don't provide it!).

But indulgence is really more an attitude. When you agree to believe a child who is dishonest or pretending to be helpless, you are indulging him disastrously. Allowing yourself to be manipulated is indulging him into thinking that is a viable and honorable way to deal with the world. Indulging your child implies you believe in his or her inability to deal with the real world. Indulgence is a way to protect your child from life. You will never succeed in that.

2. Placing the Responsibility Where It Belongs

Mike is thirteen, a "badge item" kid who will wear only particular brands of designer clothing and whose life is dedicated to skateboarding—any-place and everyplace. His last report card was disappointing.

"I'm disappointed in your report card, Mike. Your mother and I know you can do better than this. If you only put one-sixth of the effort into your schoolwork that you put into that goddamn skateboard, you would be a straight-A student!"

"My grades aren't that bad. I got two B's, and C's in everything else. And skateboarding is my life."

"Skateboarding—now that's going to take you far in life! A career a fa-ther can be proud of!"

"You don't know anything about it."

"I know enough to know that skateboarding is out of your life for now."

"Wanna bet?"

"Yeah, I'll bet. I'll bet you just lost your skateboard for a month."

"Wanna bet. You can't do that."

"Wanna bet?"

"You can't stop me!"

"Oh, yes I can."

"What are you going to do? Break my legs?"

"If I catch you skateboarding, you won't get that board back for six months!"

"You suck. I don't care what you do. You can't stop me from skate-boarding. It's my life."

"You're not skateboarding until I say it's okay. And if I hear about you skateboarding, you have lost it for a year. You hear that? One year. And I have ears and eyes all over this town."

"Fuck you!"

"Don't you speak to me that way. You show some respect."

"You show me some respect. And skateboarding, too. It's a real sport, just like bowling, only a lot better."

"Bowling is a respectable sport. Skateboarding isn't. We don't wear those stupid pants that hang down to our knees. We're an organized team."

"Fuck you, Dad. You don't know anything. I'm joining a skateboarding team."

"I know you're going to do as I say. Those grades will come up, and there will be no skateboarding."

"Wanna bet?"

"I'm telling you, that's the way it is."

"I'm gonna keep on skateboarding, and I don't care what happens to my grades. What are you going to about that?"

FALLOUT

This is a no-win situation; this argument could go on forever because you have come down to the level of your thirteen-year-old son. You and your son will just keep upping the ante on each other. In fact, you cannot control your son's behavior, so making more and more threats only brings your son to weigh every one and decide if the threat is bad enough to make him comply. He may decide that thwarting your demands is a worthwhile end in itself. Realistically, how are you going to follow through on the punishment you threaten while you concurrently risk losing credibility with your son?

YOUR JUSTIFICATION FOR YOUR RESPONSE

You are embarrassed to have your son seen wearing those clothes and skateboarding around town. Now that he has disappointed you with his grades, the embarrassment increases. It's not even possible to talk to this kid, you think. He always starts an argument, then you get caught in it and quickly become too angry to stop yourself from making threats. Because your threats are mainly unenforceable, you feel you have to keep upping the ante to be in charge.

CONSEQUENCES OF YOUR JUSTIFICATION

Your way of dealing with your son mainly teaches him to up the ante to the point where your threats become outrageous enough for him to ignore or even to ridicule them. Mike will begin to weigh and measure every threat against having another fight with you and will most likely decide that another fight isn't that big a deal. Anyway, from Mike's point of view, you are going to fight with him no matter what, and that may ultimately cause him to lose respect for, and distance himself from, you.

INSTANT REPLAY

Mike is a "badge-item" kid whose life is dedicated to skateboarding—anyplace and everyplace. His last report card was disappointing.

"How do you feel about your report card, Mike?"

"It's okay. I mean, yeah. It's okay," Mike said, trying to be as nonchalant as possible.

"You and I both know you can do better than this. If you gave some of the energy to your schoolwork that you do to skateboarding, your grades would be fine."

"Come on, Dad, they're not that bad. I got two B's, and C's in everything else. You know that skateboarding is my life, and I'm pretty good at it."

"Saying your grades aren't 'that bad' won't make them good. I do understand you are good at your skateboarding. Why don't you try to be good at two things instead of just one? Are you proud of this report card?"

"But my report card is okay, right? Skateboarding is all that really matters to me."

"Well, be that as it may, you didn't answer my question."

"What was the question?"

"You know."

Mike shifts uncomfortably from foot to foot. If he could only get his father angry, it would be easier not to feel so bad about the grades. "Uh, well. Are you going to ground me or something?"

"Your grades are your own. They are about you and your future. I already have my education. But I do think that doing well in school is likely to bring you more than skateboarding will. In the long run, I mean."

"What happens if my grades don't get better?"

"You may not pass into the next grade. Now that would be a drag! For you."

OUTCOME

Because you didn't get angry, you didn't get sucked into lowering yourself to the level of your thirteen-year-old son. You placed the responsibility of Mike's grades squarely on Mike's own shoulders. You didn't turn Mike's grades into a bone of contention but made it clear that you didn't think they were the standard your son should have for himself. You didn't waste your energy attacking Mike's skateboarding, which, though you don't necessarily like it, wasn't the issue anyway. You have helped Mike to feel his own shame in proportion to what happened. He will not need to displace it into anger about something else. You not only didn't lose credibility, you increased it. You have helped your son to grow emotionally.

ANGER

Perhaps the most common and greatest teenage threat is the threat to get angry with parents: "If you . . . I'm going to get angry!" Parents who are afraid of their child, their child's displeasure, or the "punishments" they receive when they disappoint their teen, buy peace at any price. Kids (and adults) use anger as a way to make sure they don't have to deal with the real feelings.

A possible answer to "I'm going to get angry!" is "Okay. Go for it!" Suddenly you have taken the wind out of your teen's sails. You will have taken all the power out of the manipulation, all the energy out of the threat. Once you demonstrate to your teen you can live with his anger, he has very little else with which to threaten you. The new clarity you achieve allows you to get down to talking about whatever the issue of the moment really is—and the feelings underlying it.

Some kids are just enraged—not really enraged at something, just enraged. It's an undifferentiated way of scattering immense emotional/psychological energy. As soon as teens learn to focus the negative energy of their rage and turn it into a positive force, they discover an ability to succeed—and be happy—which they cannot now even imagine.

3. Using Confusion to Divide and Conquer

Brad is fourteen. He is at that age where his friends are more important than anyone else. Being accepted and being cool is what it's all about for Brad. His parents Ted and Alice have the following discussion:

"I never gave Brad permission to have a coed sleep-over. What kind of a fool do you think I am?"

"I never said you were a fool. I just said that before you go giving him permission for things you know I don't approve of, you should speak to me."

"But I didn't give him permission. And how am I supposed to know you don't approve? We never talked about it. I never knew there were such things."

"He told me you gave him permission."

"Are you saying Brad is lying?"

"How should I know. What I do know is that we are not having a coed sleep-over in this house."

"Why not? They're good kids. They won't do anything."

"What do you mean? I'm not having fourteen-year-olds having sex in my basement!"

"Who said they are going to have sex? They're only fourteen. They wouldn't know how."

"What planet did you just land from? Of course fourteen-year-olds have sex. Have you even seen who his friends are?"

"Yeah, all the kids from school. He's been with them for years. They are good kids."

"You don't even know. Those aren't even the ones he hangs out with anymore. I don't like these kids in my house. What is Allison supposed to think when they're all down in the basement . . . 'doing it'?"

"I hate when you talk that way. And I never said he could have a god-damn coed slumber party."

"Then you tell me why he said you did!"

"Can you tell me why we are having this fight when we actually agree this time?"

"So long as they don't smoke pot or anything."

"I thought you agreed we weren't letting him have this party."

"I don't care if he has this party or not!"

"There is not going to be any party."

FALLOUT

Brad doesn't even have to be in the room with his parents to control not only the conversation, but also their feelings. Brad's half-truths and outright lies to each of his parents have brought them to have an argument they don't even mean. Caught in Brad's divide and conquer, Ted and Alice neglect to notice they agree that Brad is not going to be allowed to have a coed slumber party. Their argument doesn't even make sense. An atmosphere of annoyance, if not outright anger and distrust, quickly permeates a family when teens successfully divide and conquer their parents. Perhaps most unfortunate of all the possible types of fallout is the feeling of mistrust each parent has after he or she has been manipulated by the teen before he or she is able to clarify things with the other parent.

YOUR JUSTIFICATION FOR YOUR RESPONSE

Never sure just what is going on in your house, it is easy to justify the mistrust and anger by pinning it on misunderstanding and confusion. But it is a mistake to stop there, not seeing that the misunderstanding and confusion are coming from a teen who is dividing and conquering.

CONSEQUENCES OF YOUR JUSTIFICATION

You have stupid fights over nothing. Your child is encouraged to become vicious and conniving. Your trust for each other wanes. The atmosphere in your home is always charged, ready to explode or implode.

INSTANT REPLAY

"I never gave Brad permission to have a coed sleep-over."

"I didn't think you would have. We've got a real problem on our hands because he is always saying things like this."

"Yeah. Do you notice how he picks and chooses whom he asks for what permission? If I say no, he tries to make it sound to you as though I hadn't quite made up my mind."

"I hadn't exactly thought of it that way, but you know what? You are completely right."

"That really makes me angry."

"Okay, but we can't let that get to us. Remember last week how we started to fight over when Brad would have to be home after the basketball game? We can't let that happen."

"Have you noticed that Allison seems to be picking up on that? Yesterday she came to me and said you told her she could go to the city with Julie and Michelle."

"What? You know I'd never say that."

"Exactly. We have to make sure that whenever either one of them asks for permission for anything significant, we discuss it. They can wait for our decision to be made together even if they don't think they can."

"And if they say they can't wait, we just say that is an automatic 'No.'"

OUTCOME

By working to agree in all significant matters, Ted and Alice will soon teach Brad and Allison that their parents cannot be divided. More than likely, it won't be too long before Ted and Alice will not have to confer about every detail because they will have established their unity as parents. Ted and Alice have the advantage of being parents who are not afraid to say no and who will oblige their teens to learn that instant gratification doesn't always happen.

WHAT? NO PUNISHMENT?

You have probably noticed the absence of suggesting punishment-type consequences in these scenarios as well as in the family stories in Part II. The reason is that, in my experience, too often teens weigh the punishment against the fun of doing what they were planning to do anyway and decide on the latter.

Teaching kids that their actions have consequences is one of the basics of being a parent. That actions and attitudes have consequences is one of the points most kids learn and accept before they are out of grade school. But parents of teens in turmoil often find that giving punishments (or consequences) for misdemeanors as well as for serious infractions of rules or breach of trust simply doesn't work.

Consequences work for kids who are not yet involved in outrageous and dangerous behavior. Consequences work for kids who want to do their best. Consequences work when you still have a relationship with your teen.

Grounding, reducing or taking away allowance, refusing permission to use the car or to speak on the telephone are all viable means of teaching (reminding) your teen that there are consequences to actions and attitudes. Allowing your child to feel the results of unfinished homework instead of intervening to make sure the homework gets finished can be an effective means of teaching the meaning and consequences of actions, inaction, and attitudes. Saying "No" is also a viable alternative, even if your child moans and complains, yells or intimidates.

But, if you find you have to come up with consequence after consequence, you have a clear indication that this method of dealing with your teen is not working. If your teenager *is* out of control, it literally means he or she *is out of control. That teen is outside your control, probably the school's control, and possibly the law's control.* It is important to understand that if your child does not choose to obey the consequences you give, there is almost nothing you can do.

Even more, consider the impact on you of implementing the increasingly draconian consequences you may have had to think up. Out-of-control teens easily bring their parents to dreaming up and trying to implement (or being, in fact, too frightened to implement) far worse consequences than are in concert with their principles and with their own honor and dignity.

What happens when, despite the fact you meet every "bad" action with a consequence, your child keeps on doing what he was doing, ignoring the consequences and continuing the behavior you deplore? If or when this happens to you, you may have to face that you cannot deal with your teen at home any longer. A wilderness, emotional-growth, or similar program (see listings in Part IV) may be where he or she will best learn how to become a responsible adult.

The biggest, most obvious, and powerful consequence is probably the one you are most frightened of: withdrawing your trust and respect. Parents dealing with a difficult teen lose sight of the fact that their teens love them and want their respect. Letting your child know he or she has left you no option but to withdraw trust (not love!) until his or her actions and attitudes have changed can be a powerful catalyst to change.

4. Negotiation—Who Is Really Making the Rules?

John is a new driver. He is unhappy with having a curfew.

"I'll be home later."

"When? I expect you by midnight."

"I'm going to a concert. You can't expect me by then. It doesn't even begin until ten!"

"How long will the concert last? What time will it be over?"

"I don't know. It'll be over when it's over."

"Well, can you give me an idea what time that might be?"

"No. I just said I don't know. Everybody's going. It doesn't matter to their parents. You're so overprotective. I'm sixteen; I'm not a baby. I can take care of myself. It's only a concert, for Christ's sake."

"I only wanted to know. So I wouldn't worry."

"You don't have to worry. Don't you remember what it was like going to a concert? It's so cool. You can't just leave! Everybody will think you're a dork!"

"Okay. Just, if you are going to be later than two, please call."

"Okay. Sure. That's cool. See you later." John gives his mother a kiss as he walks out the door.

FALLOUT

John comes and goes as he pleases. You will sit up and wait, worrying, eating, pretending, rationalizing, hoping. Because the conversation *seems* to be a negotiation, you don't realize that John makes the rules in the house. (In many communities, John would be breaking the local curfew laws, opening himself and you to legal prosecution.) If John makes the rules in the house, it will be hard for him to understand he doesn't make the rules everywhere in the world.

YOUR JUSTIFICATION FOR YOUR RESPONSE

You are glad he finally has friends to go out with, and you want him to enjoy the teenage years. You don't want your son to have to feel like a dork. You remember how much you loved going to concerts when you were just a little older than he is and how dear those memories are to you.

CONSEQUENCES OF YOUR JUSTIFICATION

Your sixteen-year-old son is in control not only of his curfew, but also of your emotions. He manipulates you by playing on your emotions—and your hesitance to be strict with him. He lets you know that you will be emotionally responsible if other kids think he is a "dork." Your own identification with teenage feelings gets in your way of providing the adult response to your son. The end result is that John is well-positioned to escalate his demands as he grows older.

INSTANT REPLAY

"I'll be home later."

"Whoa, buddy. You don't make the curfew around here."

"I'm going to a concert. I'll be home when it's over."

"You will be home by one."

"That's so unfair."

"Okay. You are welcome to think so, but I don't. You know that your father and I discussed this last night. We told you this is what we decided. Please be home by one. That is your curfew."

"None of the other kids' parents are that unreasonable."

"Sorry. My position is not unreasonable."

"I can't promise."

OUTCOME

Instead of falling into a defensive stance, you have calmly stated your position. You have not fallen into the trap of needing the last word. That leaves you ready to listen to your child when he or she has different opinions, but keeps you from moving away from being the adult who has, and must have, a certain authority in the family. Calmly stating your position and refusing to engage in a negotiation about details leaves you quickly ready to discern between differing opinions and manipulations, "I want what I want" attitudes, and compromise. In fact, by remaining clear, dispassionate, and on the subject, you imply reciprocity and tolerance because you demonstrate you will listen to your child's opinions when he acts maturely.

BOTTOM LINES

Dealing with a teen in turmoil is challenging. Parents find that what they were sure they believed yesterday may not be the case today, and that what they expected from their teen seems to be a moveable feast. Only the lack of trust, the yelling, the fighting, the worry, the fear remain constant.

It is time to find your bottom line: *Just exactly how do you want to live? What are you willing to accept? What are you willing to tolerate from your child?*

Your bottom line is your connection with, and devotion to, your own principles, and it is probably related to trust between you and your teen. Your principles and honor are what will carry you through this difficult, challenging time.

Finding your bottom line will let you know how you must change and how you must catalyze change in your teen enough so that trust is reestablished in your family. Decide with your spouse or partner or, if you are a single parent, on your own, what you are willing to accept or not accept from your teen. How do you want your family to live?

5. Teens Testing Parents—Will You Pass?

Jennifer is thirteen. It is Thanksgiving Day, and the family, as they do every year, has planned to go to Grandma's for the family party. You see Jennifer getting ready to leave the house and ask:

"Where are you going? We have to leave for Grandma's in half an hour."

"I'm not going. I hate going to Grandma's. We always go to Grandma's for Thanksgiving. There's nothing to do there. Thanksgiving is stupid. And you know I hate turkey, especially the way Grandma makes it. Anyway, I've become a vegetarian. And I hate Uncle Al because he always makes fun of my age."

"Don't be silly. You always have a great time at Grandma's. Just ignore Uncle Al. And anyway, there are lots of things to eat besides just turkey. When did you become a vegetarian?" In an attempt to placate Jenny, you remind her that Aunt Meg always brings apple pie, and that she loves apple pie.

"No, I don't. I hate her apple pie."

"You do not. Last year you ate three pieces."

"I did not. You did. I would never eat three pieces of pie. That's gross."

"We have to leave in fifteen minutes. Get ready. You can't go dressed like that."

"I'm going like this, or I'm not going at all."

"Jennifer, then at least change your jeans."

"I always wear jeans."

"Then just find some without holes."

"There's nothing wrong with these jeans."

"Well, at least do something with your hair."

"I suppose next you're going to tell me to take the ring out of my nose."

"You don't have one."

"I'm going to, though."

"Stop arguing. Just go get ready."

"I'm not arguing with you. You're arguing with me. I told you I'm not going."

"You know how much it will upset your father if you don't go. Thanksgiving means more to him than any other holiday."

"Whatever! I'm still not changing."

Desperately you offer, "If you change your clothes, I'll see about taking you to buy that outfit you wanted."

FALLOUT

Having been diverted from the topic, you fall easily into bickering about extraneous subjects. This diversion, like all the others you hear every day, wearies you and confuses the issue. Everyone embarks on the journey to Grandma's tense and angry, pretending to feel like a normal family. You remain poised to clean up whatever emotional mess your daughter might create. Embarrassed by Jennifer's appearance, you worry about even greater potential embarrassment if she starts a fight with Uncle Al or sneaks wine from the bar.

Jennifer is a rather normal young teen who wants to find out if her parents can be manipulated. She is testing. If Jennifer's parents pass their first few (or several) tests, Jenny probably won't bother to carry on testing them. If, on the other hand, Jenny's parents get sucked into playing by her rules, the fallout will be that Jennifer will be making the rules of every conversation. Soon she may decide her own curfew, whether she should do her chores, and perhaps one day she will borrow the car without permission.

YOUR JUSTIFICATION FOR YOUR RESPONSE

It is just too embarrassing to be fighting with your teenage daughter in front of your brother's picture-perfect family. Your mother is so quick to judge and will hold it against you that Jennifer is wearing jeans and has become a vegetarian. A new outfit for Jennifer at $75 isn't that expensive if you can get through this dinner without a scene. You promise yourself you won't ever bribe her like this again.

CONSEQUENCE OF YOUR JUSTIFICATION

Once you bribe, the ante keeps going up. Jennifer learns how to control situations to get what she wants. You don't feel very good about the way you handled the scene. Your day is ruined.

INSTANT REPLAY

"Where are you going? We have to leave for Grandma's in half an hour."

"To the video store. I hate going to Grandma's. I'm not going. We always go to Grandma's for Thanksgiving. There's nothing to do. Thanksgiving is stupid. And you know I hate turkey, especially the way Grandma makes it. I've become a vegetarian. And I hate Uncle Al because he always makes fun of my age."

"We're leaving in thirty minutes. Be ready." Leaving the room, you continue to get ready.

"I said I'm not going."

You don't answer.

OUTCOME

You passed the test. You have refused to let your daughter make the rules of the discussion. You have refused to turn a simple request into a confrontation, being too wise to stoop to an adolescent level. You haven't gotten caught in your daughter's manipulation, nor have you allowed yourself to become stuck in a "conversation web." When no consequence has been identified, it is more difficult for a teen to call your bluff. The more you escalate, the easier it is for your child to call your bluff.

Although the way you managed the conversation in the instant replay is far from perfect, by not engaging in a fight, you have made it more possible for each of you to get out of the situation. Jennifer does not have to lose face. At least in this sort of scenario, you remain the one who is making the ground rules of the conversation. You feel better about yourself because you haven't lowered yourself to bribes. You passed Jennifer's test.

There is, of course, no guarantee that your conversation with your teen will turn out this way; however, parents generally tell me they are pleasantly surprised by the response they get from their younger teen when they refuse to accept being manipulated. The secret here is not engaging in an argument (because as such you won't win it!) and remaining firm but not angry.

6. Picture Perfect—A Teen Quietly in Trouble

Anna is the perfect sixteen-year-old. Cheerleader, honor roll student, attractive, and popular, she has only one secret: She is deeply unhappy at school and with her own actions and attitudes.

"Why don't you invite Rob over so your dad and I can meet him?"

Her voice quiet and her mood apparently bored, she answers, "Mom, you just can't do things like that. Everyone would think I'm pathetic."

"I don't really know any of your friends. Even when they come over, they don't speak to me. If I ask them a question, they give me a one-word answer. Is that the way you act when you go to their houses?"

"It's nothing, Mom. Just don't make a big deal out of it, okay?" Feeling resigned but unsettled, Mom decides to change the subject.

"I can't wait until we go to Florida. Are you as excited as I am?"

"I'm not sure I'm going."

"What? Oh, honey, we planned this trip especially for you as a special treat because you did so well last semester."

"I don't know if I want to go. That's all. No big deal. Just leave it, okay? Look, I have a lot of homework before practice. Could you just please leave me alone?"

Mom goes out of the room, worried, bewildered, and hurt. An hour later when she taps on Anna's door, she finds her asleep. When she questions Anna about why she is always so bored and tired, Anna shrugs her off with "It's okay. Don't worry about it. I have to go now. I'm going to be late."

FALLOUT

Anna's secret remains intact. She is unhappy at school, disgusted at what she believes she needs to do to remain popular, but afraid not to play into what she perceives as necessary behavior and attitudes. She is unsure of herself at every level, yet too proud to ask for help. Afraid of the teasing she would undergo if she showed how excited she was about going to Florida with her parents instead of with other teens, Anna feels herself slowly sinking into listlessness. Afraid of disappointing her parents, she works to keep up her façade that everything is fine. Afraid of losing her place on the social ladder at school, Anna acts in ways she despises because she knows if she is not the one tormenting other kids, she may become the tormented one.

You see the red flags of your daughter's withdrawal, but, afraid of what you see you fail to acknowledge their significance. It is easy enough because Anna's grades remain excellent and her social life seems perfect.

In fact, Anna is becoming caught in a web of demoralization and self-deceit which no one knows enough about to be able to help her.

YOUR JUSTIFICATION FOR YOUR RESPONSE

Anna's life has always been picture-perfect. Because Anna does not seem to have any of the "usual" signs of adolescent distress, it appears as though everything is still fine with her. Although you feel something is wrong with your daughter, you rationalize that no teen wants to have her boyfriend meet her family, that most teens don't like to speak with parents, and that between her schoolwork, cheerleading, and social life, it is no wonder Anna feels tired. You don't want to interfere in her life and make her withdraw from you even more.

CONSEQUENCES OF YOUR JUSTIFICATION

Anna will continue to maintain her façade that everything in her life is okay for as long as she can. By the time she is willing to let you know something is wrong, she may have become deeply lost and demoralized. Because Anna's standards for herself are so high, as she becomes more and more demoralized and therefore less able to meet her own demands, she may begin to turn against herself in dangerous ways. You will feel increasingly isolated from your daughter and more and more panicked as you see her becoming ever unhappier.

INSTANT REPLAY

Anna is the perfect sixteen-year-old. Cheerleader, honor-roll student, attractive, and popular, she has only one secret: She is deeply unhappy at school and with her own actions and attitudes.

You have been noticing that Anna doesn't seem quite herself anymore.

Having resolved that no matter what you will not be put off again, you initiate a conversation with her.

"Why don't you invite Rob over so your dad and I can meet him?"

Her voice quiet and apparently listless, Anna answers, "Mom, you just can't do things like that. Everyone would think I'm pathetic."

"So what if they did?"

"Mom. You don't understand. Leave it, okay?"

"No, Anna. I can't do that. I see you unhappy and listless. Do you really want me to leave you like that? What is going on?"

"You wouldn't understand."

"I might. I know you aren't okay. I don't care how good your grades look; I can see you aren't okay. I won't judge you nearly as harshly as you are judging yourself. What is going on?"

Anna's eyes fill with tears and she turns away. "I can't . . ."

"You know, I won't love you less, no matter what it is that's making you feel this way."

"Please just leave me alone."

"No. Anna, you are my daughter. I just can't leave you like this. If you won't talk to me, then we have to find you someone to talk to. You just cannot keep this much sorrow inside. No one can. I love you too much to see you this way. I can help, but you will have to let me."

OUTCOME

Demonstrating to Anna that you can accept her sorrow as well as her triumphs and joys, you open the door for communication with your daughter and gently but firmly refuse to allow Anna to close it. Careful not to pry, you use your love, understanding, and warmth to invite Anna to talk about what is bothering her. Instead of trying to divert Anna's attention to happy things like a trip to Florida, you show you are not afraid of whatever emotions your daughter is feeling. Of course, not all teens will open up and tell their parents their innermost thoughts, but when parents show they can take the unhappy as well as the happy from their teens, they demonstrate that they are not judging their child only according to outward successes.

Teens Do Love and Value Their Parents

Yes, your teen loves you. Yes, your teen values you. It may be hard to believe when he or she is creating the turmoil that defines your life just now. Nevertheless, it is generally so. Beneath anger, manipulation, drugs, alcohol, depression, failure, or just plain testing the limits, teens love their parents. It may not be cool for them to say so, but it is true.

As children move into their teen years and begin the process of gaining personal, emotional, and psychological independence from their parents, many teens seem to think they must also break the bonds of love—or at least pretend to do so. They experience love as constraining instead of liberating—or at lest they feel obliged to act that way.

When parents and teens find themselves in conflict over small details of life or over much larger issues, it becomes all too easy for love to become something no one thinks much about. Remember: Your teen does love you.

Beneath the surface of all these scenarios as well as the family stories in Part II, one important underlying theme is that teens in turmoil tend to be teens in control of their families. Of course, teens are hardly equipped to be in control of the family, not to mention your life and your emotions, but when teens somehow end up in that position, the family is headed for trouble. Taking back the control is generally easier than parents think. It takes a firm resolution and the courage to persevere.

Following is a story of one mother who suddenly discovered how easy it could be.

Could It Really Be This Easy?
Libby's Story

"Where have you been, Dr. Cameron?" Sean asked Libby as he helped her off with her coat. "We missed you. Hey, you look great! Were you on an extended cruise?"

Libby smiled at the compliment. Her face lit up. "No," she smiled, "I just had a lot to do, and I did it. Getting things right in your life is the best tonic there is. How are you?"

"Oh, you know me, I'm always fine. What are we going to do today? Cut it short or just a trim?"

Libby looked at herself while Sean put a towel and plastic cover around her and combed her hair from side to side to check the color and see how she would look in a shorter style. She scrutinized herself with the special distant objectivity specific to the moment when you first sit down at the beauty shop and exaggerate all your flaws as you look down the length of the mirror. You see all the other faces staring at themselves, too, and you compare. But his time Libby didn't concentrate on her nose that she had always thought was too long, nor on her complexion, which she usually worried was sallow; instead she saw her eyes bright and intense, her face glowing with vibrancy and meaning. She couldn't help smiling at herself, even though she felt embarrassed to look at herself and believe she looked great. "I think I'd like to try one of those new short cuts," she decided.

"What has happened to you?" Sean inquired as he began to cut her hair. "You look ten years younger—not that you ever looked old," he quickly corrected himself.

Libby laughed, remembering all too well how she had looked a few months ago. "I feel younger."

"What did you do? I always love to hear everyone's beauty secrets. Did you go to one of those pricey spas in Arizona or something?"

Libby laughed. "Not hardly. You know what I did? It's so simple, but I never thought I could do it—or would have to do it—until I did. I stood up to my teenage daughter. That's really all I did."

"What?" Sean looked confused as he continued cutting. "I don't understand."

"Do you have kids, Sean? No, you're too young."

"We're just starting to think about it, you know."

"Well, listen, here's a piece of advice from someone who just had to learn the very hard way. Don't let your kids take control of the family when they're only tots. You know, I didn't have the faintest idea what I was doing when Brooke was little. I thought I was being so clever, you know, because I figured if I didn't teach her to argue, then she wouldn't argue; if I didn't say 'no' to her, she wouldn't learn to say 'no' to me. Boy, was I wrong! You know what? She had me so manipulated! I spent my life trying not to get her angry, making sure no one in the family argued. My project was for her to be happy, every minute of every day. One day I realized what I had created."

Sean looked more interested in her conversation than her hair, and Libby worried for a moment that her haircut might suffer, but she knew she could trust Sean, and she wanted to recount her triumph.

"Am I talking too much? I don't want to bore you."

"No, tell me. Usually people tell me about how much trouble they're having with their kids. This is good. Who knows? Maybe I can pass on a few tips."

"Okay. You want the whole story or just the big points?"

"I want all the details."

"Okay. Here goes. One night, maybe about four months ago, I was trying to talk to Brooke about her grades. She's thirteen. She's always done well in school, especially in math, but suddenly it seemed to me she was never doing any homework. If I asked, she told me she didn't have any or that she had finished it in school. I wanted to believe her, so I did. I had all the excuses ready whenever I began to wonder. It made life easier for me, but I don't think I let myself realize that then. Anyway, then when it came time for report cards to be coming out, I never saw one. I kept on making excuses in my head, until finally I began to get really nervous. I finally asked her if she had gotten her report card yet.

"She looked so pretty and sweet, sitting there on her bed with all her stuffed animals around, and, well, I don't exactly like the way she dresses, but she was just out of the shower and wearing her nightgown, and she looked just like my Brooke, like the daughter I knew.

"She gave me such an innocent look—you know, all wide-eyed and astonished. She said I must have gotten it in the mail. The school had changed the policy and they sent it in the mail now, or maybe they hadn't sent it yet because midterm had only just passed. But she said she was fine, and I shouldn't worry, and did I like her hair now that it was longer, and what did I think about maybe going skiing at winter break? And then somehow we were on the way to the kitchen to get hot chocolate. I remember, she was holding my hand, leading me down the hall to the kitchen, when all of a sudden it hit me—it was like someone knocked the wind out of me. There she was, diverting my attention, so we wouldn't have to have a fight, so we wouldn't have to deal, just like I had always done with her. I had taught her that avoiding issues is a perfectly viable alternative. I was horrified and furious at myself and at her and . . ."

"I never thought of it that way," Sean said. "You know, that's exactly what my sister does with her little son. Whenever he starts to cry or to fuss, she does something to make him think about something else. Wow, I never realized . . ."

"I had never realized it either. I had had this sort of idea that fighting isn't necessary, you know, that it can and should be avoided, that it never brings anything. I realized in that moment what I had taught my daughter. Not because I ever *said* it, you know, but because I lived it, and I taught her to live it. I never had had the courage to stand up to her and say, 'That isn't okay.' It was one of those great 'AHA!' moments in my life. I felt guilty and angry. I really felt I had not served her very well as a mother. I was really afraid of fighting with her; I was afraid she would get angry at me. I was afraid she might not be happy! I was afraid to take a stand with my own daughter— my thirteen-year-old daughter. I was simply not doing my duty to her as her mother.

"I pulled my hand from hers and stopped, right there in the middle of the hall—in my old pink slippers and flannel bathrobe, I just stopped there.

Brooke didn't know what had happened because I became completely quiet. She asked me if I was okay, and I told her 'No,' that we had to go to the living room to talk, and that we weren't going to schmooze over hot chocolate.

"She was completely taken aback, and started to get petulant." Sean nodded and gently pushed Libby's head to one side to get a better angle for cutting the sides.

"Okay?" Libby asked. He nodded, and she continued, "So, anyway, I said to her that I realized I was partially to blame for what was happening, but that couldn't really be the issue. I just said that we had to be ready and able to discuss issues with each other even if they were going to be unpleasant—even if we had to disagree or argue. All of sudden I was, well, it sounds really cheesy, I know, but all of a sudden I was overwhelmed with a sense of courage. I could feel energy passing through me. I felt so powerful. I know it sounds corny, but it's true. You know, I haven't told anyone this whole story like this before.

"So, anyway, well, maybe it's almost anticlimactic, but I simply told her that I wanted to see her report card. And as she tried to divert my attention over and over again, I just stuck to my point. I think the most frightening moment for me was when she began crying and telling me I just didn't understand. Then she looked up at me through her tears and said with such accusation in her tone, 'You don't even trust me!' I could feel myself almost instinctively getting ready to deny that, to tell her of course I trusted her *except*—but then I thought, *No, that's just getting diverted again. That's just avoiding the issue.* And she was right, I didn't trust her. I realized that if I fell into that trap even once, before I knew it I would be apologizing to her, and there we would be, drinking hot chocolate and schmoozing, and I still wouldn't know what happened to her report card. And I would have failed her. I just couldn't do that to either of us any more.

"I looked her straight in the eye, and I said, 'No, Brooke. Frankly, right now I don't trust you very much. We have been sitting here for about twenty minutes, and that's after the ten minutes in your room before we started on our hot-chocolate mission, and I have asked you one and only one question, 'Why haven't I seen your report card?', and I still don't have an answer. 'So, you tell me, why should I trust you?'

"I wanted to go on, but I stopped to let her answer. Her answer was to cry and tell me that I must hate her. I had to take a deep breath to keep myself from collapsing, but I did it. I resolved to keep the focus. 'I have spent the last half hour—not to speak of the last four months—trying to find out what is going on with you and school, and the fact is, I don't have a clue. You know, when you are evasive, it doesn't build trust. Where is your report card?' It took another twenty minutes of talking back and forth before she finally told me she had thrown it away because she was embarrassed."

"So what happened then?" Sean asked.

"A lot. I told her I was far more upset that she had lied to me than I ever could be about grades. She told me I didn't understand, and I told her she had a responsibility to make me understand. You know, the usual. We had some rip-roaring fights during the first few weeks, but as I changed and became a mother who raised her expectations for her daughter instead of lowering them, my own self-respect soared. I had to stop accepting her lies, and I did. As all that happened, I found I had more and more courage to fight the battles, and all of a sudden, we weren't fighting as much. Since Brooke knew much more precisely what was expected of her, she found it easier to be honest and open about her life than to divert my attention from all sorts of things she had been doing or thinking of doing. You know, standing up for myself was the key. All of a sudden I realized I had been using up all my precious energy trying not to get her angry, making sure everything in her life was as picture-perfect as a teen's life could be, but still feeling there were things I had to say to her, problems I felt I saw, and things I had to do as her mother. My own conflict was sapping my energy. Which is why I looked the way I did. You know, she hadn't shown me her report card because she wasn't very proud of it. I helped her to face herself and her own laziness and disappointment in herself.

"You know, I had looked in the mirror one day just a little while before my great 'AHA!' moment and thought how old I was looking. I thought, well, it happens to everyone, and I felt sort of resigned until I remembered that I am only thirty-nine. I don't think there is anything that takes more out of you than trying to pretend to yourself that things are all right when you know they aren't. And when you use all your energy on that, plus you have a career, and you try to do other things, too, well, you know, Sean, the result is that you look terrible!

"That's my miracle cure," she finished with a laugh.

There really aren't any miracle cures for dealing with teens in turmoil, but the decision to become the agent of change in your family comes close to being one. It can bring you the peace in your home and joy in your family that you seek. You can become that agent of change because you now have a deeper understanding of what is going on in your teen's world, in her life, and how it affects you and the rest of your family. You see now how you play into, and sometimes even help to create, the turmoil. You understand how you have justified what you have done. This is not a time to feel guilty about what has happened up to now, but rather a time to feel excitement and energy because you know you are ready for change—and you can make it happen.

Finding solutions to problems is always based upon a thorough knowledge of the problems—and you have that now. Some of you will find solutions in your own home, through your own efforts, and without professional help. However, many parents feel they need the help of a professional to support and focus their decision to become and remain the agent of change in their family. Whether you are already consulting with a professional or just beginning to consider it, the next chapter will help you to evaluate the help you are seeking or already receiving, as well as to reconsider some generally accepted ideas about how to help your teen.

Chapter 10 ✿

Getting Help in Order to Change

The goal of this book is to help you to understand your situation so well that you become able to find your own solutions to the problems which beset your family. Self-help, however, does not mean that you never seek outside help and support. There is a saying in self-help therapeutic communities which goes: "You have to do it by yourself, but you cannot do it alone," and it is never more true than when families are working toward change. You may be wondering how much you can do on your own and how much you need help.

What you can do is a lot. What you cannot do is everything. What you can do is change yourself; what you cannot do is change someone else (at least not directly). What you can do is decide you will not lose hope, that you will not give up on yourself or your teen. What you cannot do is guarantee that everyone will live happily ever after. What you can do—and probably already have done by now—is allow yourself the luxury of knowing what you know.

Look through the following list. We hope you will feel a sense of personal and parental empowerment as you recognize how much you have accomplished emotionally, psychologically, and practically. Please do not worry or feel guilty about any of the items you know you have not yet internalized. Each individual has his or her process and rhythm, and there is no competition here. Change is a process. You can change only as fast as you can change, although you realize you have no time to waste.

WHAT YOU CAN DO (OR HAVE ALREADY DONE)
- Begin the process of change.
- Realize and accept that to change, you will have to change.

- Break through your denial.
- Give up your feelings of resignation.
- Stop being frightened of your teen.
- Stop being manipulated and lied to.
- Give up your wish for a quick and easy solution to the problems.
- Accept that your teen did not grow up in a vacuum.
- Take distance to maintain the objectivity of your clarified and focused family portrait.
- Stop rationalizing, excusing, and justifying your teen's behavior—and yours in response.
- Reclaim your emotional authenticity.
- Know that you will carry this process through to the end.
- Get rid of your own guilt.
- Rediscover the other relationships in your life.
- Let your child grow up in an age-appropriate fashion.
- Act instead of react.
- Become the catalyst of change in your family.
- Set standards of integrity and human dignity in your home and vow to keep them no matter what.
- Rediscover yourself as an individual.
- Reclaim your life, rediscover your passion.

You now have a clearer understanding of yourself and your family. You may not like what you see, but the only way to create change is to know what has to be changed. The next step is the how. You may decide you need outside help and support to effect the changes you know you and your family need.

Often when parents turn to outside sources for help, they are unsure what to expect. Understanding what therapy can and cannot do, understanding the meaning of the psychological diagnosis your teen possibly has or will receive, and questioning the use and meaning of medication will allow you to assess the help you need as well as the help you may already be receiving.

Before examining those topics, we would like to offer one more general caution: Beware of the power statistics can have on your outlook about your teen, particularly in relation to his or her life in your community.

As a society, we are inundated with statistics, and because "numbers don't lie," it is easy to find comfort in some statistics while becoming overly worried by others. No matter what statistics you read, if they relate to something about teens, you may find you experience an emotional reaction to them. But as the parent of your child, the most important point for you to remember is that statistics always refer to groups. We fully understand a parent's wish to take comfort from statistics that imply your community does not have a drug problem, but that fact (if it is one) is unimportant to you if your teen does do drugs. The other side of that coin, of course, is when parents become concerned because the statistics report an increase in teenage sexual activity in their community while there is no reason to be concerned about their teen.

Statistics about what teens in general are or are not doing really don't do much more than provide a picture resembling what you see when you look through the wrong end of binoculars. Neither group behavior nor any "norm" is your concern right now. Yours is not a social question, it is a personal one about your teen and your family. *Statistics cannot tell you anything about your teen and your situation.*

Setting Realistic Goals

On a good day, living with a teen in turmoil is a challenge. On a bad day, it's hell. Parents may find themselves wishing for that magic cure, that someone or something that will somehow, suddenly, return life to the way it used to be. Unfortunately, that isn't going to happen. This is a process requiring action, but considered, well-paced, and appropriate action. Whatever actions you try, having realistic goals is an important step toward realizing the change you seek.

Review your journal. Pay particular attention to margin notes you may have made as you read because they may well suggest the short-term and longer term goals for yourself and your family that will be catalysts for your actions now. Here are a few questions to focus your thinking:

- What changes would you like to see in your family and in your teen in six months? In a year?
- What sort of relationship do you hope to have with your son or daughter?
- What do you think *your teen* wants to achieve in school? In life?
- How do you hope he will feel about himself in six months? When he is an adult?
- How do you want to feel about yourself and your family situation in three months? In a year? In two years? Five years?

Now, without allowing yourself to romanticize, imagine and write down the description of a scene a few months in the future; then imagine a scene one, two, and five years in the future the way you would like it to be. Those pictures will help you to discover your goals and your ways to achieve them.

It has been said already, but it bears repeating because it is so important: Throughout this process support is crucial to you and to achieving your goals. Some of it will come from family members, a spouse, friends, someone in the clergy, or another parent who has had a similar experience, and some of it may well come from a professional. The support and help you get from a professional is different from that of a personal friend, and it is important to be able to judge wisely what kind of professional support and help you need and are getting.

In times of crisis, many parents find it difficult to find and maintain direction as they encounter the maze of psychological language, diagnosis, therapy, and medication which may become (or have become) a part of their everyday lives. The rest of this chapter is designed to help you negotiate that maze. Because I often encounter parents and teens who have become overwhelmed by the mountains of information, therapies, strategies, tactics, diagnoses, and medications, I have written this section specifically to help you focus your needs and your teen's needs in relation to the professional help available to you.

Everyday English Is Good Enough

A first step is to look at the words you use and hear when discussing your teen and the turmoil in your family. The language we use to describe our thoughts and feelings often defines our ways of understanding, explaining, and living our lives. Classifying your child's outrageous behavior and irrational attitudes under the rubric of "mental health" (but really, the lack of it—"unhealth") automatically categorizes feelings as mental processes. That approach confuses feeling with thought and may create a situation where a struggling teen is suddenly categorized as being "unhealthy." (Did you ever hear of someone expressing sorrow as a "broken brain"? How often have you thought to yourself that your heart is broken?)

The professionals most people turn to for help with their troubled teens are usually in the medical (psychiatric) or psychological/psychotherapeutic professions. These professionals use medical or semimedical terms and concepts to describe your teen's behavior and attitudes. The language used by professionals in psychology was conceived as a sort of professional-to-professional code to enable clinicians to communicate about their clients in a meaningful way. That language, however, has become increasingly common in the media and among laypeople and parents and has resulted in many oversimplified labels and concepts.

If you use mental health terms to define the situation in your family, you will likely discover one of two things. Either your situation isn't as threatening or ambiguous as you had thought because it has a name and others suffer from it too, or it is more threatening because the name implies some inborn malady or abnormality for which neither you nor your adolescent can be held responsible. A description of your situation in everyday English is clearer and more useful to you. The result may be that you and your teen recognize that the solutions to problems are mainly within your grasp. Either way, at a feeling level you will experience your situation differently.

Here is an example of what I mean. "He's been diagnosed borderline personality disorder" sounds so very different from "He's so impulsive—he drives too fast, especially considering he's only had his car for three months, and I worry he might be using drugs. One day he is close friends with his buddies, the next, he never wants to speak to them again. He breaks up with his girlfriend thirteen times a week, but when they are together, they are like Romeo and Juliet. When I tried to remind him he was supposed to mow the lawn, he got furious and yelled and cursed at me. And then there are the clothes he wears—and that new haircut—he looks so menacing . . ." "He's been diagnosed as borderline" has an ominous ring; the mother's description in everyday English makes clear what kind of changes this teen and mother need to make.

Everyday English not only provides words descriptive enough to explain the complexities and simplicities of life with a teen in turmoil, but it also helps to explain both your teen's and your experience of it. Using everyday language often clarifies what otherwise seem to be impenetrable problems, suggesting lifelong maladies or conditions requiring medication instead of the acceptance of personal responsibility.

Therapy

Finding a therapist is tricky. It is always useful for you to interview the therapist and to inquire about how she works with teens, whether she has experience working with a teen like yours, and what sort of time frame she usually uses for therapy. You will want to inquire if she generally favors using medication or does not. If you know someone who has seen a therapist and felt satisfied with the relationship and process, it is always worthwhile to ask for the reference.

Once your teen has begun in therapy, of course you will want to know if the therapy is being helpful. Confidentiality laws differ from state to state and even from issue to issue (abortion, HIV, and drug use, for example), so therapists probably cannot share some information with you. Many therapists believe that they would jeopardize the therapeutic relationship with your teen were they to share with you what goes on in the sessions. Some teens will not speak openly with a therapist if they think all the information will just go right home to Mom and Dad. If you trust the therapist (and if you do not, you should look for another), you must trust her to do her work, even if that means you know little about it. Remember, this therapy is your teen's. You do not need to know the details of what he is dealing with— after all, that is why you hired a therapist. If, however, you feel you are mainly being maligned in the therapy and being turned into the culprit or the bad guy (and that does happen), it is time to change therapists. If you feel your teen is just using therapy as a way to placate you or feed you information through the therapist, again, it is time to change therapists.

However, it is also important, even if difficult, for parents to question themselves about their interest in the substance of the therapy sessions. Sometimes parents try to maintain their overinvolvement with their teen's problems by wishing to be a sort of cotherapist or just remaining caught in the web of the teen's turmoil. If you feel uncomfortable about the therapy, schedule a joint appointment for you and your teen to discuss your feelings.

It is a therapist's responsibility to contact you if she has reason to believe your teen might harm himself or others or be ready to engage in violent, illegal behavior. If the therapist has reason to believe that your teen is planning to commit a violent crime (and that does not usually include smoking marijuana), it is her responsibility to contact law enforcement authorities.

There is no exact way to judge if therapy is being useful for your teen and for the family in general. Sometimes it takes a while (weeks or a few months, but don't wait half a year or more) for changed attitudes to begin to be internalized. Beware of suddenly compliant behavior from your teen because it may be a sham. The best rule of thumb is, once again, observe your teen; you know him best. If, mainly intuitively, you feel that lines of communication are being opened, that life is not just a series of conflicts, that you find yourself not being hesitant to ask your teen to take out the garbage or whatever has been a major bone of contention, then things are changing. If the tension in the house is going down, therapy would seem to be helping. If your teen's attitude toward himself seems more even, if grades begin to improve, if you see your teen seeming just calmer and happier, then therapy is probably helping.

However, like many parents I work with, you may already have your adolescent in therapy but haven't seen the kinds of results you hoped for. This may mean that the therapist is unwilling or unable to confront your teen. Sometimes, in an effort to establish a relationship with a teen or because of her own preconceived notions or theoretical bent, a therapist may choose to believe whatever stories the teen chooses to tell about the parent. Suddenly, not only do you find that things aren't getting better for your teen or for you, but that you have become "the bad guy." If that has been or becomes the case for you, find another therapist. Rethink whether therapy is a solution for your particular problems. You are, after all, the expert on your child. It is easy for parents to think the professionals know more than they do about their child. They don't. Trust your own instincts.

Good, effective therapy can be a place for teens to work out problems, either alone or with their parents. In most cases, the therapy usually need not continue for too long. However, if you find the therapy to be going on and on and on, it is valid for you to question its value. I do not think that long-term psychoanalysis tends to be useful for teens.

Don't forget that many people other than professional therapists can provide the same type of help for your teen. Clergy, teachers, adult friends, or a family member who is in recovery from substance abuse are just a few possibilities. Your community may be full of people who can, and would, gladly help, but you may have to network to find them. Sometimes teens find their own "adult lay therapists" such as a boss or the mother of the family where your daughter babysits. In my community there is a shopkeeper who functions as such for many teens.

In addition to individual and family therapy, some therapists offer group therapy sessions for teens. These can be less expensive (and if you are paying yourself, that may matter a lot) and just as helpful as individual or family sessions. Many parents, too, find that groups specifically designed for couples, men, women, or parents of adolescents are helpful. The group format allows parents to see other parents struggling with similar issues, and they can offer support to one another. Giving and receiving support to and from other parents can help bolster your courage and give you a renewed faith in yourself as a parent and as an individual.

I believe therapy is mainly a discovery, recognition, and realization process with change as the goal. Therefore, one of my most important functions as a therapist is to act as a mirror for my clients, to help them see what is really going on in their lives. When therapy is working for your teen and/or for you, life just seems to be better. You begin to feel you can find ways out of the turmoil and solutions to your problems.

Diagnosis

Nearly fifty years ago the professional psychological and psychiatric community decided to create a system to try to standardize a profession that had relied upon anecdote, intuition, and experience to "diagnose," and therefore treat, patient's symptoms. There have been several revisions of the original document, and the most current result is the *Diagnostic and Statistical Manual IV.* The stated purpose of the *DSM-IV* is "to provide clear descriptions of diagnostic categories in order to enable clinicians and investigators to diagnose, communicate about, study, and treat people with various mental disorders" (*DSM-IV*, p. xxvii).

Psychological diagnoses are different from medical diagnoses. Psychological diagnoses are descriptions of symptoms that have been grouped together because of the statistical frequency with which they occur in individuals. Each group of symptoms has been given a name that is then known as a certain type of disorder. (That "D" at the end of a diagnosis stands for "disorder," as in attention deficit disorder or borderline personality disorder.)

If or when your child enters therapy or counseling, one of the first actions many professionals will take is to order a series of psychological tests. Using these, in addition to information gathered by meeting with your child, they will categorize your child's symptoms into a "diagnosis" specifying one or more "disorders" as defined by the *DSM-IV.* One of the reasons your son or daughter is likely to be labeled with a "diagnosis" is that insurance companies (and HMOs and PPOs) require a diagnosis to authorize treatment. Many therapists comply in name only, assigning the least odious diagnosis. With a tidy diagnosis such as conduct disorder (and which adolescent wouldn't fit into that one at some time or other?), two things are accomplished: Psychotherapy will be covered by the insurance company according to their policies, and there is no stain of a terrible-sounding diagnosis on the teen's medical record. Other professionals, however, believe that the diagnosis is crucial in order to be able to treat the client, and will therefore assign the diagnosis or diagnoses believed to be most descriptive of the individual's condition. It is for you to decide which way makes better sense for your teen.

Your teen may have a variety of "disorders" assigned to her. Some therapists (often those who are working in an HMO) then follow a course of treatment from a manual which has been developed to fit the diagnosis, while other therapists will proceed with treatment according to their own (usually eclectic) methods and strategies.

Sometimes the therapist will recommend that your child be tested further. If she suggests neuropsychological testing, you may begin to wonder just how serious the problems are. If the therapist suggests an appointment with a psychiatrist or psychopharmacologist, or even with your own family physician in order to obtain a prescription for some type of medication, you may find yourself feeling either relieved ("There is a solution!"), or more concerned than ever ("Oh, my God, there must be something really wrong with her!").

When all the information is read and interpreted, your teen will be "diagnosed" with a "disorder." That means that he or she exhibits a certain number of the symptoms (different numbers for different disorders) to a maladaptive degree and for an extended period of time. This means, for example, if your child has been "diagnosed" with ADD, he or she exhibits six of the nine criteria for "inattention . . . to a degree that is maladaptive and inconsistent with developmental level" (*DSM-IV*, p. 83). In other words, when you take your child to a psychologist, what he or she is doing is giving a clinical name to what you have already observed and what you live with on a day-to-day basis.

The current trend is to conceptualize the behavior and attitude of your teen more in terms of biochemical causes rather than historical, cultural, and/or personal influences. Generally, when a professional says a teen "has a disorder," the implication is that the problem is part of his or her biological inheritance. This implies that the brain and its biochemical structure and functioning are what need treatment. The result of that interpretation of the information is not necessarily bad or wrong, but it does have the disadvantage that it does not seek to teach personal responsibility for actions and attitudes. "Having a disorder" is also sometimes misinterpreted to sound like a physical disease, which can get worse if not treated, or better, even cured, if treated.

You may first encounter semimedical psychological diagnostic terminology from a friend or colleague when you confide your son is having problems in school. "Oh, I know what you mean. My son was just like that. We took him to a therapist. She tested and found out he has ADD. She gave him Ritalin."

Suddenly you are catapulted into a different realm. Your heart beats faster with anxiety, but there is some comfort in the succinct definition. Your child "has" a "disorder." In your mind you may hear "disease" or "abnormal." The whole picture of life in your home suddenly got summarized into a diagnosis and a treatment. "Is it that serious? Can it be that simple?" you ask yourself at once. "Can he be cured? Is there a support group?"

Instead of defining your teen's life by means of a diagnosis, I urge families to describe things as they see them. As I discussed in the "Everyday English Section," see how powerful changing your language can be: What if your friend said, "My son doesn't pay attention to anything he doesn't want to pay attention to." That sounds and *feels* very different from "My son has ADD." (Just to clarify: ADD isn't something that can "show up" later in life. Experts agree that ADD, when it is really a serious problem, is evident by the time a child is seven. If your child did not manifest real and specific problems keeping his or her attention on tasks at hand before that age, it is unlikely he or she "is ADD" or "gets ADD" at fourteen. ADD isn't something kids "catch" like chicken pox.)

"My son doesn't pay attention . . ." denotes a behavior and an attitude that can be changed. It is not hopeless, and it doesn't necessarily go on for the rest of his life. It doesn't need all sorts of special handling and medication. It cannot be used as an excuse. "Having ADD" has an ominous ring and sounds like a disease. For the child who is not paying attention, psychotherapy and some real changing at home may help to solve the problem, although first everyone may have to be brought to accept that it is more an attitude and behavior problem than a biological problem.

For the teen who is excused from responsibilities because he "has ADD," medication, the victim role, and continued excusing for the rest of his life may be the best solutions that can be offered. Think about the effect of that on your teen's future. What do you think will be the result when he is twenty-five and tells his potential boss in a job interview that because he "has ADD," he probably won't be able to concentrate very well in meetings?

As explained above, using everyday English can be a liberating experience. Try the following exercise: Write down all the aspects and instances of your child's behavior and attitudes that worry you, upset you, frighten you, anger you, make you cry and feel hopeless, then give those actions and ways of being in the world a name. Here are some I have used when working with teens:

- ABD (acute boredom disorder)
- DPD (disordered priorities disorder)
- LD1 (laziness disorder)
- LD2 (lying disorder)
- PMD (pathetic me disorder)
- EEPD (everybody else's problem disorder)
- NOCD (needer of chaos disorder)
- OD (obnoxious disorder)
- THTCOTWD (thinks he's the center of the world disorder)
- PD (princess disorder)

Some of these may seem very familiar. Some may even make you smile. But after reading this list and making your own, suddenly you will find yourself feeling that you are back in manageable territory where you can act and begin to find solutions to the problems in your family. It isn't that the problems have been minimized but rather that they have returned to everyday reality where we all have more chance of change than we do in a "disordered" world.

Remember, just because your child is horrible to live with does not mean he or she is sick or disordered. It is likely that, among other things, he or she is reacting to the environment in which adolescents live today. That does not mean you don't have to step in, but there are more and less effective ways. Keep in mind that psychological diagnoses are mainly a professional-to-professional language that has crept into the everyday vernacular. You do not want to crush the spirit that enlivens your child, nor do you want anyone or anything else to do so. "Having disorders" or "being disordered" suffocates the spirit and does not necessarily have a positive effect on behavior or attitudes.

Psychopharmacological Medications (Meds)

The decision to allow your son or daughter to be medicated is a difficult and important one and should not be taken without consulting at least one or more physicians, psychiatrists, psychopharmacologists, and/or therapists whose opinions you trust. Neither diagnoses nor medications come without the possibility of emotional and psychological consequences and physical and emotional side effects. Although media hype sometimes leads us to believe in "miracle" cures, it makes good sense to scrutinize such claims carefully.

The medications that can be prescribed following a psychological diagnosis are not substances which can cure an illness, but which can, at best, ameliorate or minimize symptoms. They do not and cannot cure the way antibiotics cure an infection nor even act as does radiation or chemotherapy, putting a disease into remission. Nevertheless, these medications are powerful substances and do have effects and side effects.

What causes any particular individual (to decide) to self-destruct, to feel depressed, to exhibit maladaptive behaviors and attitudes (at least in relation to the adult world) remains unknown. Many people as well as many experts choose to conceptualize "psychological problems" or "mental disorders" as mainly spiritual questions and human paradoxes with historical, personal, and cultural roots. Others, and this is more common nowadays, believe that the underlying causes are "chemical" and therefore within the purview of medical science. (That may help to explain why between

500,000 to 1,000,000 prescriptions for antidepressants are written for children and adolescents each year.) It is important for you to decide which of the two views you believe to be more accurate. In a way similar to the requirement for diagnosis, many insurance companies and HMOs are more amenable to paying for medication than for longer-term "talk therapy."

With the exception of Ritalin, however, most of the medications prescribed for teens are only now undergoing the first clinical trials on adolescents and children, and results are not yet known. (There are, of course, serious ethical concerns involved with testing these medications on adolescents.) This means that knowledge of the usefulness, effectiveness, and the side effects (especially long term) for adolescents remains anecdotal and experiential. We do not know what effect any of these medications could have upon the still-developing brain and/or the whole body.

Because these medications are powerful substances, it is important for the prescribing physician or psychiatrist to be aware of other medications—and illicit drugs or alcohol—which your teen is taking—or using. Responsible doctors will ask that question, but let's get real: If you have had to send your teen for therapy or testing or diagnosis because things are not working well in the family, because your teen is failing in school, is depressed, secretive, dishonest, and may be abusing drugs or alcohol, do you really believe that same teen is going to be open and honest with the psychiatrist or your family doctor? Do you really believe your son or daughter will ask the physician if it is safe to take the medication when he or she is high on an hallucinogen or in combination with beer and vodka? I don't.

Keep in mind also that there is a very nice market for Ritalin at school and on the street. Kids do fake ADD to get the prescription to sell it. Don't be certain that because your teen has been prescribed a medication, he or she is necessarily taking it. Even if you see "improvement," you will be well advised to wonder if you are actually witnessing a placebo effect—or, in everyday English, a snow job from your teen.

If your child is prescribed some sort of medication, you or the physician may be faced with the difficulty of explaining (read: rationalizing) its efficacy to your son or daughter. You or the physician will have to explain why the street drugs your teen already knows makes her feel the way she likes to feel and experience what she wants to experience are "bad" and "evil," while this other sort of mood-altering chemical substance, prescribed by a physician, is okay. It is going to be tough to carry off such an explanation with any credibility to a teen for whom hypocrisy is akin to a federal crime.

Ask your teen which he or she prefers, Prozac or marijuana. I think you already know the answer. But do *you* have an answer as to why Prozac is okay and marijuana isn't?

You also need to consider that there are possible important and long-term psychological consequences to your teen taking medication—consequences for each of you. For your teen, the concept, if not the medication, may help to absolve him of responsibility for his acts. It can create in him a feeling of being a victim of a disorder who needs medication. It may make her feel like a freak who needs pills to be able to function. It may reinforce his feeling of dependence. From the parent's point of view, having your child on medication can make you feel less guilty because the problem is a "chemical imbalance" and therefore doesn't have anything to do with you as parent. Allowing your child to be medicated can also be a refined form of you rescuing your teen. It may also make you think of this child as somehow defective. It can be a way of maintaining a subtle control over your teen. Medication can also become a new and terrible family battleground. Not taking the medication is a powerful way for a teen to be defiant. Overdosing on it is another way, although a dangerous one, to get a lot of very negative attention. Most of all, it is important to consider all aspects of medication before you agree or disagree that your teen should receive it.

Taking the Hardest Step

With all you have learned, the pieces of your puzzle are probably beginning to fall into place. You don't have all the answers, nor even all the questions, but now you know you have the ability, the courage, and the perseverance to find them.

For some of you, what you have learned has shown that you can make the changes you and your family need yourselves. For others, you know your solutions will definitely involve some outside help, maybe in the form of short-term therapy, or, for some families, a residential program, whether short-term (three weeks) or longer-term (up to two years).

One of the hardest decisions any parent is ever forced to make is deciding that the situation with their teen has gone beyond their ability to deal with it at home. Fortunately, there are many quality residential programs that are specially designed to help those teens. As you ponder the question whether the best option for all of you would be for your teen to go away for a while, it is important for you to remember that the question never was deciding *if* your child was leaving home, because all children leave home eventually anyway but the how, why, and when. The sad part for parents of teens in turmoil is that their child may be leaving sooner and under more difficult circumstances than they would like.

How can you know if it is time to send your teen away? There is no measuring stick and no litmus test. Ask yourself whether, if you were Ryan's parents or Danny's parents, it would make sense to investigate using one of the many short- or longer-term programs for teens in turmoil. Look back at the third-person version of your family description and ask yourself if that teen and his family would be better off if he were sent to a wilderness program or an emotional growth school. Then look through Part IV for a better understanding of the range of programs available and what they do.

All the work you have done until now which has helped you to clarify your situation will be the material you use to decide if you need to send your teen away. If you have decided that you do need to do that, please make sure you believe that sending your child away is not an admission of failure or guilt, but rather an acceptance that it is a better way for your teen to finish her growing up process. Many parents Leslie or I have worked with have told us, "I had to send my son away in order to get him back."

Exactly how a parent can tell if it is time to send a teen away varies from family to family, but many parents tell us, "When it was time, I just knew." For most, that time came when their child's behavior had become so unbearable they couldn't live in the same house with her. For others it happened when the pain of watching him sink deeper into alcohol and drug use was overwhelming, or when the teen's grades dropped so quickly they could see his future slipping away. In some families it was when their child's behavior was so violent the family lived in fear of the teen and for the teen. For many parents, it was when they began to feel like prison guards in their own home and realized they still had no control over their teen. When parents realize they can no longer function in their jobs, or they see their marriage falling apart, riddled with arguments over the teen, they know the teen cannot remain in their home.

There are as many scenarios as there are families who have sent their teens away. In each case, the parents had reached a point where they said "Enough!" because they had to acknowledge that their child, on many levels, endangered both themselves and their families. For some parents the catalyst was the realization that they would not be able to live with themselves in the future if they could not say they had not done everything possible to try to force their child to change.

Many parents tell us they are afraid that if they send their teen away, they will sever the relationship they have with him or her. We tell them that what they have with their teen now may not be very worth having—and surely there is no future in it. By sending their child away, they may be creating the best chance to forge a new relationship with the person they used to know—with the sweet child they remember who has temporarily gone into hiding. And even if that does not happen, they can know that at the very least, their child will be safe for his or her remaining teen years. They will have done what they could.

Try not to let your anger, frustration, pain, hopelessness, despair, and grief control your decision. There will be time to let your child know how angry you are and how much pain he or she has caused, but now is not the time. To make a good decision about your teen, you will need the clear view of your family, grounded upon your own courage, moral authority, and human dignity that you now have.

If you do send your teen away, you will most likely enter something akin to a grief process. Most parents truly mourn for the life they had hoped for—both for the life they had imagined for their child and with their child, and for themselves as parents.

But the grief will pass more quickly than you expect because when you send your teen away, you know it is to create a second chance for him or her.

You Can Have Your Child Back

No parent dreams about his or her child becoming a troubled adolescent, but, because you love your child, you know you will do whatever you can—and whatever is necessary—to help your teen restore his or her future. It isn't your fault (nor anyone else's) that your situation is what it is, but it is your problem. It is tempting to want to solve the problem(s) for your teen, but you cannot. You know that now.

You will no doubt wonder, in moments when the going gets tough and you are tempted to revert to your old ways to placate your son or daughter, whether you really must break out of this cycle. When you find yourself wondering that, spend five minutes imagining how it will feel in five or ten or fifteen years if you do *not* implement the changes you know you need to make. Think about how you will feel if you are not able to look back to assure yourself you did everything in your power to help your child restore his or her future and reclaim your own life.

Remember: There is no absolute right way to conceptualize your teen's problems and the solutions to them any more than there is a wrong way. The only way that makes sense for you is the one that allows you and your teen to change the status quo. You know your child better than you think you do. Trust your instinct and your heart. Trust yourself. Trust your love for your child.

You can have your child back. You can have your family back. You can have your life back. It may not be quick or easy, but now you know in your heart you don't really have any choice but to work toward change.

Epilogue ✿

The Inner Shift

Some parents know the moment it happens. Others only realize it has happened long afterward. Suddenly people start telling you how good you look, how much younger, more vital, thinner, happier. You will find yourself being asked if you had your hair cut or if you are working out, and yes, you may have had your hair cut in a new style because suddenly it seemed okay to think about yourself instead of just worrying about your teen. Maybe you did start working out because you found you not only had the time and energy, but also the self-confidence to get back into shape. Friends may wonder if you just found the man or woman of your dreams, or suppose you suddenly rediscovered you are in love with your spouse—and they will be right because you are once again able to have an emotional relationship with someone other than your child. You kicked the crazies and the chaos and the turmoil out of your life. You changed who is in control in the family. Life just got better.

An inner shift is your goal. Not your goal for your son or daughter—he or she has to achieve that for him or herself. It is *your* goal—your goal for you. You will know it is happening or has happened when you feel a certain calm inside you haven't felt for months or years. You will know it is happening or has happened when it makes sense to walk over to your partner and give him or her a kiss. You will know when you have accepted that you cannot control your child's life. You will know it when you have agreed to let your son or daughter grow up and accept responsibility for his or her actions. You will know when you are okay with being the parent of an adult child. You will know when every day is no longer darkened by anxious dread. You will know when you are no longer terrified for and of your child. You will know when you see a star and make a wish, and the wish is about you, not about your child.

The inner shift is when you declare your own independence from being your child's emotional first-aid kit. It is when you no longer abdicate your parental responsibility to your child, to the therapist, to the medication, to the school, or to fate. In a positive and ordinary sort of way, you are back in control of your family. You are back in control of your life. No, it doesn't mean life is suddenly perfect and that problems won't happen; it means that you know you will deal with whatever comes your way.

You had begun to doubt everything about yourself, but you know you are capable of facing your fears and conquering them. When you have done it once, it gets easier and easier every time. You have entered into the parenthood that lasts for the rest of your life. You have become wiser and stronger. It isn't that you won't still worry about your child; *that* is ridiculous even to imagine because in a way, parents always worry about their children. Instead, no longer ready to panic at every ring of the phone or at every word your child says, believing you have to save and rescue and control, you worry from the love in your heart. You trust yourself, and so you know when to trust your child.

An inner shift is not a gift. You must work for it. You will not reach your inner shift just by reading this book. It will take you as long as it takes you, though there is no time to waste. When you have reached it, you will know that you have earned it, and you deserve it.

Suddenly life will feel better. Optimism will make sense. The future will be exciting. Laughter will come easily and your tears will be tears of joy.

PART IV

Resources and Programs

Making Decisions ✣

We recognize that some parents will turn to this section first, and, of course, that is fine. If you believe your child and your family will benefit most from using the information in this section, do not hesitate to read through it first and make the decisions you need to make. If you know your teen needs some type of professional help immediately, this section will provide you with the information you need to get started finding and evaluating the type of help or the program most suitable for your teen's and family's situation. We encourage you to take action quickly but thoughtfully, and we offer suggestions how to do so. However, we strongly believe that after you have placed your teen, it will be in your best interest and that of your teen and your whole family for you to take the time and effort to work through the process explained in this book.

For many parents this section provides information they do not need or do not need yet. Donna, thirteen-year-old Maria's mother, explained it this way: "I feel so confident now that I have this information. I don't think I will ever need it—at least I hope not. But if I do, I have everything I need to get the help I need for my daughter. It is like an insurance policy."

Take some time to look through these options to see which would be best for your teen and for your whole family. If you are in a crisis, you may not feel like you have extra time to make your decision, but try to ensure that your decision is not a hasty one.

Even though choosing an intervention option will no doubt be difficult, you know you are going to do what you must because deep down, you know you don't have a choice. Your teen's future, perhaps his or her life, may be seriously at risk. There is no choice but to work for change. Now, for the first time in a long time, you are going to out-strategize your teen be-

> **If at any time you believe your teen's life is in danger, act imme-
> diately. Do not hesitate to call 911, your physician or your therapist,
> or to take your child to your local emergency room if you suspect he
> or she is in immediate danger.**

cause that is what he needs from you. Armed with what you have learned from this book, you have the knowledge, strength, and courage to do it.

There is no one right way to select an intervention, and anyone who tries to give you that impression should be seriously questioned. There is no magic or correct formula to determine which intervention is the best one for a particular adolescent or even "type" of adolescent. There is no one program or professional that is right for all kids. Each adolescent and family *must* be looked at on an individual basis.

Be forewarned: When you insist upon significant change in your teen's life or plan an intervention—whether going to a therapist or placing him in an emotional growth school away from home—your teen may react by being unhappy to enraged. Remember that at a deep level your teen is terrified of facing the world without her defenses, and she will likely use whatever lies or manipulations she can to keep you from forcing her to change. Your teen is used to running the show, so it is not surprising that when you reclaim control of your family you will meet with resistance.

Don't give up, don't back down, and do seek support to help you stay the course. Later, like so many kids who have come through this process, your teen may well thank you for not giving up or giving in.

Whether you have made the decision to act, or you are still mulling it over, always base your actions on your clarified and focused picture of your teen, yourself, and your family. *Act, don't react, to your teen.*

Keep these guidelines in mind:

1. **Know who your adolescent is now.** Be sure you have a very clear understanding of your teen.
   - Be clear and honest about the lies, manipulations, and behavior you have been living with to protect yourself from being cajoled out of your decision to intervene.

2. **Realize that you must be in charge.** You are the parent and you must make the decisions concerning intervention.

- Your adolescent can be given *few*, if *any*, choices. You are making these decisions now because the choices your teen has been making have not been good ones. Now is not the time to think he will suddenly demonstrate good sense and agree with your plan.
- Be aware that if you give your teen choices regarding your intervention plan, whether the plan involves therapy or a residential placement (or in some cases even tell him about the intervention first), there is a risk he may run away before you are able to carry out your plan.
- The only kind of choice you can give your teen at this point could be, for example, that she may select one of three programs you have screened and approved.

3. **Know that you have a bottom line.** When you know what you are (and are not) willing to live with you can take a stand and hold firm to your plans for an intervention.

4. **Set goals for yourself and your teen.** If you don't know where you intend to go, you won't know when you get there.
   - Talk with another parent who has done what you are doing. If you don't know one, enlist the support of a family member or close friend who understands what is going on in your family.

5. **Know your options.** See the listing of schools and programs later in this section.

6. **Consider hiring a professional,** such as an educational consultant, as a guide through this process. This type of consultant often has a background in guidance counseling, admissions, teaching, school administration, social work, psychology, or related fields. He or she works specifically with families and teens to help find an appropriate school or program for the teen. She often specializes in one or many types of placements, including college, traditional boarding schools, vocational schools, or special-needs schools including those focusing on emotional growth, therapeutic, or residential treatment. Call the Independent Educational Consultants Association (IECA) at 703-591-4850 for a referral in your area (be sure to ask for those specializing in Special Needs Placements) or check the Yellow Pages for those listed in your area.

7. **Know that support is available. Seek it.** This road may be a bumpy one for you, and love and support will be vital.

8. **Know that you can slow down and make the right decision.** Although you may be in crisis, do not make a hasty decision about long-term plans regarding your teen. To make a rational, informed decision, consider slowing down the process by using a short-term intervention that will keep your teen safe while you have time to research and think.

   In the short term you could send your teen to:
   - A family member's home—preferably in another town
   - A wilderness program
   - A holding agency or "safe house"—which you can locate through your local social services department, through your therapist, by asking other parents, or through an escort agency trained in dealing with in-control teens (see page 211 for information on escort agencies). Many longer-term programs and some wilderness programs will "hold" a teen for several days before a program begins.
   - A hospital where your teen could be admitted for a psychiatric evaluation. (This quickly eats up insurance funds, but should always be considered if your teen is harming herself, is violent, suicidal, or threatening your safety.)

Making a Plan

Most teens who are in trouble think the only one in the family who has a problem and needs help is you. That is not news to you, but do keep it in mind as you formulate a plan for an intervention. When confronted with an intervention, your teen may:

- Suddenly seem to pull her life together. Many teens will do this long enough for you to back off, then life spins out of control again once the immediate threat of an intervention is past.
- Refuse to accept a plan or stay in a program.
- Go placidly to a program.
- Work with a plan for a while to placate you, then spin out of control when the pressure is off.
- Instigate (or try to get someone else to instigate) legal proceedings against you.
- Run away.

It is, therefore, always wise to formulate more than one intervention plan. Certain programs require that your teen be agreeable and willing to participate. If she refuses to do that, you must be ready with plan B, C, or D—a selection of more restrictive programs that do not require your teen's willingness to stay. It is not uncommon for parents to find the first intervention is not their last, either because their teen progresses through a series of plans or programs as he is getting back on track or because it may take a few tries to find the right place for their teen.

Getting Your Child to the Program

The more outrageous or dangerous your teen's behavior, the less you may want to tell him in advance about the intervention. If your child presents a run-away risk, it may be best to keep your plans secret from him. Here is where really knowing your child and his or her likely reactions is crucial.

If your teen is headed to a residential program, it is always best to take your teen to the program yourself. When a parent accompanies an adolescent to a program it sends the powerful message that the parent is back in control and serious about stopping the teen's unacceptable behavior. And although it will most likely be uncomfortable and distressing to both parents and teen, it sets the whole family on an openly acknowledged path to change.

If you don't think you can manage that emotionally, psychologically and/or physically, there are other options. Family members, family friends, or a special adult (such as a Scout leader or a teacher) with whom your teen has a good relationship may be willing to help. In extreme cases, there are professional services that specialize in transporting teens. These are called professional escorts, and they are often trained in nonviolent crisis intervention and/or a technique called Management of Assaultive Behavior (MAB). They will transport your teen from your home to a school, wilderness program, or other care facilities. You can find them through the IECA, and any program and most therapists you decide to use can recommend one. (Legislation now pending in California may significantly curb parents' ability to employ professional escort services for teens living in that state.)

Families who use escort services are coached by the intake worker and the escort service at the program for every step of the intervention from the first phone call to the pickup of the teen to the delivery of the teen to the program. Escorts stay with the teen from the moment of pickup to arrival at the program location. Female agents escort girls; male agents escort boys.

Contracts

Some therapists and most programs will require you to sign a contract. Be sure to read the contract carefully, and be sure you understand all clauses. Don't stop asking questions until you are satisfied with the answers:

- Is there a length of stay requirement?
- Are you responsible for costs if your child leaves the program? What if your teen is expelled?
- What liabilities does the program accept?
- Is there a clause that gives the program permission to use physical punishment on your child?
- Are you required to pay a deposit?
- Are you responsible for damages?
- Is there a pursue, detain, and hold clause?
- Is there anything you should know about confidentiality laws pertaining to your child's situation and/or treatment and/or aftercare?

Stand By Your Decision

If you are using an intervention beyond therapy, such as sending your teen to a residential program, be prepared to defend your decision. Even sending your teen to therapy sometimes brings a negative reaction from others. People who don't really know your family situation may accuse you of abdicating your role as a parent. Friends and even family members may tell you that you are being too strict, that you are not being understanding enough, or even that you don't love your teen. You know none of that is true. You know you are acting because you love your teen deeply. Hold firm to your decision to act.

Sorting Out the Issues

No matter what kind of placement or program you choose, there are certain issues you must be aware of.

1. Legal issues
- Every state's laws concerning the age of majority and the legal rights of a minor differ. Inform yourself before you proceed, either through an attorney or your own research.
- Ask that any contracts you will be expected to sign be sent to you for your review (and that of an attorney) **before** you deliver your child to the facility.
- Have someone else read any contracts or legal agreements you make. (If you are under pressure or in crisis, your judgment may not be at its best.)
- Adjudicated youth may not be accepted into every type of program. Check with the program before you assume they will take your teen.
- Most programs require that *both* parents admit their child, even if they are divorced.
- Laws relating to teens are often confusing and distributed throughout your state's legal code. If you and your teen are involved in any way with the legal system, seek professional legal advice.

2. Medical issues
- Policies on the use of psychoactive medications vary widely from program to program, from encouraging their use to not allowing them at all. Check before you send your child.
- In some programs, your teen will be considered a patient, therefore "sick"; in others he will be considered a student struggling with adolescent issues. Carefully consider the implications before you choose.
- Many programs will not accept teens who have been diagnosed as having thought disorders or who are psychotic.
- Some programs exclude teens who have epilepsy, Tourette's syndrome, and other specific medical/psychological disorders.

3. Academic issues
- Most long-term programs offer an academic program, but they vary in quality. Some are on-site, others are by correspondence.
- Placing your teen in any program is likely to affect college placement. Not placing him in a program may be worse. If college placement is of major importance to you or to your teen, look for programs where academics are stressed and college placement counseling is provided.

4. Policy issues

- Most programs have a dress code (or uniforms). Some allow teens to wear what they like.
- Programs vary in their tolerance for romantic and/or sexual relationships between students. Ask questions so you will know their policy.
- No school or program is immune to the influence of drugs, alcohol, and tobacco. Ask about security and substance abuse policies.

5. Financial issues   There are a variety of ways to fund treatment:

- **Apply insurance benefits** to the treatment plan or program. Coverage is of course contingent on the type of health care plan you have and the people reviewing your case. Call your benefits manager to find out exactly what your plan covers and how to maneuver through the system, then ask for a written statement from him or her detailing coverage. Be persistent; you may eventually win compensation that was refused you on the first, second, and even third try. *Sometimes insurance companies will cover the therapeutic portion of the program costs, lowering the rest of the cost to reasonable levels.*
- **Check with your local school district.** Federal law mandates that all public schools must provide the cost of educating the residents of the school district, regardless of handicap, up to the age of twenty-two or until graduation from high school. If you decide to explore this option be aware that:
    - Getting the district to cooperate can be a difficult, lengthy, and costly process.
    - Schools often deny they have any responsibility beyond academic. You may get them to pay the academic portion of the program's fees, especially if the program you choose is on a state-approved list.
    - Federal law sets basic standards, but procedures are different state by state, school district to school district. Seek advice from someone who understands the procedures in *your* state or school district, such as an attorney who specializes in disability laws or a professional advocate.
    - Even though the state is responsible for educating your child, it may be especially difficult to get your district to pay for out-of-area placement.
    - In some states students automatically qualify for aid equivalent to the cost of the education if they have been placed in a spe-

cial school or treatment center. Check to see if this is true in your state—don't assume it is.

- **Take out a loan.** Some programs and schools offer their own financing or work with a particular company. Other options include a second mortgage; using college funds (now may well be the time to use them); borrowing against a retirement plan; borrowing from relatives.
- **See if your costs are deductible.** You may be able to offset some or all of the cost of a program on your income tax return. Check with an accountant.
- **Government sources.** Call your local Social Security (SSI benefits), Medicare, or Medicaid offices to see if you or your teen might be eligible for these benefits.

Special Problems for Parents of Older Adolescents ✿

Parents of adolescents who are seventeen and a half years old and older are in a different and unique position. Although their children are not yet of legal majority, most programs will not admit a teen within six months of his or her becoming eighteen. Once a teen is eighteen, parents cannot place him or her in any program without the teen's consent. (The only exception to that rule is when parents have legally extended their custody over the adolescent. That means that parents have arranged through the courts to have the teen under their legal custody for an extended period to prevent him from making legally binding decisions. Extending custody in this way is difficult to do, and there are severe ramifications to doing so, among which are that it can remain a part of your teen's record all of his/her life. This option should only be considered as a last resort and with legal counsel. It can also take quite some time to accomplish, so if this is the option you choose, make sure you begin long before the teen turns eighteen.)

The only control you have over an adolescent once he has reached the age of seventeen and a half is financial or based on your moral authority and the love she has for you—even if she isn't exactly showing it. You can:

1. **Offer the opportunity to attend a program voluntarily.** This can work if your teen:
   - recognizes he has problems and he wants help;
   - has been threatened with expulsion from high school or college unless she agrees to attend a program or rehab;

- is mandated by the court system to attend a program or rehab until it is successfully completed.

2. **Offer to continue financial support only if he agrees to attend one of the treatment options.** This will work only if you make it clear to your teen that being on his own means you will supply no car, no computer, no money, no ATM or credit card.

To carry through on either of these options requires that you be completely committed to your plan—and very tough. If you decide to push for your teen entering a program, you must convince her she will not be allowed to live at home anymore if she refuses to *participate* in treatment (simple compliant attendance will not suffice).

Because your teen may call your bluff, you must think long and hard before you decide to take measures as extreme as these. You must think about what will happen if your teen will not go to a program and won't adhere to your conditions for staying home. Could you tell your teen he is no longer welcome at home (without treatment) and allow him to sleep on the streets, at the Salvation Army, or in a shelter for a few nights or weeks in the hope that he may realize you are serious? If you cannot, do not make the threat.

Considering that your only other option is far from good—allowing your teen, who is becoming a young adult, to live in your home without requiring him to change—you may discover a resolve you didn't know you had.

What You Need to Know About Schools and Programs ✿

Be aware of these issues as you choose a school or program for your teen:

• The goal of any intervention is to motivate your adolescent to change his or her attitude and behavior, grow up, and become a responsible, independent adult. You (in conjunction with the child's other parent or stepparents) must be the one to determine how and where that can best happen.

• Be aware that it isn't very hard for a therapist or a program to get your teen to comply and look good for a while; that is not the same as real, internal change. You must have patience to let the intervention you choose have time to work. At the same time, do not mistake patience for procrastination, obstinacy, or defiance. You, and *perhaps at a later stage, your adolescent,* must evaluate if the option(s) you have selected are creating the change needed in your adolescent and in your family situation. But also ask yourself if *you* are afraid of change or if the process is becoming too hard and gut-wrenching for *you* before you seek another program—or withdraw your teen from one.

• Many programs dealing with troubled adolescents rely mainly on confrontation as a therapeutic tool, and many parents react with horror at the idea that their teen will be confronted over and over about his or her attitude and behavior. Confrontation, when used therapeutically, is not demeaning, vicious, or cruel. It is a powerful and motivating tool for breaking through an adolescent's image, arrogance, and secret fears.

Choose a program or school based on:

- your goals
- a thorough understanding of how serious your situation is
- the treatment philosophy of a program
- their stated goals for completion
- their academic curriculum
- size
- length of stay required
- the qualifications of the treatment team
- your knowledge of your teen

- Evaluate and/or visit the programs or schools you are considering using the questions listed under Category 3. These questions are specific to residential programs, but you can adapt them to less intensive programs.

- And remember, if the first option you try doesn't work, there are many others to choose from. Keep trying until you find one that does.

How to Use the Schools and Programs Listing ✿

We have divided available programs into seven categories. The categories are not mutually exclusive, nor are they self-contained.

- **Category 1** is "not restrictive" and often allows the teen to remain at home.
- **Categories 2–6** are progressively more restrictive and are appropriate for the progressively more troubled to out-of-control adolescent.
- **Category 7** is specifically for seventeen-and-a-half to twenty-five-year-olds.

Within each category there is a range of programs from which to choose. Each type of program is presented with a short description followed by the purpose, type of adolescent for whom it is suited, length of stay, cost (for some programs, costs change from year to year), and a short list of pros and cons about the program. Deciding which are positive attributes and which are negative attributes of a program is highly subjective, so use these to get a feeling for the nature of the program. You must decide for yourself whether the attributes will help or hinder your teen's progress. In some cases you will see certain attributes listed as both positive and negative attributes. That means you must decide for yourself if that particular characteristic counts in the positive or negative column for you and your teen.

We have chosen to list types of programs rather than specific businesses that offer the programs or specific programs. We do not endorse any particular program. Once you find a type of program that suits you and your teen, you will need to research it further on your own. You can network with friends, therapists, school guidance counselors, or social workers, or call the Independent Educational Consultant Association (IECA) for a referral to an educational consultant who may be able to help (ask for one who specializes in Special Needs Placements).

Check the Internet. When using any search engine on the Internet, some key words (use quotes) to use are:

- "troubled adolescent"
- "troubled teens"
- "defiant teen"

To find wilderness programs, key words to use are:

- "wilderness therapy programs"
- "wilderness treatment programs"

Make sure you browse through the Web page matches, too, as there are many programs listed within these pages. Many programs will be listed but *we caution you to research thoroughly any program you find before sending your child.*

There are two directories which are published for professionals and parents that offer a great deal of information. They are *Woodbury Reports* and *Bridge to Understanding* and can be found in most libraries and on the Internet as well (www.woodbury.com and www.bridgetounderstanding.com). Most professionals, such as therapists, counselors, or educational consultants, may also have a copy of one or both in their offices. Another resource is *Peterson's Guide to Private Secondary Schools,* which can be bought at local bookstores, found in the research section of your library, or on their Web site (therapeutic schools are listed in the back of the book, but not all programs that are available are listed).

This chart provides an overview of the range of interventions available and a general overview of the types of kids for whom these interventions are suitable.

CATEGORY 1 Not Restrictive	CATEGORY 2 Slightly Restrictive	CATEGORY 3 Short-Term Restrictive	CATEGORY 4 Restrictive	CATEGORY 5 Very Restrictive	CATEGORY 6 Locked Facilities	CATEGORY 7 18-Plus-Year-Olds
Therapy Day Schools	Intensive Out-Patient Programs	Drug Rehabs Psychiatric Hospitals	Religions Outreach Programs	Emotional Growth Programs	Residential Treatment Programs	Residential Young Adult Programs
Alternative Day Schools	Day Treatment Programs	Wilderness Programs	Ranch "Family Style" Programs			
Boarding Schools	Group Homes					
Summer Wilderness Programs						
For:	*For:*	*For:*	*For:*	*For:*	*For:*	*For:*
• Kids for whom life is not working out very well.	• Kids who are moderately defiant and oppositional.	• Kids who are definitely in trouble who need a quick and decisive intervention.	• Kids who have had some problems in the past but who have made a firm commitment to change.	• Kids who are definitely in trouble and need a longer-term residential situation.	• Kids under 18 who present significant danger to self or others, with a history of run-away behavior.	• Kids who are over 18 and need a structured environment to finish high school and/or learn a vocation to become independent.
• Kids for whom peer, academic, or family problems exist.	• Kids who are possibly in need of substance abuse counseling, aftercare from hospital, or rehab.	• Kids with substance abuse problems.		• Kids with substance abuse problems.	• Kids with substance abuse problems.	

CATEGORY 1

In this category you can combine several options to give your child the opportunity to "start again." For example, transferring to a new school and bolstering that with individual and/or family therapy may be all that is needed to get him or her back on track.

Therapy

Local psychotherapy—individual, family, group, or any combination, whether short-term or longer-term—is often the first intervention to which parents turn when their child is experiencing difficulty at home, school, or with peers. Many therapists specialize in a specific treatment model such as cognitive, behavioral, rational emotive, reality, or person-centered, but most use a mixed (eclectic) approach. Many therapists work with specific populations such as people needing substance abuse counseling, adolescents, families, couples, etc. Even if you first decide to send your teen for individual therapy, the therapist may recommend that you and your child begin family therapy. Typically a different therapist would provide the counseling for the family. Some therapists provide group therapy for teens. It is generally less expensive than some other interventions, but can surely be as powerful as individual therapy.

PURPOSE

To help an adolescent and/or family address, understand, and work on issues that are having a negative impact on their lives. To improve communication and deal with anger.

TYPE OF ADOLESCENT

Teens (or preteens) who have begun acting out, are moderately defiant, experiencing low self-esteem, family conflict and/or poor peer relationships, have behavior and/or academic problems at school, or appear depressed or demoralized.

LENGTH OF TREATMENT

Varies according to insurance coverage and may be terminated before you feel it has been successful or even that any real progress has been made. Treatment should be entered upon with a realistic time frame in mind. If you self-pay (out of pocket) you can determine the length of treatment. If you use insurance, the treatment is usually time limited.

COST

Varies greatly in different parts of the country and according to professional credentials. Insurance reimbursement depends on policy and coverage. Coverage is usually for predetermined length of service with preselected professionals. Some policies have lifetime caps for mental health coverage. Health Management Organizations (HMOs) or Preferred Payment Option (PPOs) may require preapproval before your adolescent can see a therapist. Always check your policy or with your benefits manager before initiating service. Many times a diagnosis must be obtained before insurance companies will pay for services. If you decide to self-pay, you may be charged a different fee than you would be under insurance coverage. Ask for the hourly fee and discuss sliding scale fees (based on your ability to pay).

POSITIVES

- May help to avoid issues festering because not addressed
- Families can be involved
- Little negative connotation in community
- Can be a useful first intervention
- May provide a neutral place outside of the home to deal with issues
- May be enough to get child and family over stumbling blocks

NEGATIVES

- Can deplete mental health insurance benefits
- Can be a waste of time and money for an adolescent sent against his/her will
- Can be a waste of time and resources if the therapist is being manipulated by the teen
- Can waste time and energy if you need to try out a few therapists before finding one who works well with your teen
- Can be a waste of time for an "in your face" defiant teen

Day School Programs

In most communities there are a variety of day school programs from which a family can choose. These range from private day and parochial schools, to alternative school environments that are outside the traditional high school environment although still a part of the local public high school.

Private and parochial day schools follow the nine-month school calendar. They tend to have regular (and sometimes lengthy) holiday periods. Schools vary in their academic programs from very challenging to less challenging. They provide a smaller learning environment with more individualized attention. Most are coed. They pride themselves on creating the well-rounded adolescent but some have a special focus such as the arts, sports, religious affiliation, science and/or math, or cater specifically to students diagnosed with learning differences. Many are known for their ability to place students in top colleges and universities. Some offer specialized services for the student who requires extra help in academics or who has special learning needs.

PURPOSE

To complete academic requirements for a high school degree and to prepare for college.

TYPE OF ADOLESCENT

Bright or average student who is academically oriented or who would benefit from a smaller, structured environment with added support systems or specific types of teaching.

LENGTH OF STAY

Nine-month school year (typically September–June) for four years of high school.

COST

$6,000–$15,000 plus per school year. Financial aid is generally available at most schools, and tuition is not always inclusive of other fees.

POSITIVES

- Opportunity for adolescent to start over in a new environment
- Small academic and athletic environment with structure
- Individual attention in small classroom size
- Can be more academically challenging
- Can provide more of a sense of community than larger environments
- Many cater to different learning styles

NEGATIVES

- May not offer as many courses as a larger public high school
- May not offer as many extracurricular activities
- May have limited sports activities
- Can be expensive
- Does not provide therapy or therapeutic support

Alternative Day Programs

All public schools must comply with the Individuals with Disabilities Act (IDEA, PL. 101-476, formerly the Education for All Handicapped Children Act, PL. 94-142). This law was enacted to provide a free, appropriate public education to all children ages three through twenty-one with disabilities. Although you may not believe your child has a disability, the law specifies that children with discipline and behavioral problems are considered to have a disability, and your public school must provide an appropriate environment (regardless if it is in your district or not) to meet your child's needs.

If you want to know about alternatives, you'll have to ask. To find out more, contact a social worker or guidance counselor at your teen's school. However, if an adolescent is in need of a different environment, he or she usually has been having problems and is already known by the guidance counselor or social worker. Often they believe they are all the help your teen needs, which may not be the case. That may be why they haven't already suggested alternatives to you.

Public alternative day programs are established by many public high schools within the larger school as a way to comply with IDEA. Parents are usually not aware their local public school offers such an alternative, and schools rarely advertise that they do. Some schools also offer special programs in the evening so students can work during the day and attend classes (usually modified) at night. Each high school's program differs in its requirements, and you should be careful when researching this option and before deciding if this is appropriate for your teen. Ask your local school about the alternatives in your district about the standards and expectations for the students. The academic expectations are often much lower than you might want for your child. Before accepting this type of alternative, ask yourself some very important questions: "Why isn't my child attending school like other kids?" "Why doesn't my child want to go to school?" "What is getting in the way of my child succeeding at a 'regular' high school?" Think through your answers before you settle for lowering your expectations and accepting an alternative school as an option.

Private learning centers are alternative school programs where adolescents can complete high school academic credits while working at a computer in an office setting. These programs are structured so that students are mainly self-taught and self-paced with some professional educational guidance. Most programs are licensed, and the awarding of completion of high school degrees varies depending on the center and the school your child attends. Some school districts may recommend this option and thus will pay for it and accept the credits. Many schools offer this as an alternative for hard to handle students. There is no counseling offered with this option.

Home schooling is another option families look to when dealing with a child who refuses to go to school. This is a form of self-tutoring, sometimes with a teacher who will come to your house to help with the work. Work is mailed to the organizing institution. Some questions to ask yourself before you agree to this alternative (which many teens favor): "Will your child remain home during the day to learn?" "Can you enforce this option?" "Why does your child prefer this option?" "What are the academic standards for home schooling?"

Since you may be the one who will be teaching your child, you must ask yourself if you feel qualified and have the time to do this. Since you will be the one to enforce the individualized standards, consider whether you want to undertake this additional responsibility. Further, it is useful to consider if this will increase or decrease conflict with your teen and in your family.

If one of these program types is the intervention you have chosen, you must raise your expectations of your child because it is too easy for your child to slide by, learning and accomplishing little. You must set expectations for academic standards, what you expect grades to be, number of hours spent per day studying, etc.

PURPOSE

For public alternative day programs, private learning centers, and home schooling, the purpose is to complete academic requirements for the high school diploma or to make up incomplete work and credits outside the usual academic setting.

TYPE OF ADOLESCENT

For the self-motivated student who works better in one-on-one or small group learning situations, who has not been able to maintain or succeed in regular public school. Many are over-eighteen teens who have dropped out, or others who have been asked to leave the regular school setting. *Not* appropriate for teens who require structured learning environments. This is not a substitute for a therapeutic program. *Not* recommended for teens looking for the easy way out.

LENGTH OF PROGRAM

Until the student completes high school courses or specific credits or has begun to show that he or she can be mainstreamed to finish high school.

COST

Public school alternative programs are free of charge. Some school districts will pay fees at private facilities, but usually only if they refer the student to the program. Private programs usually charge by the hour or the credit. These costs vary program by program and city by city. The cost of home schooling varies according to the issuing institution. The fee is usually per credit.

POSITIVES

- Student can complete unfinished course work or degree
- Programs can be used in conjunction with a day treatment program (see Category 2)
- Provides a viable educational alternative for the very bright, very motivated student
- Avoids negative peer interaction (home schooling only)
- Student works at own pace

NEGATIVES

- Lowers expectations for students (particularly possible with home schooling)
- Provides little structure and accountability
- Will not change situation at home
- Provides no peer interaction (home schooling or private learning center)
- Does not address reasons teen refuses school
- Places teen with others who think like him or her, reinforcing negative attitudes (public alternative day programs)

Boarding Schools

Boarding schools provide a residential environment following the nine-month school calendar, often with long holidays. They run the gamut from the most challenging academic programs to less challenging programs. They provide an opportunity for a child to work in smaller learning environments and to live away from home. Most are now coed. They pride themselves on creating the well-rounded adolescent, but some are particularly focused on sports, arts, religious affiliations, or another area, or cater to students with learning differences. Many are known for their ability to place students in top colleges and universities. A limited number offer specific services for the student who requires extra help in academics or has special learning needs. They offer the receptive teen the opportunity to mature and gain independence. If family issues seem to be the main problem, this opportunity for the teen to live outside the home is sometimes a good solution. However, drugs and alcohol are just as prevalent on prep school campuses as they are at your local public high school.

"Traditional" boarding schools are not for the student requiring a therapeutic environment. If your child has had behavior, conduct, or academic difficulties in school, it will be very hard to place him/her in a good quality traditional boarding school. A few schools will take a chance on a student who has graduated from a wilderness experience and shows real determination to turn his or her life around. Often a professional educational consultant can aid this process.

Military boarding schools provide a very structured environment. They will gladly accept the challenge of a student who has had some less serious behavioral or academic difficulties, but they do not want the out-of-control teen. They may be useful for a floundering teen, but they are not known for warmth of community or therapy. Strong discipline, structure, athletics, and military-style training are hallmarks of these programs. Many military schools are coeducational today. As with traditional boarding schools, do not count on an alcohol and drug free campus. Be sure to check on hazing practices.

Schools specializing in learning and attention issues cater to students who need specialized teaching for their specific learning or attention disability. These schools seek to develop a well-rounded individual despite his or her disability. Central to their philosophy is accepting the student as a "normal" teen.

PURPOSE

To acquire a high school diploma and to prepare a student for college living outside the home environment.

TYPE OF ADOLESCENT

Adolescents who would benefit from a "fresh start" or who are caught in family relationship issues. Also, students with learning differences or needing structure and discipline (military).

LENGTH OF STAY

A nine-month school year (typically September to June with very long holiday periods). Offers full four years of high school and college placement.

COST

$18,000–$30,000. Financial aid is available at most schools and tuition is not always inclusive of all fees.

POSITIVES

- Adolescent can have distance from family conflict
- Student will have more individual responsibility and independence
- School may also offer a summer term
- School usually provides resources to deal with learning differences or mild behavioral problems

- Academics are often highly valued
- Student will be separated from current friends
- School can provide depressed, demoralized, or socially inept teen with a smaller community in which to function

NEGATIVES

- Drugs and alcohol typically are as accessible as at public high school
- Strong structure not part of the program (except military)
- Therapy not part of the program
- Depressed, demoralized, or socially inept teen may fall through the cracks
- Little support or discipline for aggressively defiant students
- Little supervision over which friends teen chooses. Adolescent may gravitate to negative peer group but there is no one to notice it
- Can be very expensive

Summer Wilderness Programs

These programs are primarily a preventative for the younger teen who may have begun showing worrisome behavior and attitudes. In these moderately intense programs, teens experience some of the challenges of the wilderness with a therapeutic component. They are not as confrontational as Category 3 wilderness programs. Because teens are removed from the everyday distractions in their lives, they are provided the opportunity to re-evaluate their behavior and attitude before they spin out of control.

PURPOSE

Based on the wellness model of preventative therapy, and generally using a softer approach, these programs offer younger, but also sometimes older, adolescents a place to evaluate their behavior and attitude to prevent further emotional, psychological, and academic decline.

TYPE OF ADOLESCENT

Younger teens (11–14) as well as older adolescents who may have experimented with marijuana, cigarettes, drinking, or begun to hang around with kids who are not appropriate. Also useful for teens whose behavior has started to become negative and/or who may have begun to exhibit a poor attitude at home or at school.

LENGTH OF STAY

Generally two to six weeks but can be extended.

COST

$2,500–$6,000.

POSITIVES

- Early preventative intervention
- Removes teen from everyday environment
- Usually drug and alcohol free
- Structured environment
- Younger teen accepted

NEGATIVES

- Not always drug, alcohol, and tobacco free
- May not be as intense a program as needed
- Not covered by insurance
- Does not provide substance abuse counseling
- No parental involvement

CATEGORY 2

These are intensive out-patient programs and day treatment programs for teens who are moderately defiant and oppositional or who may be in need of substance abuse counseling or aftercare following a hospital or rehab placement.

Group Homes

These are small, single-sex facilities, licensed for 6–12 teens. They function as an extended family in a caring community and a safe environment. Staff is licensed and holds a contract from the state to run the home (regulations differ from state to state). Many are operated by social service agencies. Schooling usually takes place at the local public school, but that varies. The home does not usually provide therapy, but it can be contracted. "Therapy" is considered to be the community itself. Many times a group home is used as an "aftercare" program for a teen who has just finished rehab or a day treatment program. Although they are not really restrictive, they do maintain specific curfews for the teens and hold them accountable for following the rules. Kids are required to participate in chores and daily living activities. Research the home(s) you are considering before placing your child there. Each group home is different, some are much better than others. There are some group homes where you will not want to place your child.

PURPOSE

To provide an alternative setting for teens needing a caring environment or a place to live away from home.

TYPE OF ADOLESCENT

Teens who are traumatized by family issues, need to be removed from the home due to family conflict, who have been (or alleged to have been) sexually abused. Also useful for teens who have been through a short diagnostic/therapeutic intervention, but who, for whatever reason, should not return to their homes.

LENGTH OF STAY

Six months to one year or more.

COST

$850–$1,000 or more per month.

POSITIVES

- Comparatively reasonably priced
- Provides community/family atmosphere outside the home
- Provides some emotional/psychological independence
- Provides a calmer, less chaotic atmosphere
- Provides a residential alternative for child experiencing family conflict

NEGATIVES

- May provide a negative peer group; i.e., many of the other residents are experiencing similar family/personal difficulties
- Parents cannot oversee academics
- Many kids smoke
- May not be a drug/alcohol free environment

Intensive Out-Patient Programs

Also called IOPs, these are usually community based. They are operated by hospitals, private corporations contracted by a hospital, or local social service agencies. These programs provide a structure for the teen who has just finished a rehab or day treatment program or who has recently been discharged from a psychiatric hospital. They specialize in teaching anger management and communication skills to the teen and the family, and provide substance abuse counseling as well as AA and NA meetings. Individual and/or group therapy, cognitive, behavioral, and activity groups are usually a part of the program. To be admitted and remain in the program, teens must agree to remain sober and submit to drug testing at the discretion of the staff. However, many teens merely comply or "look good" while they attend the program during the day, but when they leave the program at the end of the day, return to old behaviors, attitudes, and friends. Staff are licensed therapists, psychologists, nurses, doctors, social workers, educational specialists, and psychiatrists.

PURPOSE

To provide support to the motivated adolescent, mainly as an aftercare program to continue therapy in a semistructured environment. Anger management, communication skills, family therapy, and substance abuse counseling are central to the program.

TYPE OF ADOLESCENT

Best suited to teens who have strong motivation to change. Often chosen (inappropriately) for defiant, angry, unmotivated, depressed teens, or those experiencing peer or family conflict, school and learning issues, drug and alcohol abuse issues, or who have been diagnosed ADD/ADHD. IOPs can be good for the teen who has experienced physical and sexual abuse since they provide an intense therapy/counseling component. IOPs can be an appropriate choice for the adolescent who does not require a full day program (such as day treatment or in-patient hospitalization) but requires medication management and/or therapy more than once a week. These programs are not recommended for out-of-control violent teens.

LENGTH OF STAY

Two to four hours per day, two to five days per week, a few weeks to a whole school year.

COST

IOPs are often covered by health care provider. Costs vary from state to state, within states, and program by program. Check with the program to ascertain if they work with your insurance company. Insurance companies have negotiated preagreed-upon rates. Health Management Organizations (HMOs) or Preferred Payment Option (PPOs) may require preapproval before you can admit your adolescent. Always check your policy or with your benefits manager before initiating service. Many times a diagnosis must be obtained before insurance companies will pay for services. Programs are usually willing to work with a family to secure payment of services. Self-payment is likely to be expensive.

POSITIVES

- Adolescent can remain living at home
- Can provide an effective aftercare program
- Sends message to adolescent that parents are serious about behavior change
- Teaches insight into family issues

NEGATIVES

- Can teach outward compliance without inward change
- May not break through adolescent's defenses
- System can be manipulated by the kids
- Program cannot enforce its rules when the teen is away from the site
- Can deplete insurance benefits
- Parents must function as the de facto enforcers of rules and sobriety

Day Treatment Programs
(Also Called Partial Hospitalization Programs)

Day treatment programs are usually community based, operated by a hospital or other private corporation contracted by the hospital. They are typically located either in a hospital or in a free-standing building on the hospital grounds. They offer programs almost identical to Intensive Out-Patient Programs (page 234) except that the teen spends the whole day there. Some offer additional evening support groups.

PURPOSE

To provide therapeutic and psychopharmacological treatment and management. They also provide transition back into family, school, and community life.

TYPE OF ADOLESCENT

These programs work best for motivated youths, seriously interested in reclaiming their lives. Teens who have invested in real change while in a hospital or rehab may find these programs good as a transition back into their school, family, and community. They are not recommended for street-savvy, manipulative teens. They are often recommended for defiant, depressed, angry teens subject to violent outbursts, drug/alcohol abuse, eating disorders, or who may have physical and/or sexual abuse issues. They are also appropriate for teens who have been diagnosed ADD/ADHD, with motivational problems, school and learning issues, peer problems, or who are involved in family conflicts. Teens in need of an aftercare program may benefit from this type of program.

LENGTH OF STAY

Usually determined by insurance benefits, but generally two to three weeks.

COST

Very expensive, although fees are often covered by health care providers. Self-pay can be very expensive and varies program to program. Check with your insurance company. Insurance companies have prenegotiated rates. Health Management Organizations (HMOs) or Preferred Payment

Option (PPOs) may require preapproval before authorizing payment. Always check your policy or with your benefits manager before enrolling your teen. Many times a diagnosis must be obtained before insurance companies will pay for services.

POSITIVES

- Provides statement to teen that parents are serious about changing the situation
- Provides continuity after discharge from hospital or rehab
- Can be used as a good first step intervention
- Gives respite to parents for eight hours a day
- Allows child to live at home
- Teaches responsibility, self-confidence
- Helps teen identify self-destructive behavior
- Provides drug and alcohol-free atmosphere
- Allows for family involvement in the treatment process
- Provides family and child with anger management and conflict resolution skills
- Provides counseling as part of the therapeutic intervention
- Provides psychological testing and diagnosis
- Allows teen to continue to work on academics (during school year with a tutor, local alternative day school, or private alternative programs)

NEGATIVES

- May deplete all insurance benefits
- Teen continues to live at home, sees old friends, etc.
- May not break old, bad habits, patterns in family
- Has some negative connotation in community
- Teen may not follow rules even in program and get away with it
- Teen may learn new unacceptable behaviors from other participants
- Often not strict enough
- Parents must become de facto enforcers of program rules and sobriety
- Not always drug and alcohol free

CATEGORY 3

These are short-term residential and nonresidential programs for teens who need intervention with behavior and/or drug and alcohol problems.

You should know everything you can about a program to which you are going to entrust your son or daughter. *All programs will require you to sign a contract. Ask to see it before you deliver your child to the facility so that you will have sufficient time to peruse it. Read it well, understand everything it says, and question it!*

When speaking to a program over the phone or when you visit the program, do not hesitate to ask questions. *When you are entrusting your son or daughter to a program, no question is silly, unimportant, repetitious, superfluous, or unnecessary!* Keep asking questions until you feel you know everything you need to about the program and the staff.

Here is a list of questions to guide you through the process of interviewing schools and programs. Place a check mark by each question after you feel satisfied with the answer and make other relevant notes for yourself. If you are going to visit a program, take this list (and the one that follows) with you. You will probably find other questions to ask, but do be sure to satisfy yourself on all of these.

1. What is the daily routine?
2. Describe a "typical" kid at your program.
3. May my child make phone calls? To whom? How many?
4. May I call my child? How often?
5. May I visit my child? How often?
6. Do you suggest/require me to be involved in family therapy through the school or outside of the program? How often?
7. When may my child come home to visit? Must he/she bring a friend with him/her?
8. Does my child need an allowance? How much? What if he/she calls for more money?
9. Am I allowed to send care packages? What am I allowed to send?
10. Where did last year's graduates attend college? How are they doing? What about the year before and the year before that?
11. Are there any civil lawsuits or criminal charges pending against the program or any individual working there? Have there ever been?
12. Describe your academic program. Describe your athletic program.
13. What do the students do for "fun" or recreation?
14. What types of discipline are used?

15. Are romantic/sexual relationships allowed between students? If not, how do you prevent them? How do you deal with infractions of those rules?
16. How do you get the teen to do homework?
17. Do kids have access to the Internet?
18. Do all students interact together or do you separate them? If so, according to which distinctions?
19. Who will be my teen's therapist? What are his or her qualifications?
20. What are the specific confidentiality laws regarding my teen's treatment?
21. How often do you update parents?
22. Describe the clinical intervention methods.
23. Is therapy individual, in a group setting, or both?
24. Is the therapy based on the Twelve-Step model?
25. Do you provide Twelve-Step meetings or chemical dependency meetings?
26. What is the procedure for a runaway? Do you use restraint?
27. Has anyone ever committed suicide while attending the program? How was it handled?
28. Are there any extra fees associated with your program, or is tuition all-inclusive?
29. Do you serve kids like mine?
30. May I speak with parents of present students? Graduates?
31. May I interview some students?
32. What are the credentials of the staff?
33. What is the staff-to-student ratio?
34. What is the turnover rate of the staff?

If you feel, after asking questions and visiting, that no matter what the program's stated goal is, all they really want from your child is compliance and conformity instead of real change, this may not be the program for you. If you feel the program is mainly interested in getting you to sign a long-term contract, look elsewhere.

Even after you feel satisfied with your conversation with the admissions staff at the program, it is still extremely important for you to interview parents of students currently at the program and parents of graduates, as well as program or school officials and to feel comfortable with what they say.

What to Look for While Visiting Programs, Schools, or Facilities

Visiting a program or school can give you a sense of the campus to help you decide whether it would be a good place for your child. Make sure you keep written notes about what you see. Compare programs you visit and think it through before you make a decision. If you are unable to visit each program, make sure your phone call to them is thorough and ask for names of someone who has visited or whose child has graduated from the program to whom you can speak about their experiences.

If you do visit, use these questions as your guide to evaluating the campus. Be sure to write down your answers because after you have seen two or three programs, you may find it hard to remember details of each one.

1. What does the atmosphere feel like to you?
2. How does the staff interact with the students? How do they interact with you? With others?
3. How do students seem? Are they smiling? Laughing? Nervous? Angry? (Some may be angry and unsmiling because they may have just arrived.)
4. Is the atmosphere respectful? Do students treat others with respect? Do teachers or counselors treat students with respect?
5. Do students make eye contact with you, with staff?
6. Are you only allowed to talk to certain students or staff?
7. Is there a stated philosophy of the school/program and do the staff and administration demonstrate it?
8. Do the staff seem stressed or relaxed?
9. Do the staff have their own lives outside and away from the program?
10. Do the staff set clear boundaries and limits? Are they consistent? When they say "no" do they mean it?
11. Do the kids answer your questions with rote answers or do they seem to be honest, candid, and open in their responses?
12. How do you feel (in your gut) as you walk around the campus or facility?
13. Would you be comfortable knowing that your child would be living with these people?
14. How do the academics look to you? Sit in on a class and watch the interaction in a classroom setting.
15. Do you feel there is any sort of cultlike atmosphere?

Drug and Alcohol Rehabilitation Programs

Drug and alcohol rehab programs are assessment and treatment facilities for people with substance abuse and addiction issues. There are both residential and nonresidential programs based on one of two concepts:

1. the medical model of disease
2. the self-help model

In each model, therapy takes place mainly in a group setting and primarily addresses addiction issues but also includes anger management, women's issues, sexual promiscuity, adoption issues, peer relationship issues, dishonesty, and cravings. Although there are significant theoretical differences in the approach of the two concepts, in most programs, the differences are beginning to blur. Staff is a mixture of licensed therapists, master's level social workers, as well as psychiatrists (for medication management) and nurses to monitor health issues. In the self-help model, recovering addicts are key to the theraputic work.

The Medical Model

This model regards addiction as a disease beyond the individual's control. Medical model programs are usually based on the Twelve-Step model of treatment and tend to be associated with a hospital. Although theoretically voluntary, most programs are in one sense involuntary: Depending upon age and state laws, parents may be able to admit their teen, but the teen must agree to stay. Teens can leave at any time or be expelled if they disobey rules or refuse to do the work asked of them. They may also leave once they have changed their behavior and attitude. Laws concerning confidentiality in a drug rehab environment are different from those in other programs, and you should research them carefully and understand them before admitting your adolescent.

PURPOSE

To break the denial of addiction and begin the recovery process.

TYPE OF ADOLESCENT

Teens for whom drugs and alcohol have become a central focus.

LENGTH OF STAY

Determined by insurance coverage and individual insurance policies. Most stays are about 30 days. This period of time does not suffice for true recovery—it is only a beginning. Programs often provide halfway house opportunity for aftercare, which may not be appropriate for all teens. A halfway house may be appropriate for a teen whose only issue is with drugs and alcohol but not for a teen whose issues are more with emotional growth and behavior issues. Do not let anyone try to convince you to place your teen in a halfway house if that is not the option you think best for your child.

COST

Very expensive, if you must self-pay. Costs are often covered by health care providers. Costs vary from program to program, state to state, and even within states. Insurance companies have prenegotiated rates. Health Management Organizations (HMOs) or Preferred Payment Option (PPOs) may require preapproval (and referral from a psychiatrist) before you can admit your adolescent. Always check your policy or with your benefits manager before enrolling your teen. A diagnosis may be required from a psychiatrist or attending physician before insurance company will pay for services.

POSITIVES

- Can help teen begin to break through the denial of addiction
- Typically teaches Twelve-Step recovery model
- Focuses primarily on addiction
- Most offer some voluntary family involvement
- Placement is voluntary but can sometimes be effected by parent
- Teens can continue academics during the school year
- Teen can be remanded by courts or told to complete program in order to return to boarding school or college

NEGATIVES

- Placement is voluntary
- Teen often continues or begins to smoke cigarettes
- Typical term of treatment may not be long enough to enact real change
- May deplete all insurance benefits

- Focuses primarily on issues of addiction and not enough on underlying issues such as defiant behavior, aggressive, out-of-control attitude
- Teens often do not buy into the "higher power" concept of Twelve-Step programs
- Teens can learn how to be compliant instead of really changing
- Some facilities have their own aftercare program and recommend only those

Self-help Model

These programs often seem strange and frightening to the uninitiated. Loud, aggressive confrontation is the hallmark of the therapy style. Originally based upon the work of British psychiatrist Dr. Malcolm Jones, the U.S. version primarily uses recovered addicts as therapists and does not allow for the placing of blame or fault on others. The individual must face him/herself as the one and only person responsible for his/her problem. Self-help model programs are often found in urban settings and are always voluntary. Individuals seeking admission to these programs must convince the program of their intense desire to change. Parents cannot admit their children. After being admitted to the community, individuals can be expelled if they disobey rules or refuse to grow and change.

PURPOSE

To end addiction and examine the issues that brought the individual to it.

TYPE OF ADOLESCENT

Teens who really want to change their life and are able to make a real commitment to sobriety. These programs are better suited to the older adolescent and young adult.

LENGTH OF STAY

Up to nine months, with halfway house possibilities for another three to six months.

COST

Some programs do accept insurance reimbursement. If you must self-pay, amounts are determined on a sliding-scale basis.

POSITIVES

- Placement is voluntary
- Adolescent must be serious about, and dedicated to, recovery
- Adolescents cannot easily get over on staff and peers as they can in hospital programs
- Peer confrontation
- Teens may continue academics
- Therapy is constant, rooted in the community
- Teens are confronted about their responsibility in their addictions
- Positive peer pressure

NEGATIVES

- Placement is voluntary
- Most teens smoke
- Most programs do not take younger teens
- Teens who cannot take confrontations may find the program difficult
- Kids who do get over on the staff and peers will be asked to leave if it is discovered

General Hospital with Psychiatric Unit or Psychiatric Hospital

A general hospital with a psychiatric unit provides medical attention upon admission. Free-standing psychiatric hospitals are able to provide only psychiatric treatment. Any patient needing medical treatment (such as for a suicide attempt or drug overdose) would have to be stabilized at a medical facility before admission to a freestanding psychiatric facility.

In-Patient

Therapists and/or parents may decide to place a child in a psychiatric hospital or in a psychiatric unit of a general hospital if the child is physically out of control and/or presents a danger of harming him or herself or others. They may also choose this if the child has suicidal ideation, has repeatedly run away, or if parents suspect extensive drug or alcohol abuse. This type of intervention allows for a psychiatric assessment. Personnel are medically trained and use a team approach. Professionals on the team include doctors, psychiatrists, psychiatric nurses, nurses, and psychiatric or clinical social workers. It is often the case that, after a diagnosis, psychopharmaca may be prescribed for your adolescent. If medication is prescribed for your teen, you must decide whether to allow it or not. *If your child is in extreme crisis, go to an emergency room!*

TYPE OF ADOLESCENT

Teens who have exhibited suicidal or self-mutilating behavior or ideation or are harmful to others. Also teens who are prone to violent outbursts, severe mood swings, depression, excessive running away, extensive drug and alcohol use or abuse, victims of sexual or physical abuse, or adolescents needing intense intervention.

LENGTH OF STAY

Generally determined by insurance benefits.

COST

Usually carried by healthcare provider (check with provider before admission). Costs vary from state to state and within states: Check with your insurance company. Insurance companies have prenegotiated rates for each hospital. Health Management Organizations (HMOs) or Preferred Payment Option (PPOs) may require preapproval before you can admit your adolescent. Always check your policy or with your benefits manager before initiating service. Many times a diagnosis must be obtained before insurance companies will pay for services.

PURPOSE

Crisis intervention for an out-of-control adolescent. To begin to address suicidal behavior or ideation, self-mutilation, harmful behavior to others, violent outbursts, sexual or physical abuse, severe mood swings, depression, excessive running away, extensive drug and alcohol use or abuse.

POSITIVES

- Provides a safe refuge for a teen in severe crisis; safer than being out on the streets or at home if child is violent, abusing drugs/ alcohol, or engaging in risky sexual behaviors
- Provides psychiatric evaluation/assessment
- Provides prescription of medication to stabilize teen
- Provides drug testing and evaluation/assessment
- Provides complete look at teen's physical condition
- Provides testing for pregnancy and HIV (some states only with patient's and/or parents' permission)
- Makes the statement that parents are seriously worried about child
- Offers chance for adolescent to begin the recovery process
- Allows time for parents to check out their options
- Offers serious wake-up call to adolescent to change

NEGATIVES

- Can use up all available insurance money; two weeks in hospital may cost as much as a year in other programs
- Tight time limit; usually too short a time frame for child to re-evaluate self and internalize change
- Relatively easy for adolescents to conform and look good without really changing
- Relatively easy to play the patient, hopeless, victim role
- Discipline may be lax
- Patients often are allowed to smoke
- May offer no aftercare plan, or the plan is time limited
- Aftercare plan may be difficult to enforce, so child returns to old way of life and friends
- Medication is often prescribed
- Diagnosis can stay with a teen for life

Wilderness Programs

Wilderness programs are therapeutic adventure experiences that are physically and emotionally challenging. These programs evolved from adventure based and survival programs such as the National Outdoor Leadership School (NOLS) and Outward Bound. (NOLS and Outward Bound offer wilderness and team building experiences but do not offer the intense therapeutic component needed to reach out-of-control adolescents.) Almost all therapeutic wilderness programs have intense group and individual therapy, but different programs use them in different ways and in different proportions. The philosophy includes the idea that when a teen has learned basic survival skills he no longer needs to fear for his own survival, which raises his self-esteem. By removing the adolescent from everyday distractions in his or her environment, the meaning of consequences, goal setting, decision-making, and personal responsibility can be learned more quickly. Being placed where most adolescents do not feel comfortable and are psychologically disarmed and dependent upon their leaders is a quick and often successful way of breaking through the arrogance and defiance which has characterized the adolescent's attitude.

Many wilderness programs are well respected and do the job they promise, but you must use caution when choosing one for your child. Because the situation is in itself potentially a dangerous one, if the staff is underqualified or careless your child could be placed at risk.

Questions to Ask When Checking Out a Wilderness Program

Use the guidelines listed at the beginning of this section (pages 238 and 240) to guide your search. Remember: Read the contract well, understand what it means. Ask questions until you do. Also ask:

1. Who is the on-site director? What are his/her qualifications?
2. Are there any civil lawsuits or criminal charges pending against the program or anyone involved with the program? Have there ever been?
3. How is the program licensed? By whom? Will they provide you a copy of the license?
4. Is the program insured? For what and by whom?
5. What credentials and experience do the staff have?
6. What is the ratio of staff to students?
7. How many students do you have per session?
8. How does the program handle a runaway situation?
9. What, if any, are the additional costs?
10. Has any student been hurt, killed, or committed suicide while there?
11. How can I contact the program once my child is there?
12. How frequently does the program brief the parents?
13. What is the parent involvement?
14. Is there a graduation ceremony? What is my role at that graduation?
15. Do you use deprivation or starvation techniques?
16. How do the kids get water and food?

17. What happens after my teen completes the program? Do you counsel us on the next step?
18. May I have the names of parents whose teen has recently graduated?
19. Does your program have any arrangement with any other programs, especially school programs or aftercare?
20. Will the program support me in a decision to have my child attend a therapeutic/emotional growth program afterward or do you solely advocate kids return home or find care in programs which are a part of your system?
21. Does your program specialize in any one particular area (i.e., substance abuse)?
22. Do you offer a special summer program for younger teens?
23. Do you advocate/encourage medications or do you discourage/prohibit them? Can my teen remain on medication? Must he?
24. How do you deal with infractions of the rules?
25. Are romantic/sexual relationships allowed among the participants? If no, how do you prevent them? What do you do with individuals who break that rule?
26. How do you deal with the absolutely noncompliant adolescent?

There are two types of wilderness programs:

Short-term wilderness programs tend to be highly confrontational in order to penetrate the outer defenses of the adolescent quickly. Their primary goal is to intervene swiftly and dramatically in seriously oppositional, defiant, and/or self-destructive behavior.

Long-term wilderness programs offer the adolescent the same type of program but not in the "stark" wilderness. Because the programs are longer in duration, they offer the adolescent a chance to continue his/her academics at school facilities at the program.

TYPE OF ADOLESCENT

Oppositional and defiant teens, experiencing family conflict, involved with drugs and alcohol, with a history of truancy, running away, violent, and/or depressed behavior. These programs can be useful for self-absorbed, self-centered teens with entitlement issues.

LENGTH OF STAY

Three to twelve weeks for short-term programs; up to one year plus for long-term programs.

COST

$3,000–$30,000 or more.

PURPOSE

To break through adolescents' denial that problems exist and move them to a place of change. To emphasize responsibility and care as a member of a group. To undo the narcissistic and arrogant attitudes pervading most troubled adolescents' thinking.

POSITIVES

- Demonstrates to child that parent is back in control and plans to stay there
- Teaches teen responsibility
- Promotes self-confidence and experience competency
- Assures drug and alcohol free environment. (Many programs strip-search teens and their belongings on arrival for drugs, alcohol, weapons, etc.)
- Environment assures there are no distractions from the task at hand
- Teaches teens to reevaluate actions, beliefs, choices
- Teaches teens to care about others
- Gives parents time to think about and decide what the next step should be
- Provides a safe place for child
- Offers a high ratio of staff (instructors) to students
- Can be a cost effective alternative

NEGATIVES

- Not a cure-all
- Strip searching teens and belongings on arrival for drugs, alcohol, weapons, etc. is objected to by some teens and parents

- Usually too short to enact long-term, internalized change of sabo-taging, self-destructive behaviors
- Kids can avoid doing emotional work
- Kids usually need long-term program afterward
- May teach only outward compliance
- May not break through kids' defenses
- Can be expensive, especially if an extended program is required

CATEGORY 4

Programs listed here are for teens who have had some problems but who have made a firm commitment to change. When you are finding out about these programs, use the same questions for researching programs listed under Category 3.

Religious Outreach Programs

These are programs supported by religious groups or denominations. Although most offer the possibility of residential living, some also offer a day program. Some have on-site academic programs, while others use the local public school system. These program offer adolescents support to ameliorate emotional and behavioral issues in order to achieve academic success. Programs of this kind may require the youth to participate in a community service component as well as a Christian-based education. The therapeutic component is usually the community itself. Most of these programs can be accessed through police social workers or agencies dealing with runaways or through your state department of mental health (the name for this agency is different in each state). They vary greatly in the populations they serve as well as in the structure of each program. Many have waiting lists because they have contracts with state agencies. Police social/family workers often refer teens to these types of programs.

PURPOSE

To provide a structured living arrangement in a specifically Christian atmosphere emphasizing important life skills such as problem-solving, honest communication, moral and ethical behavior, taking responsibility for one's actions, responsibility for others through community service projects. They also provide an opportunity to finish high school academic requirements.

TYPE OF ADOLESCENT

Angry adolescents with attachment issues, family relationship problems, teens exhibiting poor self-control and judgment, poor personal responsibility, and self-esteem. Although appropriate for those who have minimal drug-related issues (not addiction/abuse issues), teens with gang involvement are most appropriate for these programs.

LENGTH OF STAY

Six months to one year or more.

COST

Programs supported by religious orders or denominations usually have a sliding-scale fee based on a family's income. Some programs begin under $1,000 per month going up to $1,500 per month.

POSITIVE

- Sliding-scale fee makes treatment affordable
- Program requires community service
- Program requires religious education
- Offers family living setting
- Opportunity to get away from gang involvement

NEGATIVES

- Usually has long waiting list to enter program
- Does not offer structured therapeutic intervention
- No help for the drug/alcohol abusing adolescent
- Adolescent must be a willing participant in the religious community.

"Family Style" or "Ranch" Programs

These programs are patterned after the group home or foster home model. They provide a structured, family-oriented living arrangement to emphasize important life skills such as problem-solving and honest communication. They stress moral and ethical behavior and taking responsibility for one's actions. A few have on-site academic programs, but most use the local public school system. Many are situated on ranches or large tracts of land to encourage participation in chores and to discourage running away and unacceptable behavior such as involvement in drugs and gangs, etc. Program size is usually small with all members learning to become a part of the community. Staff is seen as "parental" figures, and they use this role to help guide the adolescent in effecting change in behavior and attitude. Positive peer pressure is also used to effect change.

PURPOSE

To provide a structured, family-oriented living arrangement and an opportunity to finish high school academic requirements. These programs provide a safe environment away from inappropriate friends and distractions. They can be used as a next step after a wilderness program.

TYPE OF ADOLESCENT

Adolescents for whom it has been difficult to form attachments in the family, who are involved in family conflict, exhibit poor self-control, lack of personal responsibility, self-esteem, and/or who have minimal drug related issues, but not addiction/abuse issues. Can be good for self-centered, self-absorbed teens with entitlement issues.

LENGTH OF STAY

Minimum one year to two years or more.

COST

$2,000–$4,000 per month.

POSITIVES

- Students study in a local public school, by correspondence, or they attain their GED (General Education Diploma)
- Students may be assisted by individual tutoring and independent study courses as needed
- Placement is voluntary
- Provides family setting, homelike environment

- Requires community involvement
- Teaches team building
- Builds sense of responsibility through chores and activities

NEGATIVES

- Students study either at a local public school or through correspondence course
- Program may not offer the level of academics parents desire
- Usually will not take adjudicated youth
- Facilities are not locked
- Addiction programs not available
- Students may have access to drugs, alcohol
- Teens can gravitate to the "wrong" crowd
- Placement is voluntary

CATEGORY 5

Category 5 programs are for adolescents who are truly out of control. These are for teens who are in serious trouble and need longer term residential treatment. You will want to visit the campus before you send your child—use the guidelines listed under Category 3.

Emotional Growth Schools and Programs

These programs are based on the idea that by providing a structured, healthy, therapeutic environment combined with a strong academic component adolescents could make substantial academic, emotional, psychological, and personal progress. They provide an opportunity for kids to "redo" the growing up that didn't work out well at home. Adolescents attending these programs profit from confrontational therapy and raised expectations to change their habits of failure into a search for success. Emotional Growth Schools are self-contained environments offering academics with an integrated counseling and therapeutic component. The curriculum stresses personal values, moral integrity, and positive self-image with the goal of producing socially, emotionally, intellectually, and physically well-rounded individuals. The community itself intensifies the therapeutic atmosphere. Peer intervention is combined with, but is not a substitute for, adult, professional intervention. Positive peer pressure is an integral part of these programs.

Staff are known as mentors and teachers, students are known as students. These schools are year-round, twenty-four-hour, seven-day-a-week residential programs.

The structure and process of these programs varies greatly. Some programs emphasize academics more than others. Some are truly voluntary while others almost resemble a locked facility.

PURPOSE

To force the out-of-control adolescent to stop his/her self-sabotaging behavior and attitudes while providing an academic program.

TYPE OF ADOLESCENT

Passively noncompliant, oppositionally defiant, depressed, demoralized, or underachieving teens, many of whom have drug and alcohol abuse problems, or who are involved in family conflict.

LENGTH OF STAY

Twelve to 30 months; year-round programs. May require parents to sign a financial commitment for first year.

COST

From $30,000 to $70,000 per year. Tuition usually is not covered by insurance, yet there have been circumstances where parents have been able to negotiate with their insurance company to cover expenses. Therapeutic expenses may be covered by insurance under the mental health coverage part of your insurance policy; school districts may cover costs for the academic portion. Costs may be tax deductible.

POSITIVES

- Provides safe environment
- Promotes a drug and alcohol free environment
- Most are involuntary, but not locked facilities
- Often situated in extremely remote parts of the country to deter runaways
- Teens can continue academics
- Provide college placement

- Limited parental contact in beginning gives parents a break
- Most promote family involvement
- Uses positive peer pressure

NEGATIVES

- Can be expensive
- Most are involuntary, but not locked facilities
- Not all have quality academic facilities
- Some academic programs are through correspondence courses
- Limited parental contact in beginning
- Not necessarily drug and alcohol free
- Some promote compliance as opposed to internal change
- Many want a long-term (circa 30-month) commitment

CATEGORY 6

Category 6 program are for adolescents who present significant danger to themselves or to others and those who are likely to run away. These are locked, residential facilities. Use the questions listed under Category 3 if you are checking out one of these for your teen.

Residential Treatment Centers

These handle the most serious adolescent problems, including self-mutilation, suicide attempts, heavy drug/alcohol abuse, eating disorders, and runaway risk. Residential treatment centers can be hospital based or free standing facilities. Many are based on the medical model of treatment, and adolescents who are admitted become patients. These are not the terrifying hospital wards of yesteryear. Emerging new breeds of residential treatment programs are multidisciplinary in nature and emphasize all aspects (psychiatry, therapy, education, recreation, and environment) of treatment. Academics are provided year round. In most cases programs deem family involvement critical to the success of the child's treatment. Staff at these schools/programs are known a counselors. These types of programs tend to be more staff run; patients are given little or no responsibility to bring about and direct each other's behavior and attitude.

Staff are medically trained and usually use a team approach. These facilities provide psychological assessment, diagnosis, and often prescribe medication.

PURPOSE

To provide psychological assessment, diagnosis, intervention, and care for the very out-of-control teen.

TYPE OF ADOLESCENT

Teens who present the highest runaway, self-mutilation, or suicide risk. Those who are severely oppositional or depressed, as well as those who seriously abuse drugs and alcohol.

LENGTH OF STAY

Minimum of six months; up to a year plus.

COST

Approximately $300 or more per day. Most insurance companies will pay for services from programs approved by the Joint Commission on Accredited Heath Organizations. Many will require a diagnosis. Programs contracted with JCAHO affiliated insurance companies will help parents secure coverage.

POSITIVES

- Provides safe, locked environment for out of control adolescent
- Placement is involuntary
- Addresses drug and alcohol issues and addiction problems
- Handles most serious psychiatric issues in a more user-friendly environment than a hospital
- Offers confrontational approach
- Can maintain medications (if needed)
- Offers intense therapy
- Requires shorter length of stay than emotional growth programs
- Teen can continue academics
- Family involvement is part of program

NEGATIVES

- Requires shorter length of stay than emotional growth programs
- Not all programs have adequate academics

- Shoes are taken away every night in order to prevent running away, although some runaways still occur
- Adolescents seen as patients
- More apt to medicate or encourage medication

Boot-Camp-Style Programs

These have become another alternative available to improve adolescent antisocial behavior. They provide strict discipline for the out-of-control adolescent. Boot-camp-style programs are based on the belief that in order for a child to stop his or her bad behavior he must be broken down before he can be rebuilt into a caring human being. The adolescent must accept the belief that he is rotten to the core before he can accept his own behavior and change.

Most programs are run by the judicial system, and youth are court mandated to attend. This may be the type of program your child will be mandated to attend if he or she is or becomes involved in the judicial system. It may be more appropriate to find a wilderness program or a therapeutic school as an alternative. You can offer this option to the judge, as many are unaware that these alternative programs exist.

CATEGORY 7

Young Adult Transitional Programs

These programs target the eighteen- to twenty-five-year-old population and are community based. Every year more young adults who are not able to emancipate, many of whom have not finished high school, are in need of these programs. Programs of this kind are appropriate for the young adult looking for a safe place to develop the motivation and courage to live independently. With the help of compassionate staff and a curriculum that empowers them to leave their past behind and move positively into the future, young adults can turn their lives around. These programs use a "level" system. The first level is the most structured, and the last level is self-structured, allowing the young adult to learn gradually to take responsibility and become accountable for his or her actions.

PURPOSE

To provide a young adult a safe, structured place to develop the motivation and courage to live independently and empower them to leave their past behind and move positively into the future while finishing high school, acquiring a GED, or attending a community college.

TYPE OF ADOLESCENT

Older teens and young adults needing educational support in completing a high school diploma or educational and tutorial support in pursuing a college education. Also appropriate for those needing support to overcome the emotional issues standing between themselves and successful emancipation, and for those who do not assume personal responsibility, display learning differences, have distressed family relationships, or who make unwise choices could benefit from programs like these.

LENGTH OF STAY

One year to eighteen months.

COST

$3,000 or more per month.

POSITIVES

- Teaches independent living skills
- Provides opportunity to finish high school
- Provides opportunity to begin community college with structured support
- Offers services at program
- Offers an alcohol and drug-free environment
- Offers a structured living environment
- Provides peer interaction with others who are serious about turning their lives around
- Provides vocational training
- Offers limited family involvement

NEGATIVES

- May seem punitive to an older teen/young adult
- Can be expensive
- Offers limited family involvement
- Possibility of negative peer interactions
- Programs based on young adult's behavior
- Won't work for young adult who is not determined to turn his life around

Where Else to Find Help ❀

Even as we finish this book, more and more programs and even new and different types of programs to help teens and families in turmoil are being started. Like everyone, we are saddened that it needs be so, but our minds are also eased because we realize that the needs of families are being met in more and more different ways, in more and more different parts of the country.

A new organization, NATSAP (National Organization of Therapeutic Schools and Programs), has recently been founded. Their goal is to provide information to parents, enhance communication among programs, and to set ethical standards for the types of programs listed in the previous pages. They can be contacted at 805-687-5825.

New Web sites appear on the Internet all the time. While many of them provide interesting and helpful information, parents should be wary of any grandiose claims or outlandish ideas.

Carol's List

Whenever I am asked to suggest something to help people in any sort of turmoil, I find my first and best suggestion is always the same: Mozart. Listening to Mozart soothes the spirit, calms the mind, and somehow brings optimism to the heart. A few of my favorites are: Cosi fan Tutte (KV 588), Mass in C minor (KV 427), Exultate Jubilate (KV 165), and Piano Concerti Nos. 21, 23, and 24. I also find Gustav Mahler's Symphony No. 2, "Resurrection," to be moving and inspiring.

There are a plethora of books available about teens, but I don't think anyone has ever explained teens more accurately than did J. D. Salinger in

The Catcher in the Rye and *Franny and Zooey*. Although written almost half a century ago, each of these books remains timely and meaningful. I recommend them especially to parents who feel they just don't quite understand where their teen is coming from, but I have also recommended them to numerous teens.

Shakespeare's *Hamlet* is always timely for adolescents and parents. (I know it's not quite a mainstream idea, but I have often thought of Hamlet as a struggling teen—"To be or not to be . . ." —one of the main questions teens ask.)

Joseph Campbell's *Hero With a Thousand Faces* can be helpful in understanding the journey from childhood to adulthood. The hero's journey, in many ways, parallels that of each adolescent.

I have often read the Grimm Brothers' fairy tale "Mary's Child" to teens who would not stop lying.

"The Little Matchgirl" by Hans Christian Andersen is a good story for a child who loves to feel sorry for herself.

The Razor's Edge by W. Somerset Maugham and *Demian* by Hermann Hesse are two excellent books for teens who are searching for meaning in their lives.

Oscar Wilde's *The Picture of Dorian Gray* is short, engrossing, and sometimes provides teens with enough of a fright about what happens to dissolute people to bring them to reexamine their own lives.

Shouting at the Sky: Troubled Teens and the Promise of the Wild by Gary Ferguson will help parents to understand the experience of teens in a wilderness program.

Am I Crazy or Is It My Shrink by Larry E. Beutler, Bruce Michael Bongar, and Joel N. Shurkin helps to identify if a therapist is the right one, and if not, what to do to find a right one.

Back in Control: How to Get Your Children to Behave and *Parent Back in Control* by Gregory Bodenhamer present a somewhat different approach than does this book. Many parents have found Bodenhamer's approach very useful.

For parents wondering about medication, I recommend *Toxic Psychiatry, Talking Back to Ritalin*, and *Answer to Prozac* by Peter Breggin, M.D. Although outside the mainstream approach, Dr. Breggin's books are well researched and written for the layperson.

An excellent article contextualizing out-of-control teenage behavior appeared in the May 1999 issue of the *American Psychologist* (available in university libraries and many public libraries or by contacting the American Psychological Association at 800-259-2666). The article is entitled "Adolescent Storm and Stress, Reconsidered" and was written by Jeffrey Jensen Arnett.

Because it is so easy to become overinvolved with a teen in turmoil, I like to advise parents to read far afield—whatever is their own particular bent. I usually suggest literature because I think we can learn as much from literature as from anything. I think Dickens's *David Copperfield* provides one of the best pictures of the dangers of being an overinvolved parent—and it is wonderfully entertaining.

Martin Buber's *I and Thou* remains one of the most meaningful books I know. It is about relationship at the most profound level.

A great resource for parents looking for help funding any of the programs listed in our book is *Wrightslaw: Special Education Law*.

Many parents and teens have been grateful to me for introducing them to the writing of Rabindranath Tagore. His work fills volumes, and you can find them listed on the Internet or in good local bookstores. His work has the wonderful advantage that you can start almost anywhere, read for only a few minutes, and feel deeply enriched.

Almost more important than which books to read is a caution about what not to read. Don't read *DSM-IV*. Most nonprofessional readers find it terrifying because it seems as though everyone you know has one or more of the disorders. Don't try to read professional journals about the disorders your teen has ascribed to him; unless you are trained to read such data, these articles, once again, may be more alarming than helpful.

Be wary of books, speakers, and media productions that seem facile and give too easy an answer. Unfortunately, there is a lot of that available nowadays, and such things are rarely helpful to you. Keeping in mind that complex problems never have simple answers is a good idea.

Leslie's List

Using stories about girls and their families with whom she has worked, I found *Reviving Ophelia* by Mary Pipher, Ph.D., helped to put into focus the issues so many young girls are dealing with. It gives a clear and often eye-opening view of the world our daughters are living in and the impact that world has upon them. Pipher does the same for families in *The Shelter of Each Other: Rebuilding Our Families*.

Real Boys by William Pollack, Ph.D., is the *Reviving Ophelia* for boys. Dr. Pollack helped me understand why so many boys are struggling. He has a great deal of insight into the fact that, even when they present a very different persona, so many boys today are in fact sad, angry, lonely, and confused.

We all changed when we become mothers, and in her book *The Mother Dance: How Children Change Your Life,* Harriet Lerner had me both chuckling and recognizing myself in her anecdotes. Her stories helped me see through the trials and tribulations of being a mother.

I, too, found Gregory Bodenhamer's books helpful. (*Parent In Control: Retore Order in Your Home and Create a Loving Relationship with your Adolescent,* and *Back In Control: How to Get Your Child to Behave.*) They are both hard-hitting and straightforward. Many families I have worked with have told me these books helped them gain strength and an understanding of the role they need to take to regain control of their families.

Iron John and *The Sibling Society,* both by Robert Bly, are two of my favorites. In *Iron John,* Bly describes how the role of older males to young boys in our culture has shifted dramatically. He clarifies the loss of relationship with their fathers that so many young teens I've worked with have spoken about. In *The Sibling Society,* Bly asks, "Where have all the grown-ups gone?" He shows how, in our culture, adults have regressed toward adolescent behavior and adolescents are refusing to grow up. Understandably, Bly calls for the "rediscovery of adulthood."

In *The Dance of Anger,* Harriet Lerner has written a guide to help women understand and deal with their anger in constructive ways. Chapter 8 on triangling was especially helpful for me. After reading it, I understood how I was being pitted against my husband and not working in concert with him in dealing with our children.

When the Drug War Hits Home: Healing the Family Torn Apart by Teenage Drug Abuse, by Laura Stamper, explains the issues behind adolescent drug abuse, as well as the basics of intervention and treatment. She also describes what families can expect after treatment. Also helpful in this area is *Choices and Consequences: What to Do When a Teenager Uses Alcohol/Drugs,* by Dick Schaefer.

Straight Talk about Psychiatric Medications for Kids by Timothy E. Wilens, M.D., is aimed at parents and can help you discern if psychiatric medication is right for your child.

Alice Miller's *The Drama of the Gifted Child* provides insight into our parenting and ourselves, as does *The Moral Intelligence of Children: How to Raise a Moral Child,* by Robert Coles.

Last, I had to step back and reassess my own life and that of my family's after reading *The Hurried Child: Growing Up Too Fast, Too Soon* by David Elkind. He describes in detail the negative effects on our children of hurrying them to grow up too fast.

*   *   *

As a last word, make sure your own life is becoming even richer and more differentiated. You will know your own best resources to make that happen for you.

We wish you Godspeed.

Acknowledgments

I would like to express my deep gratitude to:

The woman whose name I don't know with whom I spoke more than three years ago whose plaintive cry "But isn't there a book to help me get through this?" catapulted me into the realization that, since there wasn't, I would have to write it.

Leslie York, for so generously sharing her story to enrich this book, as well as for the wonderful times we spent together during our marathon working sessions.

The teens, parents, and colleagues from whom I learned enough to write this book.

Susan Ginsburg, my agent, and Janet Goldstein, my editor at Viking Penguin, for believing in the project when it was no more than a five-page proposal and then for helping to mother it through its very many stages.

Pam Novotny for her expert cutting and pasting.

The friends, acquaintances, and friends of acquaintances too numerous to name who so generously gave their time to read drafts of the manuscript and whose critiques were always so helpful.

My brother, Steve, for his care, support, and sage advice in these last difficult months.

My deep and humble gratitude to:

Leahi, for her calming presence and constant inspirations

and

Jack, for teaching me so much.

*   *   *

My debt to my parents and my daughters is greater than words can express. Without their love and support, this project could never have come to fruition.

And a very special extra thank-you to Maya, Kala, and Bama for their tireless reading and editing of page after page, draft after draft—and for never being afraid to say when something was not good enough.

—CM

Before I ventured into writing a book, I always took books for what they seemed to be—words on a page that someone had written. Never did I realize how much went into producing a book. I now know that writing a book takes more than simply putting words on a page. A book is only as good as all the people who have had a part in making it come to fruition. As a result, there are many people to whom I owe so much and whom I would like to thank.

First, I would like to thank my agent Susan Ginsburg for believing in the ideas presented in this book and having enough faith in two unknown writers to represent us.

To Janet Goldstein, my editor at Viking Penguin: This book would not be what it is today without her guidance, direction, and support. Thank you.

To Pam Novotny, I will forever be grateful for all the time, effort, and energy she spent on the manuscript and especially for keeping my sense of humor alive when I thought it was impossible.

Without the support, guidance, and belief in my ability to help families as she helped ours, I would not have had the courage to change careers and become an educational consultant, and so I thank my mentor, friend, and colleague Jeanette Spires.

To all the professionals, program heads, admissions directors, therapists, teachers, and educational consultants who have shared their knowledge and taught me so much about adolescents and this field, thank you.

I would also like thank Jim Feldman and the staff at Haven Youth Services for believing in my ability to work with adolescents and their parents.

I wish to thank the following people who have supported me from the beginning and to the end of my process of change: Carolette Turner for the support she offered as I struggled with my son; Lisa Young for providing long-distance encouragement, friendship, and love; Meredith Adams for being there when I just needed a friend to cry, laugh, and walk with; and my brother Sloane and his wife Dani, for all the help they gave my son and for believing that our family would make it.

And to everyone who encouraged me to write when I thought it an impossible task, I thank you for helping my dream become a reality.

There are so many people who read the manuscript at various stages that it is impossible to list them all, but to each and every one of you, thank you.

I would like thank my mother for instilling in me the faith that I could become anything I wanted, and for all the support, love, and guidance she gave during each phase of the book.

And to Carol Maxym for asking me to share my thoughts and insights into what it was like to go through the process of change and to bring to the project my expertise as an educational consultant, thank you.

To my sister, Allison, I love and thank you from the bottom of my heart for being the best sister a person could have, for helping when you could, for listening whenever I called, and for accepting my situation unconditionally.

I would not be a part of this book had it not been for my son Tom. Although it was not a journey that I relished making, it was one that has made each of us a better person. Thank you for allowing me to share it with you and for the wonderful relationship we now have.

To my daughters Sloane and Catherine: Thank you for being who you are. For loving our family with all our imperfections and for having the ability to forgive, forget, and move on. I love you each with all my heart.

And finally, I would like to thank my husband, Dick, for his love, encouragement, support, guidance, understanding, laughter, and sense of humor and passion throughout the writing of this book and before. Without you by my side, my life would be so empty.

—LBY

Biographies ✿

Dr. Carol Maxym is a psychotherapist and educational consultant who divides her time between western Massachusetts and Honolulu. A native of Denver, Colorado, Dr. Maxym earned her B.A. from Sarah Lawrence College, her M.A. from Antioch University, and her Ph.D. from Saybrook Institute. She has also studied at the Leningrad State University, the Sorbonne, and the Jung Institute. She lived and worked in Europe for almost two decades; returning to the United States in 1992, she became dean of students in an emotional growth program for troubled teens. Now in private practice, Dr. Maxym also offers process workshops for teens and their parents. She is working on her next book, which explores the language of sadness. She is the mother of two adult daughters. She can be reached through her Web site at www.drcmaxym.com

Leslie B. York is an educational consultant specializing in alternative placements for out-of-control adolescents. She holds a Master's degree in Social Service Administration from the University of Chicago and a Bachelor of Arts degree in Human Services. During the past thirteen years Mrs. York and her husband have been foster parents to more than eighty runaway or throw-away adolescents. She is a member of the Independent Educational Consultant Association, the Association of Educational Therapists, and the North Network Coalition, a Chicago-area organization working to develop and promote programs for teens.

Leslie York is the mother of three children and she lives with her husband in Wilmette, Illinois.

Index